Matthew Smith graduated from Manchester University and is a successful scriptwriter, producer and author. He has written extensively on the Kennedy administration and assassination and was consultant to Central Television's *The Men Who Killed Kennedy* and German ZDF television's *John F. Kennedy: Der Jahrhundertmord*. Matthew Smith lives in Sheffield.

VICTIM
THE SECRET TAPES OF MARILYN MONROE

Marilyn Monroe's death in August 1962, apparently a suicide, shocked the world. With fame, fortune, powerful friends and lovers, and the world at her feet, why would she have killed herself? Looking back at thousands of documents, some of them never published before, Matthew Smith argues strongly for a startling new version of events. His argument is based not only on these documents and on the complete forensic evidence, but also on the secret, confidential tapes Marilyn made for her psychiatrist in the weeks leading up to her death — tapes that portray a woman in charge of her life and looking forward to a busy, bright future. Here, from the transcripts of the tapes, are the most private thoughts of Marilyn Monroe.

MATTHEW SMITH

◆

VICTIM
THE SECRET TAPES OF MARILYN MONROE

Complete and Unabridged

CHARNWOOD
Leicester

First published in Great Britain in 2003 by
Century
London

First Charnwood Edition
published 2004
by arrangement with Century
The Random House Group Limited
London

British Library CIP Data

Smith, Matthew
    Victim: the secret tapes of Marilyn Monroe.—
Large print ed.—
Charnwood library series
1. Monroe, Marilyn, *1924 – 1962*
2. Monroe, Marilyn, *1924 – 1962*—Death and burial
3. Motion picture actor and actresses—Biography
4. Large type books
I. Title
791.4'3'028'092

ISBN 1–84395–245–9

Published by
F. A. Thorpe (Publishing)
Anstey, Leicestershire

Set by Words & Graphics Ltd.
Anstey, Leicestershire
Printed and bound in Great Britain by
T. J. International Ltd., Padstow, Cornwall

This book is printed on acid-free paper

This book is dedicated to Peter, Martin, JoAnne, Stephen, Tracey and Michael

Contents

Foreword

by Donald O'Connor

Though I had previously met Marilyn Monroe, it was only when we co-starred in *There's No Business Like Show Business* that I got to know her. Our other co-stars were Ethel Merman, Mitzi Gaynor, Dan Dailey and Johnny Ray and there was room for all our talents in a movie full of Irving Berlin's delightful songs.

I remember the time well, but as far as Marilyn was concerned those were not the happiest of days. She was involved in divorcing Joe DiMaggio and things were difficult, for it appeared he had her watched constantly, every move she made.

When the bombshell of Marilyn's death came along and they said she had committed suicide I felt in my bones there was something wrong. I knew her well enough to believe she could not have killed herself; it was not in her nature. She was murdered, but by whom? There are those who have asked us to believe that John F Kennedy and his brother Robert were responsible but could such a thing have been possible? I have to say at once that, for my part, that is too much to believe.

The truth has been out there somewhere, waiting for someone to tell us what really happened, for far too long. Marilyn's death created a mystery of great proportions, but at last answers have been painstakingly extracted from among the fiction attributed to how and why she died. I welcome the depth of the investigation Matthew Smith has carried out, and find the solutions he advances fascinating.

Donald O'Connor, Arizona

Introduction

by Robert F Slatzer

Over forty years ago Hollywood's most famous glamour girl died: Marilyn Monroe.

News of her so-called suicide was trumpeted throughout the world — but when the dust had settled in the passing of years, her death was not a suicide after all. Instead there was a massive cover up which went all the way to the White House — and in a lesser way, still exists today. However, her death brought together strange bedfellows: and this is how I was fortunate enough to meet a gifted writer and investigator, Matthew Smith, plus former deputy county district attorney, John Miner, a man with impeccable credentials. Both men possess dignity and honesty and command great respect among their peers.

How did the three of us come together? It all started with a statement back in 1962 by the late and former Los Angeles Police Department Sergeant, Jack Clemmons (the first officer to investigate Marilyn's death), when he told me a few days after Marilyn had died, 'This is an out and out case of murder.' It was sometime later that, due in part to this remark, Sergeant Clemmons lost his job and pension in respect of sixteen years' service, and for a long time had difficulty finding other work.

At the time of Marilyn's death, John Miner witnessed her autopsy but maintained dignity by not talking about it for four decades.

After I heard Clemmons' remark, and had several talks with him in the ensuing months, I took it upon myself to investigate the death of the female I had known well for the last sixteen years of her adult life. In doing so I, like Matthew Smith and John Miner, found many locked doors — people that would not or could not talk. But in 1974, I published a book on my findings, *The Life and Curious Death of Marilyn Monroe*, which spawned a host of other books and which also revealed a cover up; proof that Marilyn did not die by her own hand. Meanwhile, Matthew Smith, who had studied this case for a long time, authored a book, *The Men Who Murdered Marilyn*, a vivid account of the star's death.

Throughout the years following Marilyn's death, John Miner and I, later joined by Matthew Smith, petitioned the local authorities to reopen the case and hold a special inquest. This fell upon deaf ears, unfortunately. In 1985 we nearly succeeded in reopening the case, and the LA County Grand Jury approved it, but a few days later the Grand Jury foreman was fired and the case swept under the carpet once again.

Meanwhile, for forty years John Miner kept a vow of silence he made with Marilyn's psychiatrist, the late Ralph Greenson, that he would never reveal the substance of the Marilyn tapes — secret tapes she made before her death and which now, for the first time, will come to light. Consequently, the end result of Matthew Smith's work, with the co-operation of John Miner, is an effort to erase the stigma that Marilyn Monroe committed suicide. Now the truth will be coming out, and wherever Marilyn's spirit might be, I am sure she is smiling at the friends she still has on this earth who are endeavouring to clear her name.

I am sure you as a reader will share the same feelings I have about this new book, and say, 'It's a real page-turner.'

After all, there is no statute of limitation on murder.

Robert F Slatzer, Hollywood, California

Preface

There is nothing quite as daunting as trying to solve a forty-year-old mystery. The advantages of hindsight and the ability to achieve a considered perspective are grossly outweighed by the handicap of so many witnesses having passed on and by the fact that many of the surviving witnesses will not share what they know with us. But in spite of this, in the case of the death of Marilyn Monroe, a clearing picture emerges of intrigue and cover up, lies, deceit and — murder.

I first became involved in researching the death of Marilyn Monroe through my work on the assassination of President John F Kennedy, and later, the murder of Senator Robert F Kennedy. My further work on Chappaquiddick and the near political demise of Senator Edward Kennedy convinced me there was a clear pattern running through these events, but I saw that it didn't begin with the shooting of President Kennedy. The pattern began in 1962 with the murder of Marilyn Monroe.

When I finished my first book on the death of Marilyn Monroe in 1996, I thought there was little mileage left in the investigation without some sort of major breakthrough. There are breakthroughs and breakthroughs, of course, and if a writer is fortunate enough to come by a scoop he is generally content for that to come in modest shape and form. Such was not the ease in this instance. To obtain the exclusive world rights to a transcript of tapes Marilyn made very shortly before she died consitutes a breakthrough of enormous proportions. In seeking to know what was in her mind at the time she died, Marilyn here speaks for herself. Such a windfall is unlikely ever to come again. A great many things about which we have speculated in the past are now confirmed.

The picture has become sharp and clear, and I believe we now have the answers to this forty-year puzzle. The publication of the tapes may also take us a giant step towards persuading the Los Angeles authorities to disinter Marilyn's body so that final confirmation may be obtained in a new autopsy and belated inquest. This is favoured by both Dr Thomas Noguchi, who conducted the original autopsy and who was frustrated in completing his work, and John Miner, who as Deputy to the District Attorney, was present throughout the autopsy proceedings and knows the circumstances that prevented its completion. Both Thomas Noguchi and John Miner have expressed the wish to be involved in any further autopsy investigations.

I must here record that discretion has been exercised in relation to publication of certain of the tapes' contents that were deemed extremely intimate and entirely personal. Some references have been omitted to preserve decorum. Had I published those portions of the tapes in question, Marilyn would have been embarrassed and, no doubt, my readers would have been embarrassed for her.

Matthew Smith, Sheffield

Acknowledgments

There are many people I must thank for their co-operation and kindness in assisting me with my research for this book. My special thanks go to Donald O'Connor for writing a foreword to this book. He knew Marilyn Monroe and co-starred with her in *There's No Business Like Show Business*, and was kind enough to share his memories of those days with me. I know my readers will appreciate his contribution and will take pleasure in hearing from him.

Next I must express my gratitude to Robert F Slatzer for the introduction he has written to *Victim*. If anyone is conversant with the minute details relating to the death of his long-time friend, Marilyn Monroe, it is Robert Slatzer, and since he is also conversant with my thinking on the subject, he was an obvious choice for me. I am grateful to him also for providing a number of excellent photographs of Marilyn from his collection. Thank you, also, to Debbie Slatzer, Robert's wife, for the valuable help and advice she has given me.

I am greatly indebted to John Miner for entrusting me with the transcripts of the two tapes Marilyn made for her psychiatrist, Dr Ralph Greenson, shortly before her death. They are very revealing and form the core to the new data featured in this new book. I am also grateful to him for re-constructing his memorandum, the original of which he submitted to Coroner Theodore Curphey, with a copy to the Chief Deputy DA, Manley Bowler. Both copies of the original memorandum unaccountably disappeared.

Tom Reddin, who served as assistant under William Parker as Chief of Los Angeles Police Department, and who later became Chief himself, has rendered advice and assistance which is greatly appreciated. I am grateful to Dr Thomas T Noguchi for discussing the autopsy he carried out on Marilyn and permitting me to quote from his book, *Coroner*. Dr Cyril Wecht also rendered expert opinions that I found extremely valuable. Patte B Barham also kindly consented to me quoting from the excellent book she co-authored with Peter Harry Brown, *Marilyn: The Last Take*, and gave me other assistance, and this kind help is greatly appreciated. A big thank you also to Jeanne Carmen, Marilyn's neighbour and friend, for talking to me and corresponding since.

Debra Conway of JFK Lancer in Dallas made a positive contribution for which I thank her, and Anne Lajeunesse, Greg Schreider, and William Bailey all gave me their specialist help and advice which I acknowledge with thanks. Stanley Rubin went to a lot of trouble in putting me in touch with people which was extremely helpful, and Ted Landreth also pointed me in the right direction. The kindness of Marvin Paige has also earned my appreciation. My thanks to all.

In research carried out what seems like a long time ago I spoke to Antoinette Giancana, Ralph de Toledano and Natalie Jacobs, all of whom helped me. Dr Robert Litman was kind enough to talk to me and Dr Norman Farberow took the time to write to me. My thanks also to them, and I must also acknowledge the help of Andy Winiarczyk of the Last Hurrah Bookshop and Al Navis of Almark and Co. in Thornhill, Canada, in helping me to find books I needed. I remember with appreciation the management and staff of the Hollywood Plaza Inn where I stayed while carrying out research.

Jack Clemmons was unstinting in the help he gave, and I also appreciated being able to talk to Milo Speriglio. Robert Mitchum and I talked together for hours and I am greatly indebted to him for the memories he shared with me. Sadly, Jack and Milo and Bob Mitchum are no longer with us.

Andy McKillop, at Random House, has been there for me while I have written this book and I have appreciated greatly his advice and assistance. My thanks, also, to Hannah Black and Deborah Bosley, who have made the editing process as painless as possible.

I am also indebted to Gerald N Davis MD for his kindness in contributing photographs.

I am always conscious of the help and support of my wife, Margaret, without whom there would be no book. My family are also enthusiastic and supportive and this contributes in no small measure. My sons Stephen and Michael have helped me out, as always. Stephen now regularly checks my proofs with me and helps me in the tiresome but essential task of constructing an index, while Michael assists with checking the text. Thank you both.

1

COLLISION COURSE

The year was 1962, and the set of *Something's Got to Give* had become a battlefield. The director, George Cukor, and the star, Marilyn Monroe, were slogging it out on a daily basis. Cukor was an unwilling director. The film was his last contract commitment to Twentieth Century Fox, and he really would have preferred to be elsewhere. It was thought his desires and ambitions had been taking him in the direction of making *My Fair Lady*, but Fox were having none of it and, threatening legal action, demanded he fulfil his obligation to them.

The talented Nunnally Johnson had written the script. It was a re-make of *My Favourite Wife*, which had been very successful for Cary Grant and Irene Dunne in the early forties. Marilyn got on well with Johnson and looked forward to doing the movie, which represented a change in direction in her acting career. Cukor, however, who preferred the original *My Favourite Wife*, which he had also directed, sought to demolish the *Something's* script with volumes of re-writes, so that when shooting began on the picture, it was far from complete. At one point during the production, re-writes had run riot and only four pages of the original

1

script remained. The changes that were being made were not for the better.

Fox had been having a rough time of it financially. The Richard Burton and Elizabeth Taylor epic, *Cleopatra*, had run wildly over budget. Costs had soared to $30 million, an unheard of sum in those days, and had brought the studio to its knees. To facilitate progress on *Cleopatra* Fox were obliged to transfer shooting from London to Rome, because Elizabeth Taylor could not cope with the English weather, and the movie hung like an albatross round the studio's neck. The film would eventually cost them $43 million, but at the box office it would go down like a lead balloon. To raise money in their bid for survival, they sold off their back lot and closed the talent school to reduce outlay. Between 1961 and 1962, a healthy 31-movie schedule fell to less than one third, the studio's number of contracted producers was reduced to half, and their number of employees, which had reached over 2,000, was now just over 600. During this one year the number of stars they had under contract shrunk to less than a quarter of what it had been. The company had recorded a loss of over $20 million in 1961 and it was struggling for survival.

Nunnally Johnson expressed doubts as to whether *Something's Got to Give* would ever be made. As far as Fox were concerned they were in a 'heads you win, tails I lose' situation. No-one was sure whether making the film would help or hinder their financial position. While the budget position for *Something's Got to Give* was modest to the millions that *Cleopatra* had gobbled up, it was the most expensive movie they had in production at that time. Before a foot of film was shot, the script alone had cost about $300,000, several times more than had been budgeted, and the script changes, made on a daily basis, continued to maul whatever had been approved.

Cukor was angry that David Brown had been replaced by Henry Weinstein as producer of *Something's* and suspected the new producer was favoured because of his connections with Ralph Greenson, Marilyn's psychiatrist. This caused friction, while Greenson, with his brother-in-law, lawyer Milton 'Mickey' Rudin, who had stepped in to act for Marilyn since she had no agent at that time, did not make matters any easier. Marilyn, who had worked with Cukor previously when she made, *Let's Make Love*, and had called him, 'the best comedy director in the history of Hollywood', found herself 'piggy in the middle' of all the confused and conflicting interests and influences, and was soon disillusioned if she expected an easy ride from the director.

The day's script changes were sent to Marilyn late each night, so she had little opportunity to absorb them before the next day's work. The changes were typed up on blue paper to distinguish them from the basic script, which was on white. Changes to the revised script were typed up on yellow paper, and changes to the revisions of the revisions were typed on pink sheets. Marilyn found the volume of changes

George Cukor lays it down to Marilyn on the set of
Something's Got to Give.
Photo Robert F Slatzer Collection.

overwhelming and complained to Cukor, and a
battle raged between the two. Cukor, in collusion
with Henry Weinstein, sought to pull a fast one
by submitting the changes on white paper, so
they would not be noticed, but she was not
fooled. She countered with re-writes of her own,
and chaos reigned.

The last-minute script changes had another
dire counter-productive effect on the production
of Something's Got to Give. Marilyn's ability to
give the director a take in one shot deteriorated
until there was talk among journalists of her
mental health declining and gossip about the
added complication of too many pills. But those

on the set noticed the difference between takes of scenes that were not rewrites and those which had been scrambled together hastily. She did not have a problem with the former: with the latter she sometimes could not memorise words for a close-up which she had said only a few moments earlier in a long shot. But given the task of coping with revisions delivered to her late at night, only to find they were rewritten again next

Cukor and Marilyn did have their lighter moments. Photo Robert F Slatzer Collection.

day before the shot was made, it was hardly surprising she had difficulty. And of course the cost of the re-shoots added up, increasing the mounting budget overrun.

In a lighter moment on the set she turned to George Cukor after the twentieth take of a scene which involved 'Tippy' the 'family' dog. 'He's getting good,' she laughed and Cukor shared the laughter. She was patient with the dog and loved animals in general. It was one of those golden moments in the making of a film that had so few.

Walter Bernstein was the current 'on the set' writer, whose job supposedly was to carry out the minor alterations in day-to-day shooting, and whose job had turned into a nightmare. He was seventh in line. There had been six writers who had come and gone before the picture had started shooting. Bernstein did not see the need for consultation with Marilyn on the script, nor did he understand Weinstein's dilemma, and reminded him that Marilyn's contract did not give her script approval. 'Marilyn doesn't need script approval,' replied Weinstein. 'If she doesn't like something, she doesn't show up.' The producer was nothing less than a realist.

Marilyn's besetting problem was her inability to get a good night's sleep. Without sleep she could not give of her best, and on set she was a perfectionist. Her doctors plied her with drugs of various kinds but they were having only a limited effect. As a result of the drug taking, some mornings she was dysfunctional, and there were days when the previous evening's cocktail of pills meant she was simply unable to work. It was a tribute to her finely tuned grasp of pharmacology that she survived. None of this improved matters on the set. Cukor continued to rage at her and she continued to rage back.

It was commonly reported that Marilyn was terrified of appearing in front of the camera. She delayed, using non-existent make-up problems, additional rehearsals, any reason that came to hand as an excuse to delay putting in an appearance, and she was sometimes seen throwing up before reaching the set. Producer Henry Weinstein, who was sympathetic, said, 'We all experience anxiety, unhappiness, heartbreaks, but that was sheer, primal terror.' This was nothing new. Bob Mitchum told me Marilyn suffered from the same problem when they worked together on *River of No Return*, and it was a problem when she made *The Misfits*. Said Mitchum, 'Marilyn would see her hairdresser at seven o'clock in the morning, and after that go back to her apartment. Then she would be afraid to go out. She was afraid to leave the confines of wherever she was.' This was not the only manifestation of her problem, however. 'Every time the director said 'action', to her great embarrassment she began to menstruate. This was a big problem to her. And they thought she was being temperamental,' Mitchum told me, fully sympathetic to Marilyn's problems.

But when she finally did reach the set of *Something's Got to Give*, Marilyn, to her credit, worked extremely hard. She would normally be word perfect and willing to carry out the every wish of the director. An inveterate latecomer, she

7

Marilyn recovering with the help of Agnes Flanagan and Paula Strasberg. She fainted from sheer fatigue. Photo Robert F Slatzer Collection.

more than compensated when she arrived, and re-takes, as many as Cukor wished, were not a problem. She had, after all, made 20 of her 29 films with Twentieth Century Fox, and it was not hard work that was a problem for her, though she was once known to faint on the set from fatigue. Nor was she less than respected there. Even frustrated scriptwriter, Walter Bernstein said he found her ' . . . astute, knowledgeable, shrewd and accomplished.'

On 1 June, Marilyn celebrated her thirty-sixth birthday, and, though Cukor would not allow any celebrations before the day's shooting was completed, at six o'clock the cast sprang a surprise party for her. An enormous birthday cake was produced and the partying began. The

8

distinguished cast of *Something's Got to Give* featured Dean Martin as Marilyn's leading man, her husband, who had just remarried after she had disappeared some years before and had been declared dead. The new wife was being played by Cyd Charisse, and other parts were being played by Tom Tryon and Phil Silvers. Ellen Arden, played by Marilyn, returned just in time to find her husband newly married, and the plot, which included their two children, was a delightful light comedy which took Marilyn far away from her *Bus Stop* image.

But the feuding continued and soon the budget was overspent by $1 million, with only six minutes usable footage in the can. There was talk of firing Marilyn, but Nunnally Johnson, who had stayed in touch with what was happening at the studio, cabled studio chief Peter Levathes, saying, 'If you're going to take anybody out of this picture, shouldn't you decide first who brings the people in, George Cukor or Marilyn Monroe? You should remove George because they are so antipathetic and that's what's causing Marilyn's disturbance.' Marilyn stayed, but for the time being, so did George.

Ralph Greenson, Marilyn's psychiatrist, went on an extended five-week vacation while the picture was in progress. He had promised to deliver a lecture in Europe, and then he and Hildi, his wife, would holiday abroad for the remainder of their time. Marilyn had come to lean on Greenson, and his absence threw her, though she would have been reluctant to admit it. Greenson left her with props — drugs — for the time he was away, but this was quite inadequate and placed an extra burden on her at a time she needed all the help she could get. Her main problem was the commotion being caused by her time off to appear at the President's birthday party in New York. It had all been arranged well in advance, but Fox, anxious about further delays to filming, and preoccupied with establishing its authority on what was happening on the set, told Marilyn she could not go. To disobey would attract serious penalties, the studio bosses said. Marilyn went. Marilyn was fired.

2

BUSY DAYS

It could be argued that in spite of extreme provocation Marilyn had been absolutely exasperating to Fox, especially when their financial problems were crippling. When she deigned to put in an appearance at the studio she feuded with Cukor and, in the script war, demanded one costly and irritating change after another. When she didn't turn up it cost them more and more money without any footage to show for it. Of 36 days' shooting, Marilyn had appeared on only 12 of those days, and Cukor had had to shoot the scenes 'around her', using others in the cast where he could. But when she disappeared from the set sick, and was next seen at Madison Square Garden singing 'Happy Birthday' to President Kennedy during his forty-fifth birthday celebrations, the studio, desperate to assert its authority, had had enough. Acrimony flared and they slapped a half-million-dollar writ on Marilyn Monroe Productions Incorporated for 'wilful violation of contract' and told her not to come back. The sum they were to sue for later increased to $750,000.

At one point it was announced Lee Remick had been given the part, though she had been third in line behind Kim Novak and Shirley

MacLaine, who had both turned it down. Then Dean Martin, who, in his contract, had the right to approve his leading lady, stepped in and invoked this right and said he would not play with anyone but Marilyn. Marilyn was tearfully appreciative of Martin's loyalty. In an attempt to get round the Dean Martin problem, the studio offered the part to Bob Mitchum. 'They asked me about it, asked me to step in,' he told me, 'but I heard from Dean and I wouldn't,' he said. 'She didn't get along with George Cukor. Cukor was foaming at the mouth. He was a basket case. I worked with him on a picture called *Desire Me*. Nobody desired any part of it.' Changes were then made in high places in the Fox management team, and a week after Marilyn was fired the overtures to woo her back began.

'Good riddance,' had been Marilyn's snooty response when she was fired, and, no doubt, she wished she could have meant what was merely a demonstration of her pique. She had been in a corner really, but not without ideas on how to combat her problem. She posed for a series of photographs for some of the most famous photographers in the business. Bert Stern, George Barris and Douglas Kirkland knew how to present Marilyn at her most alluring, and as far as a movie studio was concerned, her most desirable. She did not have to wait long for a Fox executive to call her. After all, a newly appointed, different set of executives reasoned, they had a part-made movie on their hands, the most expensive of their current productions — they had already invested $35 million — and

12

scrapping it would cost even more in settling contracts elsewhere. Marilyn landed sunny side up with a revised contract worth three times more than her previous one. Add to this her royalties from the percentages she owned in her films such as *Some Like it Hot* and her most recent film, *The Misfits* and she was solid gold.

Marilyn was on a high. Things were now going her way. She had bought a house, the first she had ever owned, and it thrilled her. It had wood-beamed ceilings and featured a spacious central living room and small bedrooms. She had had it carpeted throughout in white pile and, piece by piece, she was furnishing it to her liking. She was taking her time selecting the items she wanted, and though she had just received some new furnishings from Mexico, she had some way to go before she had obtained all she needed. She engaged a handyman to sort out the plumbing in her bathroom to bring the house up to par: this home of hers was going to be something else. The architecture was in the style of a Mexican hacienda and that appealed to her. Though it was modest and did not compare with the sumptuous spreads of some of her movie-star friends, it was what she wanted. She had her pool and the garden was an attraction: girls who lived in apartment blocks had no such luxuries. She enjoyed buying new plants for the garden and paid $100 each month — a tidy sum in those days — to have it kept up.

At the beginning of August everything was looking rosy. The present and the immediate future were assured. Her mind was now clear to

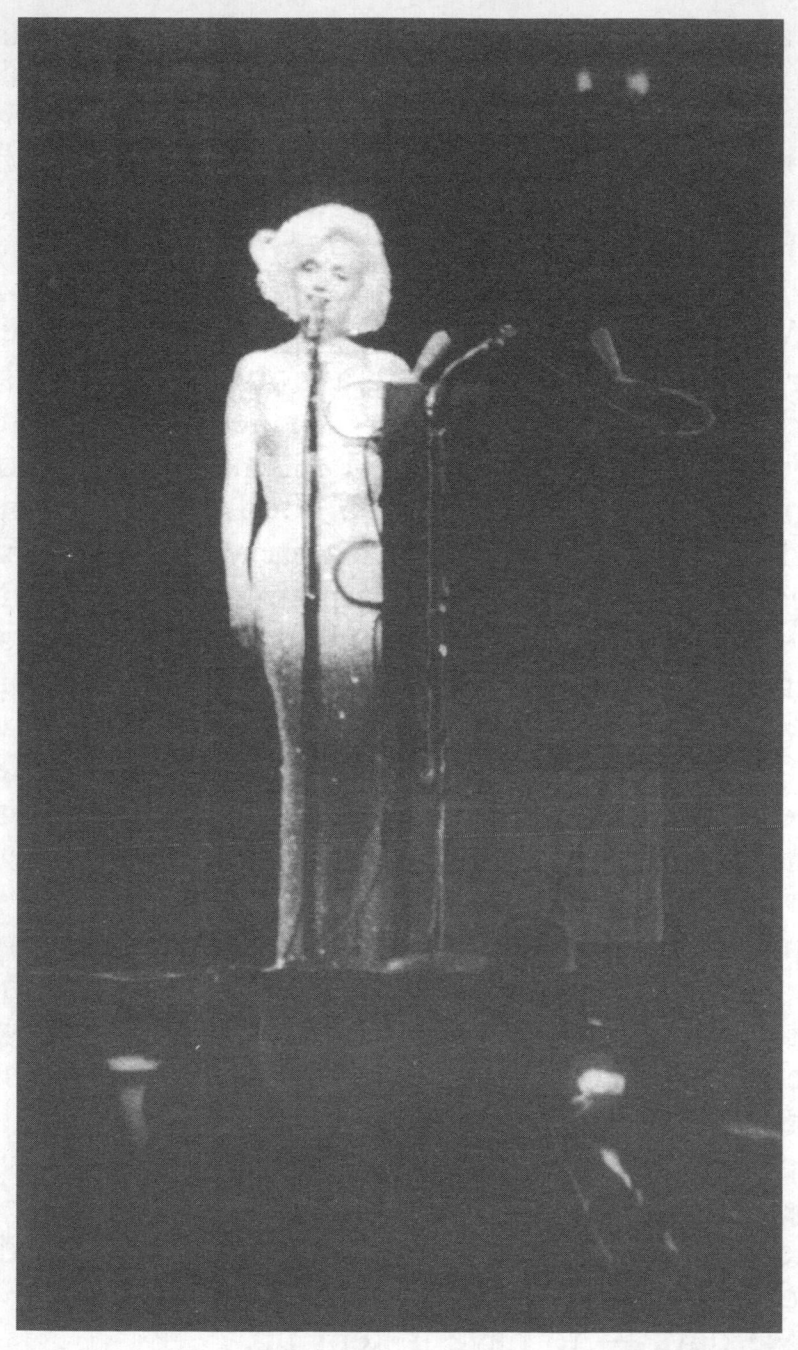

'Happy Birthday, Mr President.' Marilyn at Madison
Square Garden.
Photo Courtesy John F Kennedy Library

Marilyn's house at Fifth Helena Drive.
View from the gate.
Photo Matthew Smith Collection

look forward to other projects and she had a number of irons in the fire. Jules Styne was talking to her about the prospects of remaking *A Tree Grows in Brooklyn* as a musical starring Marilyn and Frank Sinatra. An Italian company was expressing interest in her. They wanted her for four movies and there was seriously big money in that deal.

It was Saturday 4 August. She had an appointment the following day to meet with her journalist friend, Sidney Skolsky, to discuss a movie she wanted to make about blonde bombshell Jean Harlow. Harlow had been an incredible figure to the teenage Monroe who very much admired her. To play her in a movie would be a dream come true. On Monday she had one necessary chore: to see her lawyer,

15

Milton Rudin, about changing her will. But in a more pleasant vein, later in the day she had a date to meet Gene Kelly to discuss a new movie with him. The movie, released later, was *What a Way to Go*. Life was full of promise for Marilyn.

But there was one thing that was not going Marilyn's way. Speculation about an affair between Attorney General Robert Kennedy and Marilyn has raged for years without researchers and writers being able to obtain hard and fast confirmation that it had really happened. Marilyn's secret tapes, which are featured in this book, now provide that certainty. And in the early summer of 1962, that was the one blot on her landscape. Marilyn had earlier been involved in a torrid relationship with Senator Jack Kennedy, who, after he was elected to the Presidency, switched off and didn't want to know her any more. With Marilyn the fire had not gone out, however, and she still expected her gallant hero to make his way to Los Angeles on some pretext or other so they could meet. But it didn't happen and was never going to happen again. Everything had changed now and there was too much at stake for the new President, who seemed not to know how to break off a relationship gently. For him it was instant.

Robert was despatched to make contact with Marilyn ostensibly to explain things to her and placate her, though some would challenge that these were his motives. By all accounts he fell under her spell and another affair began, just as torrid as that with his brother. Marilyn fell madly in love with the Attorney General, brother of the

16

President, who, she was convinced, would divorce his wife and marry her. They were as close as two peas in a pod. Several of Marilyn's closest friends asserted she had an abortion — probably in Mexico — shortly before she died, and that the father was probably either Jack or Robert Kennedy. Then, all of a sudden, Robert became bitchy and argumentative. The only interest Robert appeared to have left in Marilyn was in the acquisition of something she had in her possession and, it seemed, something she was not parting with.

Now it was Robert's turn to break off the relationship with Marilyn as cruelly as his brother had. Instant again. He did not come to see her and would not take the many telephone calls she made to him. The private phone number he had given her was changed and, when she attempted to go through the switchboard of the Justice Department, it became clear Robert had left instructions her calls were not to be put through. Marilyn's response, according to those who eventually came to hear the rumours of Robert Kennedy's actions, was to fall into a deep depression. A neat scenario, still subscribed to by many, but like so many neat scenarios, it was not the way it really happened. Nonetheless, Saturday 4 August turned out to be a very decisive day for a number of reasons.

★ ★ ★

Out of the blue, in the still of the night — at 4.25 a.m. on the following day, Sunday 5 August — the phone rang in the duty room of the West Los Angeles Police Department, and a voice announced to the watch commander that Marilyn Monroe was dead.

3

CURIOUS BEHAVIOUR

The watch commander that night was Sergeant Jack Clemmons. It was not his job to answer the telephone but he just happened to be nearest, and he was later glad he had. It gave him a degree of continuity in the matter from the very beginning.

'Los Angeles Police Station, Sergeant Clemmons,' began the watch commander. It was Dr Ralph Greenson at the other end of the phone. 'Marilyn Monroe is dead from an overdose,' he said. 'What did you say?' responded a shocked Clemmons. Said Greenson, more emphatically, 'Marilyn Monroe is dead. She's committed suicide.' The sergeant said he would be right over, and he left at once. It was not his job to hare out to the scene of a suicide, either, but he thought it wise to make sure the call was not merely a morbid prank. The Police Department suffered from time to time from hoax calls, and if Clemmons had passed on this news to his superiors and it eventually proved to be false, it could have led to a great deal of embarrassment. The night had been extremely quiet, anyway, and he had been fighting off drowsiness. The night air would wake him up.

He arrived at the house to be admitted by Mrs

Dr Ralph Greenson said she had committed suicide, but the evidence pointed in another direction.
Photo Matthew Smith Collection

Sergeant Jack Clemmons was officially the first Police Officer on the scene, but was he really?
Photo Robert F Slatzer Collection

Murray, who introduced herself as the house-keeper, and he was taken to see the body. Clemmons asked her who else was in the house, and the housekeeper told him there was only Dr Ralph Greenson, Marilyn's psychiatrist, and Dr Hyman Engelberg, her physician. Retrospectively, it was when he first saw the body that he knew something was wrong. Her nude body was lying diagonally face down on her bed, her toes to bottom right and her head to top left, with her arms by her sides. She had been covered with a sheet and Clemmons did not subject her to the indignity of stripping this off to look. What he saw was enough, the face said it all, with the wisp of blonde hair showing above the top edge of the sheet. He knew she was dead. Clemmons asked who had discovered the body and when. Mrs

20

Robert Slatzer conducts a rare interview with
Dr Hyman Engelberg.
Photo Robert F Slatzer Collection.

Murray spoke up and said she had found her at about midnight and had telephoned Dr Greenson at once. The sergeant's first reaction was to ask why they had delayed until 4.25 a.m. before notifying the police, but he did not receive a very satisfactory answer. 'Mrs Murray was acting as though she was frightened,' said Clemmons. 'She was solemn and withdrawn. She spoke in hushed tones.' The doctors were having little to say for themselves, but Dr Greenson appeared to have been elected spokesperson and he volunteered that they had to wait for the permission of the publicity people at Twentieth Century Fox before releasing the news. But the doctors knew very well the law relating to informing the police of a coroner's case, and Clemmons was well aware that they knew. He was not impressed.

21

'Dr Engelberg looked depressed; he seemed sad,' said Clemmons. 'His shoulders were drooping and when he spoke he spoke in a low monotone as well. Dr Greenson spoke in a low voice except for a couple of times when I couldn't understand him and I asked him to speak up. But the thing that was peculiar about Greenson's attitude was the look on his face, and the best way I can describe it, it was almost like a leer. He was leering at me, and the tone of his voice sounded sarcastic to me. Now, under the circumstances that simply did not make any sense. And I kept looking at the man and asking myself, 'What is it with this guy, what's bugging him?' ' It would be quite a long time before Clemmons would find answers to his questions.

The Sergeant looked around Marilyn's bedroom and was struck by how tidy it was. People planning to take their own lives are not renowned for their tidiness. Neither, for that matter, do they normally collapse in a tidy straight line on their beds to die. It was becoming more and more curious. He looked over at the bedside table, which she had only recently acquired, on which stood, he said, 'about eight or ten bottles that had contained prescription medicines and [Dr Greenson] waved his hand and said, 'She must have taken all of these,' and he directs my attention to them. So I walked over and the caps were taken off these bottles and . . . were laid down on the table, and I put my head over the bottles and looked straight down into them, and not a single pill or capsule was in any of those bottles. They

22

Posing for the camera? When Sergeant Jack Clemmons was shown round Marilyn's bedroom a drinking glass could nowhere be found. He also thought it peculiar that there were no letters or documents to be seen anywhere. When official photographs were taken later, however, (see above), letters and scripts were strewn around the floor and that could just be a drinking receptacle in view to the extreme right. But who dressed the place up?
Photo Robert F Slatzer Collection

were totally empty . . . 'Boy,' I thought. 'That's a lot of pills.' We looked for a glass. I said, 'What did she use to take these things with . . . Water, she'd have had some water.' And we looked in the bathroom, the adjacent bathroom, we looked all over her bedroom . . . and there was no glass there,' Clemmons said. And though the sergeant immediately thought this odd, he did not realise how extremely significant it was until later when he learnt that Marilyn always needed water with which to take medication.

The doctors and Mrs Murray helped Clemmons to search for a receptacle of some kind — any kind — but they drew a complete blank. Of course the running water in the bathroom might have at least partly solved this particular problem, but the plumbers were working on that and the water was cut off. That was as far as Clemmons' search extended: he was not an investigating officer, the investigations team were on their way. His job was to establish the authenticity of the call he had received and he had done that.

The silence he had encountered from the doctors and Mrs Murray had been deafening. They only spoke when he asked a specific — routine — question and that was unusual for those encountering suicide. People tended to be forthcoming about why they thought such a terrible thing had happened, they expressed concern for others, were anxious, or perhaps guilt-ridden. Not so here. No note had been left. And there was no one to console. Clemmons elicited from Mrs Murray that Marilyn had gone

24

to bed early and she — Mrs Murray — had gone to bed at about ten o'clock. She noticed that Marilyn had taken a telephone on a long lead into her bedroom. This was so that after her calls she could put it outside the door — with a pillow over it — before going to sleep. She had great difficulty sleeping and didn't want a telephone disturbing her once she got off.

The housekeeper said she awoke at about midnight and when she went to the bathroom she saw the light still showing beneath the star's bedroom door and the telephone lead still in place. She said she tried the door but it was locked. She knocked to rouse Marilyn to make sure there was no problem. When she got no

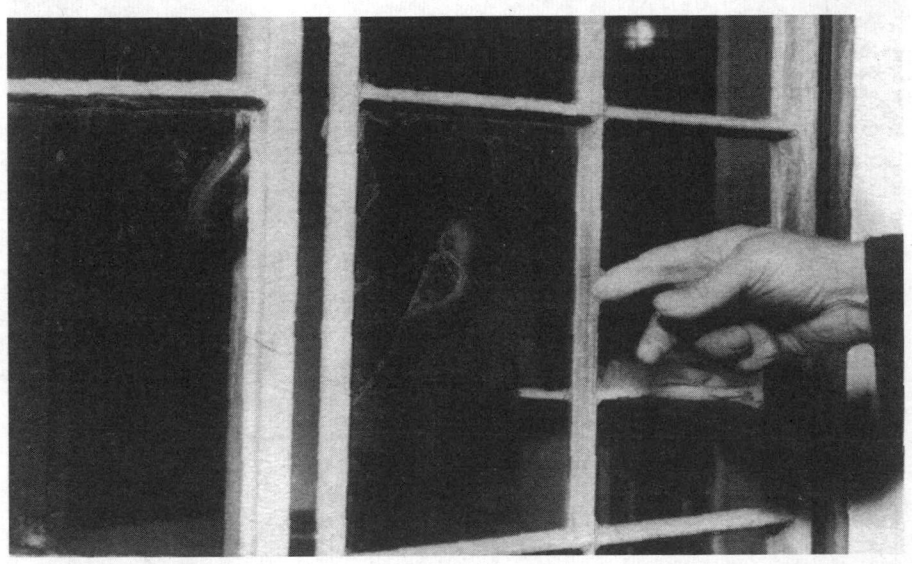

Marilyn's bedroom window. The glass was broken to gain entry it was claimed, but later evidence revealed this was unlikely. Glass lying on the ground outside the window did not support this story, either.
Photo Robert F Slatzer Collection.

answer to her repeated knocking she became alarmed. She then rang Dr Greenson, she said, and he came over quickly. Dr Greenson could not rouse Marilyn, either, and Mrs Murray told of how he then went outside, peered through an opening in the curtains and saw her nude body lying there. Next he smashed a pane of glass in her bedroom window so that he could open it and when he finally entered the room he found Marilyn dead, she said.

Clemmons had radioed for back up while he had driven to Brentwood, and he stayed until his fellow officers arrived. He was uneasy. There was

Marilyn's house pictured while her death was being investigated. When everyone had removed what they wanted, the house was finally sealed. The notice is pinned to the front door.
Photo AP Wide World

more to this than met the eye. He had been somewhat distracted by the sounds in the house: amazingly, sounds of the washing machine running and a vacuum cleaner being used. Odd sounds for that time of night and for that set of circumstances. Mrs Murray explained the need for everything to be tidy before the house was sealed. It appeared she was also loading boxes into the trunk of a car. And he had a feeling that those he had seen and spoken to were not the only ones in the house during the 90 minutes he had spent there. But he had no official justification to search the other rooms.

Sergeant Marvin Iannone, who would later become Beverley Hills Chief of Police, arrived first. His job was to preserve the scene and then go on to assist investigating officer Detective Sergeant Robert E Byron the best way he could. Byron arrived soon afterwards and began taking statements all over again, and later Lieutenant Grover Armstrong would share this task with him. Jack Clemmons would later discover that the story given to Byron and Armstrong was different from that given to him. Mrs Murray, Dr Greenson and Dr Engelberg had reshuffled the timings of events and added further embroidery for the investigating officer. Mrs Murray, for instance, now said she had noticed the light under the bedroom door at 3.30 a.m. and Greenson revised the time he had been called out to this time. This neatly sidestepped the need to explain away the delay of several hours before calling the police. In this embroidered version it was Mrs Murray who had taken a fireside poker outside to push back a curtain through an open window of Marilyn's bedroom to see her lying unclothed on the bed, though Dr Greenson was still credited with breaking a window to gain entry into the bedroom where he announced she was dead.

At this stage it is true that neither Byron nor Armstrong knew anything of the story told to Clemmons, but their perception of what was going on did not appear to be troubled by irregularities. They got no further than a gentle admonishment of Mrs Murray when Byron wrote up in his report:

It is this officer's opinion that Mrs Murray was vague and possibly evasive in answering questions pertaining to the activities of Miss Monroe during this time. It is not known whether this is or is not intentional.

But discrepancies had begun to appear in the statements taken from the doctors, which Byron and Armstrong did not pick up. For instance, Ralph Greenson said that he came straight over when called at 3.30 a.m. and that he called Dr Engelberg after he arrived. Hyman Engelberg asserted that he had dressed, driven to Brentwood, examined the body and signed the death certificate at 3.50 a.m., barely 20 minutes later. Surely this demanded investigation? Also, if 3.50 a.m. was accurate, Dr Engelberg could not have failed to see that rigor mortis had long set in by the time he reached the body. When Guy Hockett from the Coroner's Department took

Marilyn's body away to the mortuary less than two hours later it was so affected by advanced rigor that he had to bend her arms to fit her on the gurney.

Contradictions began to spring up all over the place. Marilyn had had a thick white pile carpet fitted throughout the house and regardless of Mrs Murray's assertion to the contrary, Detective Sergeant Byron did not notice that any light in the bedroom could not have been seen under the door. Another question he might have asked was what necessitated Mrs Murray passing Marilyn's door? The bedroom she occupied had its own en suite bathroom and visiting it would not have taken her past Marilyn's bedroom door. The broken window also raised questions that went unanswered, such as why was so much of the glass *outside* of the window? And why was it so urgent that Mrs Murray got in touch with her son-in-law, Norman Jeffries, to come right over and repair it?

Then later there was the case of the disappearing tablets. Clemmons spoke of all the medication bottles on Marilyn's bedside table being empty, yet when he later read the toxicologist's report he was astounded to see that differing numbers of various pills were checked present in all but two of them. If they were taken out of the bottles before he was called to the house, who had done such a thing? And then who had returned them for submission to the toxicologist? And why?

Detective Sergeant Byron's investigation was superficial at best. He did not seem to notice the irregularities and the discrepancies on display before him. And Robert Byron was not incompetent: Tom Reddin, LA Chief of Police, now retired, who was assistant to Chief Parker in the sixties, told me how highly Byron was thought of by his superiors. But how was it that in his report he wrote, 'My feeling was that . . . it had all been rehearsed beforehand,' and yet he still did not try to get beyond the superficialities? The next question must inevitably be: Was he supposed to notice anything, do anything, or did someone put pressure on him?

4

FEVERISH ACTIVITY

When Sergeant Jack Clemmons got back to his office he rang Jim Dougherty, whom he knew. Dougherty, now a police officer, had been Marilyn's first husband and lived locally. Others, no doubt, would break the news to the other men to whom she had been married: the famed Yankee slugger Joe DiMaggio, and the internationally renowned playwright, Arthur Miller. Robert Slatzer, her long-time friend, to whom she had been married for only a few days before the studio stepped in and had their union quashed, would not be told by anyone: he would learn the news from the radio. Clemmons settled down to deal with the phone calls that came from many parts of the United States and across the world.

The body of Marilyn, removed by Guy Hockett on that Sunday morning, was taken to the silence and solitude of a mortuary slab where it was prepared for an autopsy, but by the time she was placed there, her house had become like Grand Central Station. Milton Rudin, her recently appointed lawyer, was there while the police were busy. Pat Newcomb, her press secretary, said she had heard the news about 4.00 a.m. and had hurried over, and Inez

31

Melson, her business manager, was soon there. Hazel Washington, Marilyn's studio maid, called in to recover a card table and some chairs she had loaned Marilyn. The house was alive with activity.

But it was eventually learned that the house had been even busier during the hours before Clemmons had been called. Arthur Jacobs, Fox's ace publicist, was there, and two other men from the studio's publicity department arrived and began to search her files. They took some documents away with them and destroyed others on the spot. And they were not the only ones determined to get their hands on Marilyn's papers, it seems. In March of that year, barely four months before she died, Marilyn had had a new lock fitted to her filing cabinet because someone had broken into it, and by now the lock had been forced again and various people were rifling it.

Peter Lawford, husband of President Kennedy's sister, Pat, had been a friend of Marilyn for some years. He was in and out of the house during that night, and it emerged that, as a consequence of this, private detective Fred Otash was called by the actor very early in the morning and hired to 'sweep' the place. The key question in this, of course, is 'sweep it of what?' Once again, the most likely answer is documents. Otash said he was told to remove ' . . . anything which would incriminate the President.' When Lawford left he did not by any means leave empty handed, and he was not the only one who helped himself. Fred Otash later said that when his men arrived ' . . . the place was swarming with people. They

Hollywood detective Fred Otash. He was called in to 'sweep' Marilyn's house.

were incapable of sweeping the place or anything.' But however it was achieved, the place was remarkably tidy and orderly by the time Clemmons arrived. I met and talked to Jack Clemmons in Los Angeles some years before his death. He told me there were no letters or documents to be seen: 'The house looked as if it had been cleaned up.'

However, if there were strange goings on in the quiet of the night in the hours before the police were called, they did not cease afterwards. Hazel Washington was heard to say, 'Honey, those agents burnt documents in the fireplace,' and Inez Melson threw the supposed investigation into further disarray when she later told how she found a number of pill bottles at Marilyn's bedside that contained Nembutal and Seconal capsules. She flushed them all away, she said. But Sergeant Clemmons confirmed there were no capsules or pills in any of the bottles on display on Marilyn's bedside table. He was, therefore, dismayed and bewildered by a later report that bottles, part filled with pills, were submitted to the coroner's office. And it was simply not credible that there could still be bottles and pills for Inez Melson to find. So much for the house being sealed, if an investigation was in progress. Alternatively, if the investigation had by then been completed, so much for the investigation.

All the people who were in and out of the house in Fifth Helena Drive that night had an agenda of one sort or another. Those who represented the studio apparently wanted to remove all the records of Marilyn's dealings with them. They wanted her old contracts, for instance, and there were plenty of those. She had made 20 movies with Twentieth Century Fox, and it appeared they wanted to leave behind no trace she had ever been associated with them. Hazel Washington referred to 'agents' burning documents in the fireplace. It would be interesting to know who they represented and what *their* particular agenda was. Everybody was busy.

After Arthur Jacobs and the doctors had left, it appeared lawyer Milton Rudin was in some sort of a command position. Pat Newcomb said it was Rudin who called her with the news about 4.00 a.m. when she dashed straight over to the house. Sergeant Jack Clemmons, who believed he was the first to be told about Marilyn's

34

death — at 4.25 a.m., the official time of the notification of the police department — was later to piece together that the world and his wife knew before he did, and the world and his wife had access to Marilyn's home regardless of any control the police might have claimed to have had.

Away from the chaos which surrounded the death of Marilyn Monroe, the Fox publicity machine announced to the world that Marilyn

The lawn at the back of Marilyn's house after her death. Could the stuffed toy furthest from us be the tiger she received the day she died? (see chapter 17)
Photo Corbis — Bettmann/UPI

was dead and that she had died by her own hand. Her fans, with the rest of the movie world, were stunned. Not everyone believed that this was all there was to it, however, and a few reporters began to dig around. They received no help from the authorities. The police had nothing to add which did not support what had been released, and a shroud of mystery surrounded the passing of the star who had, by all appearances, been on top of the world in the days before she died. The coroner's office would later 'confirm' that she had died from an overdose by her own hand and other than that would say nothing. The lips of all the police officers who were in and out of Marilyn's house were quickly sealed, and reports eventually submitted of the 'official investigation' were of little value in relation to what actually went on in the house at Fifth Helena Drive.

The very day before she died, Saturday 4 August, came under particular scrutiny by those who found the whole thing hard to believe, and those who had been with her or had spoken with her on the telephone that day were grilled for clues. What was her frame of mind? Was she depressed? Did she leave a note? Who was the last person to see her? It was many years afterwards that the staggering fact emerged that the person likely to have been her very last visitor before she died was Attorney General Robert Kennedy, brother of the President.

5

MURDERERS! MURDERERS!

Natalie, the beautiful widow of publicist Arthur Jacobs, recalled the night of Saturday 4 August very well. 'We were at the Hollywood Bowl,' she said. 'It was before we were married. It was a Henry Mancini concert and we had lost ourselves in the music, but a young man on the Bowl staff crept up the aisle and whispered something to Arthur. He left and when he returned he told me I should stay for the rest of the concert but he would have to go. 'Something's happened over at Marilyn's house,' he said. That was about 10.30 p.m., and at that time of night it would not take him above thirty minutes to reach Marilyn's house. I never saw him the next two days.'

She said she thought the call had come from Marilyn's house and that it was Pat Newcomb who had made the call. Natalie also said that Pat later told her she had been the first on the scene. For her part, Pat Newcomb, Marilyn's press secretary and a member of Arthur Jacobs' staff, denied this and stuck to her claim she had not heard the news of Marilyn's death until about 4.00 a.m. on the Sunday morning, when Mickey Rudin, Marilyn's lawyer, telephoned her. She went straight over then, she said.

Before it gets lost in the rush, it should be noted that Pat Newcomb did admit to being in the house before the official report of Marilyn's death to Sergeant Jack Clemmons and the Police Department, and that Milton Rudin was already there, supporting the sergeant's feeling that there were others hiding in the house when he arrived. It is hard to say how many were in — and out — of the house before Marilyn's death was

Arthur Jacobs and his wife, Natalie. Natalie told how Arthur was called to Fifth Helena Drive before Marilyn died. A consummate publicist, he told the world Marilyn had committed suicide.
Photo Matthew Smith Collection.

reported to Clemmons.

But Pat Newcomb's story produces a number of problems unless she had been there when Marilyn died, had gone home and was called at 4.00 a.m. by Mickey Rudin. The trouble stems from the fact she had attended Peter Lawford's dinner party at his beach house on Saturday night, the night Marilyn died. She was seen there by other guests including producer George Durgom, who said she arrived at 9.30 p.m. Before her arrival Lawford had been involved in calling his business associate, Milton Ebbins, for advice on how to handle a possible emergency involving Marilyn that he thought he should do something about. Ebbins contacted Marilyn's lawyer, Milton Rudin, who telephoned Fifth Helena Drive at about 9.00 p.m., to be told by Mrs Murray that all was well. Did this not enter into the conversation with Pat Newcomb when she arrived shortly after? If it did, did Pat not fear for Marilyn's wellbeing?

Did Pat Newcomb not become aware of the 'panic' calls concerning Marilyn made later in the evening by Peter Lawford to Joe and Dolores Naar, who had been his guests and had made for home shortly before 11.00 p.m.? Pat had been in the middle of what has become recognised as a centre of intrigue insofar as there are numerous claims of phone calls and other activities relating to Marilyn Monroe emanating from the Lawfords' beach house that night. Could she have left for home after dinner without becoming conscious of any of it? By midnight, if not before, her host was accompanying Marilyn to hospital in an ambulance. Soon after her death he was organising the 'sweeping' of her house for any connections with the Kennedy brothers. Did all this go on without Pat Newcomb knowing about it?

Sergeant Byron plodded through his questioning, dutifully made notes and submitted a report of sorts on what he found. It stated:

Death was pronounced on 8/5/62 at 3:45 A.M., Possible Accidental, having taken place between the times of 8/4 and 8/5/1962, 3:35 A.M. at residence located at 12305 Fifth Helena Drive, Brentwood, in Rptg. Dist. 814, Report # 62–509 463.

Marilyn Monroe on August 4, 1962 retired to her bedroom at about eight o'clock in the evening; Mrs. Eunice Murray of 933 Ocean Ave., Santa Monica, Calif., 395–7752, CR 61890, noted a light in Miss Monroe's bedroom. Mrs. Murray was not able to arouse Miss Monroe when she went to the door, and when she tried the door again at 3:30 A.M. when she noted the light still on, she found it to be locked. Thereupon Mrs. Murray observed Miss Monroe through the bedroom window and found her lying on her stomach in the bed and the appearance seemed unnatural. Mrs. Murray then called Miss Monroe's psychiatrist, Dr. Ralph R. Greenson of 436 North Roxbury Drive, Beverley Hills, Calif., CR 14050. Upon entering after breaking the bedroom window, he found Miss Monroe possibly dead. Then he telephoned Dr. Hyman Engelberg of 9730 Wilshire Boulevard, also of Beverley Hills, CR 54366, who came over and then pronounced Miss Monroe dead at 3:35 A.M. Miss Monroe was seen by Dr. Greenson on August 4 1962 at 5:15 P.M., at her request, because she was not able to sleep. She was being treated by him for about a year. She was nude when Dr. Greenson found her dead with the telephone receiver in one hand and lying on her stomach. The Police Department was called and when they arrived they found Miss Monroe in the condition described above, except for the telephone, which was removed by Dr. Greenson. There were found to be more than 15 bottles of medication on the night table and some were prescription. A bottle marked 1½ grains Nembutal, prescription #20853 and prescribed by Dr. Engelberg, and referring to this particular bottle, Dr. Engelberg made the statement that he prescribed a refill for this about two days ago and he further stated there probably should have been about 50 capsules at the time this was refilled by the pharmacist.

Going back to the very beginning of this generally unimpressive document, it would seem to me that Detective Sergeant Byron demonstrated remarkable insight into the events on which he was submitting an initial report. For him, without the benefit of an autopsy or a

41

coroner's report, to indicate that this was 'Possible Accidental' was nothing short of remarkable. Here he was, apparently having no doubts he was reporting on a suicide, and expressing that it was a 'Possible Accidental', something which had yet to be deliberated upon by the coroner, with the benefit of the autopsy report and the advice of the LA 'Suicide Team', and then formalised to 'Probable Suicide.' It would be interesting to know what prompted the sergeant to make this note. What could possibly have been in evidence to support it? He gives us no clues. Could he, at the end of the day, merely have been indulging in guesswork?

In Byron's report, Mrs Murray had now revised the time of her discovering the body to 3.30 a.m. when she telephoned Dr Greenson, though not before peering through the bedroom window. Greenson, on his arrival at Fifth Helena Drive, telephoned Engelberg who, they said, went straight over. Sergeant Byron, it seems, did not think it odd that Greenson dressed and drove to Marilyn's house in exactly no time at all, and that Dr Engelberg, even more remarkably, had dressed and driven to the house in time to make an examination and declare her dead at 3.35 a.m.. A follow-up report by Byron contributed little more, although Engelberg now does not arrive until 3.50 a.m., when he declares her dead. It is decidedly odd, however, that an experienced officer can make a report and fail to draw attention to a gap of 25 minutes unaccounted for between 4.00 a.m., when the doctors said they had telephoned the police, and

42

4.25 a.m., the time their call was actually logged. This went completely unchallenged by Byron. It was as though he did not notice it.

Dr. Greenson received a telephone call from Mrs. Eunice Murray who is the reporting person, at 3:30 A.M. on 8/5/62, wherein she stated she was unable to get into Miss Monroe's bedroom, and also that the light was on. He instructed her to pound on the door and look through the bedroom window, after which she should call him again. Mrs. Murray called back at 3:35 A.M. and said that Miss Monroe was lying on the bed with the telephone in her hand, and that she looked strange. Having dressed by this time, Dr. Greenson left his home to go to the residence of the deceased, which is about one mile away. Dr. Greenson also told Mrs. Murray to call Dr. Engelberg.

It was about 3:40 A.M. when Dr. Greenson arrived at the home of the deceased. He broke the window pane and entered the home through the window and then he removed the telephone from the deceased's hand.

Rigor Mortis had set in. Dr. Engelberg arrived at 3:50 A.M. and pronounced Miss Monroe dead. The two doctors, above named, talked for a few minutes. It is the belief of both of them that it was about 4:00 A.M. when Dr. Engelberg telephoned the Police Department.

A check with the Complaint Board and

WLA Desk indicates that the telephone call was received by the Police Department at 4:25 A.M. Miss Monroe's telephone, which is GR 61890, has been checked and it was found that no toll calls were made during the hours of this occurrence. The telephone number of 742–4830 is being checked at the present time.

In this version Mrs Murray makes two telephone calls to Ralph Greenson, and it is she who calls Engelberg. Dr Greenson arrives but five minutes

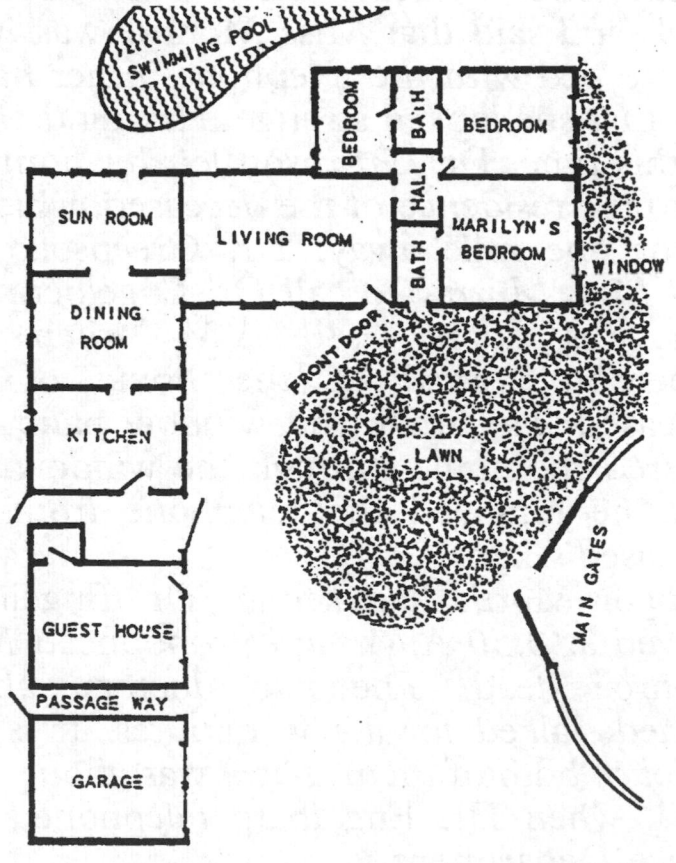

Plan of Marilyn's house.

after Mrs Murray's second call and Dr Engelberg arrived ten minutes after that. All this, timewise, even in the still of night, is fairly remarkable. Even allowing for their revisions in the timing of events as quoted to Sergeant Jack Clemmons, when there was a gap of several hours totally unaccounted for, this new version still left a gap of 35 minutes between the signing of the death certificate and the point where the police were called. In the supplementary report Byron does not think it necessary to indicate that he now revises the time Marilyn was declared dead by Dr Engelberg and that his first report was in error. Taken together, Byron's reports were loose and inaccurate versions of events and could have been of little worth. It also appeared that if any superior officer read them he did not deem it necessary or desirable to challenge them or take Sergeant Byron to task for his inadequate reporting.

Several people in the cul-de-sac where Marilyn lived said that soon after dawn that Sunday morning a woman ran from the house screaming, 'Murderers! Murderers! Are you satisfied now you've killed her?' This reached the ears of the reporters who began to gather, including the celebrated Florabel Muir, and it was confirmed that it had occurred. Muir set about identifying who the woman had been and was able to eliminate housekeeper Eunice Murray. She then turned her attentions to Pat Newcomb, who had said she did not arrive at the house until after she was called at 4.00 a.m. She speculated Newcomb was kept out of

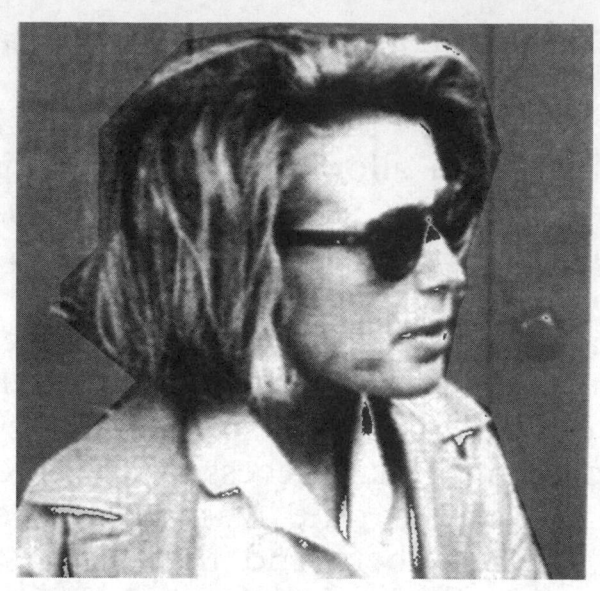

Pat Newcomb, Marilyn's Press Secretary.
Photo Robert F Statzer Collection.

it as long as possible and that when she arrived she identified what she saw as a murder scene. Florabel Muir never did get to the bottom of it and when I broached the subject in an interview with Pat Newcomb there was no comment from the lady. It would be surprising if it were not Pat Newcomb, however. She was reportedly the only woman at the house at that time apart from Mrs Murray. Another report added a tirade, directed at the newspaper people, 'Keep shooting, vultures! You blood-suckers! You vampires! You can't even let her die in peace, can you?' Florabel Muir was, no doubt, interested to learn that Pat Newcomb was quickly fired by Arthur Jacobs, the reason given being her 'dispute' with reporters, when she had become hysterical and had been restrained by a police officer.

In the few, limited, comments she made to the press, Pat Newcomb contributed a little more to our understanding of what happened shortly before Marilyn died. The issue of the *Los Angeles Herald Examiner* dated 15 August 1962 said:

Miss Newcomb attributes at least a part of Marilyn's happiness during the last hours of her life to the fact that 20th Century-Fox appeared ready to resume 'Something's Got To Give' with their star property again in the lead role.

'It pleased Marilyn very much that the picture was going back into production,' Miss Newcomb related. 'And it pleased her to know that when the completed portions of the film were shown to studio executives in New York there was a great deal of excited comment.'

There was, however, a much more basic reason for her happiness. After a seven-year absence, she had returned to California to find there a sense of peace and contentment.

Two days before the above article appeared, another piece in the same newspaper had announced:

Marilyn's personal publicity agent, Pat Newcomb, is out of a job and is reported vacationing in Hyannis Port with Mr and Mrs Peter Lawford at the presidential summer home.

Friends here said she had been fired for

her dispute with the press following the star's death.

The morning Marilyn was found dead . . . Miss Newcomb was reported to have clashed with newspaper photographers for attempting to get pictures at the scene.

NO LONGER EMPLOYED

The Arthur Jacobs Agency, who employed Miss Newcomb for the publicity on Marilyn, would say only: 'She is no longer with the firm.'

Her phone has been disconnected.

In an interview with Arthur Jacobs' widow, she told me Pat was fired following a row with her (Natalie), though, as stated in the newspaper, it tallied with at least one of the outbursts recorded above, if not both. It is also odd timing that Natalie speaks of a row they had at this time, however, since she and her husband had been good friends to Marilyn and greatly supportive to her. It was odd that Pat could both get into a row with her boss's wife *and* lose her job at this juncture, in particular.

It is also extremely interesting that Pat Newcomb instantly flew east to Hyannis Port, or more exactly, to the home of the Kennedys, then is next reported flying off to Europe for a six-month holiday. More interesting still is that when she returned we hear of her being appointed to a government department in Washington. (See documents, on following pages)

APPLICATION FOR FEDERAL EMPLOYMENT

57-10;

DO NOT WRITE IN THIS SPACE

APPLICATION NO.

ANNOUNCEMENT NO.

1. Kind of position applied for, or name of examination

Federal Administrative and
Management Examination

Announcement No.
167

2. Options for which you wish to be considered (If listed in examination announcement)

Information Specialist (Motion Pictures)

3. Primary place(s) of employment applied for (City and State)

Washington, D.C.

4. Name (First, middle, maiden, if any, last)

Margot Patricia Newcomb

5. Address (Number, Street, City, Zone, State)

2920 P Street, N.W.
Washington, D.C.

6. Home phone
452-8901

7. Office phone
DU 3-4160

8. Legal or voting residence (State)
California

9. Height without shoes
5 feet 6 inches

10. Weight
114

11. Sex ☐ Male ☒ Female

12. Marital status ☐ Married ☒ Single (Incl. widowed; divorced)

13. Birthplace (City and State, or foreign country)
Washington, D.C.

14. Birth date (Month, day, year)
July 9, 1930

15. Social Security Number
559 | 45 | 8494

16. If you have ever been employed by the Federal Government, indicate last grade and job titles

GS-13 Information Specialist
(Motion Pictures)

Dates of service in that grade
From May 6, 1963 To Present

DO NOT WRITE IN THIS BLOCK
For Use of
Examining Office Only

☐ Appor. ☐ Nonappor.

Material ☐ Submitted ☐ Returned

Entered Register:

Notations:

App. Reviewed:

App. Approved:

Option	Grade	Earned Rating	Preference	Augm. Rating
			☐ 5 points (Tent.)	
			☐ 10 points Comp. Dis.	
			☐ Other 10 Point	
			☐ Disab.	
			☐ Being Investi- gated	

Initials and date

17. AVAILABILITY INFORMATION

A. Lowest grade or pay you will accept URGENT

For or grade

B. Will you accept temporary appointment? (Acceptance or refusal of temporary employment will not affect your consideration for other appointments.) ☒ Yes ☐ No If "Yes," indicate by "X" in appropriate box or boxes.

☐ 1 mo. or less ☐ 1 to 4 months ☐ 4 to 12 months

C. Will you accept less than full-time employment (less than 40 hours per week)? ☐ Yes ☒ No

D. Are you willing to travel? ☐ Not at all ☐ Occasionally ☒ Frequently

E. Will you accept employment in Washington, D.C.? ☒ Yes ☐ No Outside U.S.? ☐ Yes ☒ No

F. Will you accept appointment only in certain locations? ☒ Yes ☐ No If "Yes," list locations: Washington, D.C. ... City

18. ACTIVE MILITARY SERVICE AND VETERAN PREFERENCE

A. List Dates, Branch, and Serial or Service Number of All Active Service

From	To	Branch of Service
NONE		

B. Have you ever been discharged from the armed forces under other than honorable conditions? ☐ Yes (Give details in Item 39) ☐ No

C. Do you claim 5-point preference based on wartime military service? ☐ Yes ☐ No

D. Do you claim 5-point preference based on service during peacetime campaign? ☐ Yes (Complete and attach Standard Form 15) ☐ No

E. Do you claim 10-point preference? ☐ Yes ☐ No If "Yes," check type of preference claimed and complete and attach Standard Form 15, "Veterans Preference Claim" TYPE: ☐ Compensable disability ☐ Disability ☐ Wife ☐ Widow ☐ Mother

THIS SPACE FOR USE OF APPOINTING OFFICER ONLY

The information given in answer to Question 18 has been verified with the discharge certificate and/or other proof which shows that the separation was under honorable conditions.

VETERAN PREFERENCE ALLOWED: ☐ 5-point ☐ 10-point Comp. Disab. ☐ Other 10-point ☐ None

Signature and title | Agency | Date

Application from Pat Newcomb for a government post which she took up soon after her return from a world tour. (This and next page.) Before she left for Europe she was a guest at the Kennedy compound at Hyannis Port.

20. SPECIAL QUALIFICATIONS AND SKILLS

A. Kind of License or Certificate (For example, pilot, teacher, registered nurse, lawyer, radio operator, C.P.A., etc.)	B. State or other licensing authority	C. Year of first license or certificate	D. Year of latest license or certificate

E. Special skills you possess and machines and equipment you can use. (For example, short wave radio, teletext, comptometer, key punch, turret lathe, transcribing machine, scientific or professional devices)

F. Approximate number of words per minute
Typing	Shorthand

G. Special qualifications not covered in application. (For example, your most important publications (do not submit copies unless requested); your patents or inventions; public speaking and publications experience; membership in professional or scientific societies, etc.; and honors and fellowships received.)

21. EDUCATION

A. Place "X" in column indicating highest grade completed

1	2	3	4	5	6	7	8	9	10	11	12
											X

B. If you graduated from high school, give date

June, 1948

C. Name and location of last high school attended

Immaculate Heart
Hollywood, California

D. Name and location of college, or university	Dates attended		Years completed	Credit hours			Degree received	Year received
	From	To	Day	Night	Semester	Quarter		
Mills College	1948	1952	4				BA	1952

E. Chief undergraduate college subjects	Semester Hours Credit	Quarter Hours Credit	F. Chief graduate college subjects	Semester Hours Credit	Quarter Hours Credit
Psychology major					
History &					
Government					
Liberal Arts Course					

G. State major field of study at highest level of college work

Psychology

H. Other schools or training (for example, trade, vocational, Armed Forces, or business). Give for each the name and location of school, dates attended, subjects studied, certificates, and any other pertinent data.

22. FOREIGN TRAVEL

Have you lived or traveled in any foreign countries?

☒ Yes ☐ No

If "Yes," give in Item 39 names of countries, dates and length of time spent there and reason or purpose (military service, business, education, or vacation).

23. FOREIGN LANGUAGES

Enter foreign language and indicate your knowledge of each by placing "X" in proper column	Reading			Speaking			Understanding			Writing		
	Exc.	Good	Fair	Exc.	Good	Fair	Exc.	Good	Fair	Exc.	Good	Fair
French			X			X			X			X

24. REFERENCES

List three persons living in the United States or territories of the United States who are NOT RELATED TO YOU AND WHO HAVE DEFINITE KNOWLEDGE of your qualifications and fitness for the position for which you are applying. Do not repeat names of supervisors listed under Item 19.

FULL NAME	PRESENT BUSINESS OR HOME ADDRESS (Number, Street, City, Zone, and State)	BUSINESS OR OCCUPATION
David O. Selznick	1400 Tower Grove Rd. Beverly Hills, California	Producer
Lois Weber	Allan-Weber Co. NYC	Public Relations Exec.
Mr. & Mrs. Peter Lawford	625 Ocean Front Santa Monica, California	Actor
George Stevens, Jr.	1330 New Hampshire Ave. N.W.	Director, IMS

50

6

AMBULANCES, MOTIVES AND HUSH MONEY

Rumours circulated that an ambulance had been called to Marilyn's house and that she was rushed off to hospital in the small hours of 5 August. A claim that an ambulance had been called first surfaced in 1982, when Ken Hunter, who worked for a big company owned by Walter Schaefer, said he had driven over to Fifth Helena Drive only to find Marilyn was already dead. He named his partner as Murray Liebowitz, who roundly denied he was ever there. Walt Schaefer himself, after denying he had sent an ambulance during all the intervening years, finally admitted in 1985 the story was true and that Liebowitz, had, in fact, been with Hunter.

Schaefer went further. He said Marilyn was still alive when Hunter and Liebowitz arrived, and she was rushed to Santa Monica Hospital. He did not know, he said, how her body had been returned to Fifth Helena Drive, though it is not surprising if he did not want to advertise he had transported a corpse in one of his ambulances. The ambulance business was very competitive and such a revelation would not have helped business at all. When asked why he

Walt Schaefer, proprietor of an ambulance fleet admitted eventually his company answered a call from Fifth Helena Drive to take Marilyn to hospital.
Photo Robert F Slatzer Collection

had kept silent for so long, Schaefer gave an explosive reply. He said that 80 per cent of his work came from city and county establishments *and since the Kennedys were involved* his business could have been ruined if he had spoken up. It is interesting, to say the least, that Schaefer was so well informed on the Marilyn-Kennedy relationship, and also that he considered the Kennedys would be embarrassed by the fact that an ambulance was introduced to the scenario.

Another ambulance story was publicised some time after the Schaefer admission. It came from a man named James Hall, who claimed he worked as a driver for Schaefer, and that he drove the ambulance to Fifth Helena Drive, with Liebowitz as his partner. Hall told of arriving at about 3.30 a.m. on the Sunday morning, and finding Marilyn in the guest-room bed. Pat Newcomb was there and was in a hysterical state, he said. She screamed, 'She's dead! She's dead!' he claimed, and got in the way while he worked. He adjudged he should carry out a CPR (cardiopulmonary resuscitation), and in order to do it he found it necessary to lift Marilyn down on the floor, since the pressure applied would otherwise be offset by the softness of the bed. He said that he and Liebowitz accidentally dropped Marilyn in the process of putting her on the floor, and this caused a bruise to her hip (which was the one, he claimed, later observed by the autopsist). Hall maintained this was evidence that Marilyn was still alive at that point because dead bodies don't bruise.

Hall claimed that mouth-to-mouth resuscitation that he was administering was working and she was responding. Before he went any further, however, his work was halted by the arrival of a man claiming to be Marilyn's doctor, so he stood back. The doctor, said Hall, could not revive Marilyn and immediately produced a hypodermic from his bag, which was already fitted with a long needle. Pushing her breast to one side, he administered an injection, though the needle stopped when, presumably, it hit a rib. The doctor pushed, Hall said, and something snapped. One minute later Marilyn was dead, he said. Hall went on to explain that he believed for a long time that he had witnessed Marilyn being given an adrenalin injection. By the time he was telling his story, however, Hall was saying he believed he had actually seen the star murdered, and the doctor was the murderer. He identified Dr Ralph Greenson as the man who had killed Marilyn.

Marilyn had died shortly after 3.30 a.m., Hall said, which, if true, threw all accounts and timing previously reported into confusion, but the highly coloured account rendered by Hall promptly crumbled when faced with all the known facts. First of all, Marilyn's body could not have reached the extreme state of rigor by 5.30 a.m., when Guy Hockett, the coroner's man, collected it, if she had died at 3.30 a.m.. He estimated she had died six hours before the time he took her away. Hall's account would render Hyman Engelberg guilty of complicity to murder, also, since he had signed a certificate of her death at 3.50 a.m. and must have been there all the time. Similarly, Mrs Murray and Peter Lawford — who Hall said was also present — were both party to the monstrous deed.

Ralph Greenson was one of America's leading psychiatrists and it is nonsensical to think of him charging in and murdering Marilyn. Why would he do such a thing? What would be his motive? He lost a great deal rather than gained by her death. After all, she was his most famous patient. Any kind of involvement in her death would have ruined him completely, let alone exposure to a charge of murder. Dr Greenson was known to be a man of considerable integrity and he would have had to have taken leave of his senses before playing the role ascribed to him by Hall. And there was no evidence from any quarter that this was the case. As it would later prove, his reputation suffered as a consequence of Marilyn being labelled a suicide. There is no worse failure for a psychiatrist than to have a patient commit suicide.

Similarly, Engelberg was a prominent physician known for his ability and with an unblemished reputation. It would have been hard even to have imagined him watching someone kill Marilyn or, for that matter, hiding in another room while Marilyn was fighting for her life. Hall really got his wires crossed. Ralph Greenson, although qualified as a physician, practised only as a psychiatrist and it was as a psychiatrist he treated Marilyn. It was for this reason Marilyn needed Dr Engelberg. It was a nonsense to think of Greenson acting the part of a physician and dramatically producing a hypodermic, especially with Engelberg in the house. Similarly, Engelberg would not have dreamed of intruding into the realms of psychiatric treatment for his patient.

Hall must also have known that doctors do not normally walk around with hypodermics fitted with needles in their bags. Quite apart from it being quite dangerous and unhygienic, the needle was also subject to damage in that state. Such a suggestion was somewhat ludicrous. The needle as described by Hall would have been quite long — long enough to transmit the adrenalin straight to the heart. No: the doctors were maligned in this unthinkable invention.

During my investigations into the death of Marilyn I interviewed Dr Thomas Noguchi, who had conducted the autopsy on Marilyn's body. I specifically asked him whether there was any damage to a rib that would have lent a degree of credence to Hall's story (the snapping sound he said he heard when the needle was driven in). Dr Noguchi told me there was no sign of an injection having been given, and that as part of the autopsy he had removed the rib cage. He had found no damage to the ribs, and he assured me he would have seen any break or damage that might have existed. When I spoke at length with John Miner, who had been Deputy District Attorney when Marilyn died, he gave me the same answer. John Miner had studied medicine before taking up law and he was present as the DA's representative throughout the autopsy.

James Hall's story does not stand up to any kind of scrutiny. In view of everything I have learned about the period immediately before and after Marilyn's death, it appears to me to be extremely inventive. No doubt at the time he spoke about these things he attracted a certain amount of attention. Perhaps that is what he craved. When Schaefer was asked about Hall he said Hall had never worked for him. This proved, in fact, to be untrue, but the fact Hall had worked for the company went nowhere to supporting his mischievous claims. As we will see a little later, as events were clarified and a more realistic time scale emerged, Hall's story was shown over and over again to be absurd.

Somewhat remarkably, the District Attorney of Los Angeles County, conducting a further 'threshold' enquiry into Marilyn's death in 1982, appeared to consider Hall's story in a degree of depth, but not Hunter's. He did not admit any reference to the ambulance as evidence. He treated it as no more than rumour, and the incredible implications of an ambulance being there, and the claim that the star was then alive, were lost.

In fact, the DA only had to ask Marilyn's neighbours to have the presence of the ambulance confirmed. They told those who did ask they had seen it. Looking for a reason for this laxity, it would appear that the politics of Marilyn's death were still fully active even 20 years after she had died. It seems the implications would have had profound consequences even then. Not least would have been that the authorities had conducted a sloppy and superficial investigation at the time of Marilyn's death, as we have already found grounds for asserting, and that the scandal of a cover up was waiting to be unearthed.

The driver — Ken Hunter — whose story of taking an ambulance to Marilyn's home did stand up, nonetheless denied ever taking Marilyn to hospital. Walt Schaefer was speaking three years after Hunter's admission when he confirmed the dash to Santa Monica Hospital, and the question raised by Hunter's denial may not take a deal of answering. Schaefer was the boss and he, therefore, was not answerable to anyone else in the company for what he said. This was not so in Hunter's case, and we have already drawn attention to the competitiveness that existed in the ambulance business. If Hunter admitted he had raced across to the hospital and it was too late by the time he arrived it did nothing for his reputation, neither for that of the company. Also, it seems that Hunter could have been leaned on to turn round and take Marilyn's body back to her home, and it was strictly a no-no for an ambulance to be used as a hearse. As long as Hunter maintained he had not taken her to hospital in the first place, the question of driving her body back home did not arise. But Schaefer knew better, even though he would not admit — even in 1985 — that his ambulance had transported the body back to her home. Presumably he could not quite stomach that. So far, but not that far.

We can be satisfied that Schaefer's ambulance was sent for and that Marilyn was rushed off to hospital. Looking at the time scale of events as suggested by the phone call to the Hollywood Bowl which sent Arthur Jacobs haring across to Marilyn's home, Marilyn had been discovered in distress by 10.30 p.m. on the Saturday night. With this in mind, we can say that Dr Engelberg dropped something of a bombshell when *he* eventually spoke of the timings of things. Through the period of the enquiries surrounding Marilyn's death he had left Dr Greenson to make statements on behalf of both of them, but later, in a little-publicised comment, he spoke up. He said the alarm was raised at about 'eleven to twelve' which would fit Natalie Jacobs' Hollywood Bowl recollections with a degree of accuracy, and introduced a whole new ball game.

Leaving aside the fluctuating times quoted by Mrs Murray, a more realistic version of events is now possible. It is likely someone at Marilyn's house called Dr Engelberg at about 11.00 p.m. and he was out. The ambulance was called and probably arrived between midnight and 1.00 a.m. Ken Hunter spoke of the 'early morning hours' and mentioned 'about one-thirty a.m.', but this may well have been the time he was leaving. Marilyn's neighbours, Abe Landau and his wife, said they saw an ambulance there at 1.00 a.m. They said also that there was a police car there and several other cars with the ambulance. Ken Hunter at first spoke of seeing the police arrive before he left Fifth Helena Drive, though he later denied this. We can be sure that the police presence at the house at about 1.00 a.m. was totally unknown to Sergeant Jack Clemmons, who heard nothing from the house for more than three hours after this time. But it gives us an enormous clue to what really happened.

Ken Hunter dropped out of making any further comments on what had happened. Murray Liebowitz would not admit to being there at all, and staunchly continued to deny any knowledge of the ambulance at Fifth Helena Drive, but a possible explanation for his denials is in the offing. James Hall, whose testimony we have dismissed, volunteered he was listening to a chat show on radio when one of Schaefer's staff rang in and was talking about Liebowitz. He told how Liebowitz drove him around as many as six car washes, and when asked why, Liebowitz said to him, 'I'll not tell you what happened to Marilyn that night, but I will tell you that after the funeral I came into a large sum of what you would call hush money. I own the car washes.'

He bought them, he told the caller, with the money he was paid to keep him quiet. 'The only reason I'm still working at Schaefers' is to keep up appearances,' the caller said Liebowitz told him. If this is true one has to wonder if this was the case with others. Hush money appeared to be spread around liberally, in fact. Immediately after the enquiry into Marilyn's death Mrs Murray, for instance, quit her apartment leaving no forwarding address, and made off to Europe for a holiday, following it with two further holidays in Europe during the sixties. Once her story had 'settled down' she repeated it consistently and on the few occasions when she blew the gaff it appeared they were instances of her being caught out telling the truth rather than volunteering it. Many years afterwards, the ex-wife of Dr Engelberg asserted he had banked money in Switzerland after Marilyn's death.

The sequence of events involving the ambulance appeared to be that Marilyn was discovered between 10.00 p.m. and 11.00 p.m. comatose but not sleeping naturally. She could not be roused. Dr Engelberg was telephoned but was not at home. Arthur Jacobs was called and he came straight to the house, and it is likely Dr Greenson was sought at this time though he had taken his wife out for dinner. Sometime between midnight and 1.00 a.m. an ambulance was called and Marilyn was driven post-haste to Santa Monica Hospital. If this is so, in the light of what we know it would seem reasonable to assume that Marilyn died on the way. If they had reached the hospital by this time they would not be anxious to have her admitted and, thereby, lose control over what was happening. There is also the point that a hospital may not have been enamoured of the idea of admitting a corpse. It would seem that she was then taken back home to become engulfed in the lies and deceptions that have prevented us knowing the truth for all this time.

The tailpiece to this chapter comes from no less a key player in the mystery than Mrs Murray. She had been interviewed by the BBC in 1985 for a programme on Marilyn's death made by noted researcher and author, Anthony Summers, and had said all the usual things to camera. After the recording had been completed, however, Mrs Murray confessed to the crew, among other things, that, in fact, an ambulance and 'a doctor' did arrive at the house while Marilyn was still alive. Just one of her little slips.

7

THE AUTOPSY

The autopsy on Marilyn Monroe's body was carried out on Sunday 5 August by Dr Thomas Noguchi. Noguchi was a junior member of the coroner's team, but exceptionally well qualified. In a book he wrote in 1983,[1] Noguchi made an enlightening statement. He said, 'A more senior medical examiner would normally have performed the autopsy. And yet Dr Curphey [the Coroner] had made a unique call early on a Sunday morning assigning me to the job.'

Noguchi pondered this. His first reaction was, 'I felt sure that this autopsy was going to present a very special scientific problem . . . ' But after further consideration, he changed his mind. 'A routine suicide, I thought. But why, then, had Dr Curphey assigned me to it? Perhaps because the autopsy wouldn't match the facts in the investigator's report.' Was Dr Noguchi suggesting Curphey had assigned him the job because he would be the easiest member of his staff to 'control' if the facts flew in the face of the suggestion of suicide? Said Noguchi, ' . . . I realised what an awesome responsibility was

---

[1] Thomas T Noguchi MD with Joseph DiMona, *Coroner*, Simon & Schuster New York 1983

ahead of me. I knew that everyone in the world would demand to know what had happened to the beloved Marilyn Monroe. With this responsibility in mind, I began my examination by searching painstakingly with a handheld magnifying glass for any needle marks which would indicate that drugs had been injected. And I looked as well for any indication of physical violence. I found no needle marks . . . ' A small inexplicable bruise was found on her hip, but this appeared insignificant. It was the kind of bruise caused by bumping into furniture, Noguchi said, and he did not relate it in any way to her death.

John Miner, who was Deputy District Attorney and who had founded and headed the Medical-Legal Section that specialised in the investigation and prosecution of crimes presenting complex medical problems, was present throughout the autopsy. He told me, 'I went to as many autopsies as my schedule permitted, amounting to several thousand over the years. Forensic pathology asks the body to tell everything it can about what caused its death: how it died, was it murdered? To get answers involves surgery, microscopic examinations and the laboratory sciences . . . The process begins and ends with the pathologist who is the autopsy surgeon. I shared the work of examining every inch of Marilyn Monroe's skin with a magnifying glass looking for any traces of needle injections. There was none.'

Dr Noguchi then took smears from her genitals, anus, rectum and mouth, which, under

Dr Thomas Noguchi conducted the autopsy on Marilyn, but the specimens disappeared and he was unable to complete his work.
This could not have been an accident.
Photo Judith Gordon

microscopic examination, would disclose if there had been any sexual activity. At the outset these proved negative. He then began dissection of the body, and the autopsy itself revealed no apparent cause of death. The next step would be a laboratory analysis of the specimens removed from the body, which included organs, brain, blood, urine, smears of genital, anal and oral areas, and stomach contents. This is where bells began to ring.

The initial examination of the stomach

contents revealed nothing. There was no sign of drugs or alcohol there, or the tell-tale gelatine, which would have indicated drug capsules having been ingested. The duodenum revealed nothing, and an examination of the kidneys, which were clear of barbiturates, tended to support that the stomach had been by-passed in the administration of the drugs. Neither had Noguchi found any sign of the yellow stain usually left behind by the gelatine in the gullet. It was the toxicologist who produced the answer. Marilyn's death was caused by a massive amount of a barbiturate, Nembutal, often prescribed for nervous disorders and sleeplessness. This was shown in the analysis of her blood and in her liver. A volume of chloral hydrate — used in 'Mickey Finns' — was also detected, and though this was not a fatal dose, it may have proved a distinct pointer to the way she died.

Even though the coroner, Dr Theodore Curphey, had found no sign of drugs or gelatine capsules in the deceased's stomach, he said ' . . . it is my conclusion that the death of Marilyn Monroe was caused by a self-administered overdose of sedative drugs and that the mode of death is probable suicide.' In a press conference he spoke of Marilyn taking the capsules ' . . . in one gulp, within — let's say — a period of seconds.' Marilyn was said to have taken something like 47 Nembutal capsules plus a whole lot more containing chloral hydrate. The adding of the word *probable* to the suicide verdict was interesting. It mercifully softened the harsh term, permitting that 'accidental suicide'

Coronor Theodore J Curphey.
Probable suicide was his opinion.

may have taken place, though this was equally unsupported by what Dr Noguchi had found. Adding the word 'probable', however, had the effect of getting Twentieth Century Fox off the hook with their insurance claim which ran to millions of dollars at a time when they were financially very fragile. It might also be said that Fox were taken out of the equation in circumstances where they might have challenged a straight suicide verdict.

Returning to the autopsy, Dr Noguchi had the job of finding out how the fatal volume of barbiturates had been administered. As has been said, the empty stomach revealed she had not swallowed the large number of capsules which would have been necessary for a volume of 4.5

milligrams per cent to have been present in her blood, regardless of what the coroner would say. Neither would the 13 milligrams per cent of pentobarbital — which also translates into barbiturates — be explained this way. Interestingly, the possibility of the stomach being empty because a stomach pump was used in an unsuccessful attempt to revive her was also ruled out by the fact the drugs had not reached the duodenum. Administration by injection had been impossible, not just because of the absence of needle marks, but because the amount of the drugs found in the liver did not admit to a power-packed lethal injection, which would have killed her instantly, long before any liver metabolism could have taken place. Marilyn had died slowly, the drugs being absorbed into her system over a period of time.

The toxicologist's report was received by Dr Noguchi some hours after he had finished the rest of the autopsy. In his book he says, ' . . . as I read it a warning signal immediately sounded in my mind . . . In addition [to the liver and specimens of blood] I had forwarded other organs, including, most importantly, the stomach and its contents, and the intestine for 'further toxicological study'. Now I instantly noted that the lab technicians had not tested the other organs I had sent them. They had examined only the blood and the liver . . . Raymond J Abernathy [the head toxicologist] apparently felt there was no need to test any further.

'Still, I should have insisted that all the organs, including the contents of the stomach and segments of the intestine, be analysed. But I didn't follow through as I should have. As a junior member of the staff, I didn't feel I could challenge the department heads on procedures, and the evidence [presence of barbiturates and chloral hydrate in blood and liver, in relation to an empty Nembutal bottle, and partly empty chloral hydrate bottle, had been reported] had persuaded me as well as the toxicologists that Marilyn Monroe had ingested a sufficient amount of drugs to cause death.' And all of this smacked of a rash statement made to gloss over obvious irregularities. But there is more to come. Dr Noguchi wanted to return to the specimens he had preserved for further examination *but they had disappeared*. The stomach contents, the organ samples and the smear material had all vanished. Microscopic examinations could not now be undertaken and, for instance, it became impossible to tell whether an abortion had recently been carried out. Abernathy said, 'I'm sorry, but I disposed of them because we had closed the case.' In all the thousands of autopsies John Miner had observed over the years he never encountered another instance of this happening. Retired Chief of Police Tom Reddin, who was assistant to Chief Parker when Marilyn died, commented that to destroy such evidence was against the law.

There is, in all this, a distinct hint that the junior of the coroner's team had been selected to carry out this autopsy because foul play was suspected — or even known to be the case — and he was the member of the team the others involved could walk all over to limit the autopsy and contribute to a cover up. Did Noguchi realise this? Was this the reason he drew attention to his junior status in the book he wrote? Whatever the case, there is nothing to detract from Noguchi's honesty and integrity. He was the fall guy in the autopsy scenario.

John Miner was left to consider how the drugs could have been administered if Marilyn had not swallowed them and if an injection was not possible. There was only one other route, and he at first thought of suppositories. This was quite impossible, however, because of the large volume of barbiturates involved. The clear memory of seeing the sigmoid colon coloured purple had stuck in his mind. When he had seen it during the autopsy he had asked Dr Noguchi to take an anal smear but this had not been carried out. In all his experience he had not seen a colon coloured purple before. Had the drugs been introduced by suppository they would not have got far enough to cause discoloration of the colon. 'Any discoloration and irritation would then have been confined to the rectum,' he told me.

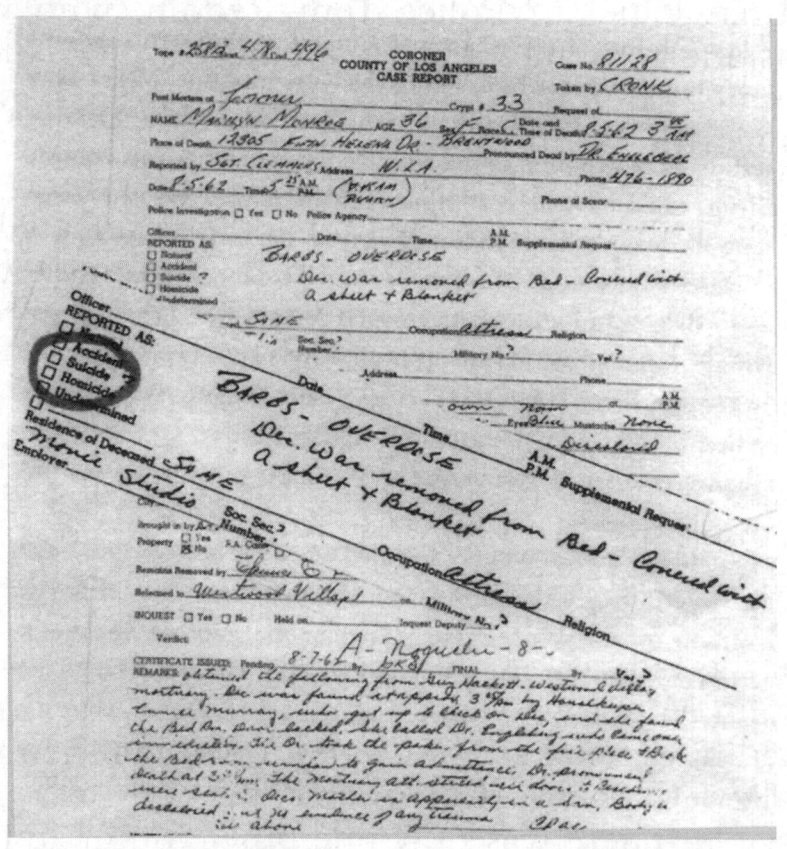

Note the question mark against suicide.

John Miner decided to consult two eminent pathologists on the question of the purple colon. He sent copies of the Monroe autopsy file to Dr Milton Halpern, the City of New York's Chief Medical Officer, and Dr Leopold Breitnecker, one of Europe's foremost pathologists. He received the same opinion from both. They said the purplish hue of the colon was a manifestation of an inflammatory response to barbiturates in the large intestine. Miner now had the answer. The drugs had been absorbed through the large intestine — not explored in the autopsy. The only way this volume of drugs could have been administered, therefore, was by enema. Nembutal was available in liquid form in the early sixties and, in any case, Nembutal powder derived from capsules readily dissolved in water. Added to this, he later learned that all the enema equipment was on hand in Marilyn's bathroom, since she — in common with other stars — took enemas regularly as part of her health and beauty treatment. She has much to say about this in the secret tapes she made for her psychiatrist, which we feature later in this book.

John Miner's work was not finished when the autopsy was over. Theodore Curphey, the coroner, asked him to interview Dr Ralph Greenson on the Wednesday following the autopsy, no doubt because of his qualifications and background. Miner informed the coroner he counted Ralph Greenson among his friends, but the coroner still insisted he do the interview. Ralph Greenson was distressed, Miner said, and they spent four hours in conversation. In spite of

71

STATEMENT BY THEODORE J. CURPHEY, M.D.
CHIEF MEDICAL EXAMINER-CORONER
COUNTY OF LOS ANGELES

Now that the final toxicological report and that of the psychiatric consultants have been received and considered, it is my conclusion that the death of Marilyn Monroe was caused by a self-administered overdose of sedative drugs and that the mode of death is probable suicide.

The final toxicological report reveals that the barbiturate, previously reported as a lethal dose, has been positively identified as nembutal by the toxicologist.

In the course of completing his routine examination, the toxicologist, Mr. Raymond Abernethy, discovered in addition to the nembutal present a large dose of chloral hydrate.

Following is the summary report by the Psychiatric Investigative Team which has assisted me in collecting information in this case. This team was headed by Robert Litman, M.D., Norman Farberow, Ph.D., and Norman Tabachnick, M.D.:

"Marilyn Monroe died on the night of August 4th or the early morning of August 5, 1962. Examination by the toxicology laboratory indicates that death was due to a self-administered overdose of sedative drugs. We have been asked, as consultants, to examine the life situation of the deceased and to give an opinion regarding the intent of Miss Monroe when she ingested the sedative drugs which caused her death. From the data obtained, the following points are the most important and relevant:

"Miss Monroe had suffered from psychiatric disturbance for a long time. She experienced severe fears and frequent depressions. Mood changes were abrupt and unpredictable. Among symptoms of disorganization, sleep disturbance was prominent, for which she had been taking sedative drugs for many years. She was thus familiar with and experienced in the use of sedative drugs and well aware of their dangers.

"Recently, one of the main objectives of her psychiatric treatment had been the reduction of her intake of drugs. This has been partially successful during the last two months. She was reported to be following doctor's orders in her use of the drugs; and the amount of drugs found in her home at the time of her death was not unusual.

"In our investigation, we have learned that Miss Monroe had often expressed wishes to give up, to withdraw, and even to die. On more than one occasion in the past, when disappointed and depressed, she had made a suicide attempt using sedative drugs. On these occasions, she had called for help and had been rescued.

"From the information collected about the events of the evening of August 4th, it is our opinion that the same pattern was repeated except for the rescue. It has been our practice with similar information collected in other cases in the past to recommend a certification for such deaths as probable suicide.

"Additional clues for suicide provided by the physical evidence are: (1) the high level of barbiturates and chloral hydrate in the blood which, with other evidence from the autopsy, indicates the probable ingestion of a large amount of the drugs within a short period of time; (2) the completely empty bottle of nembutal, the prescription for which was filled the day before the ingestion of the drugs; and (3) the locked door which was unusual.

"On the basis of all the information obtained it is our opinion that the case is a probable suicide."

A statement from the coroner.

what he had previously stated, he now confessed he was convinced Marilyn had not committed suicide. John Miner wrote a memorandum to the coroner, with a copy to the district attorney, telling him this, but it made no difference. Curphey declared Marilyn a suicide in the face of evidence given by Noguchi that she could not have died from gulping down more than 40 barbiturate capsules, plus a large quantity of chloral hydrate capsules ' . . . in one gulp . . . in a period of seconds', and in the face of a specific professional opinion which he had sought himself from Greenson and now chose to disregard. It was fairly clear that Curphey wanted support for his suicide verdict and thought Dr Greenson was the man who would give it. When this proved not to be the case he was not interested in what Dr Greenson had to say.

And then the Miner memorandum disappeared without trace. Both copies.

OFFICE OF COUNTY CORONER

File # 81128

Date Aug. 5, 1962   Time 10:30 a.m.

I performed an autopsy on the body of   MARILYN MONROE

at the Los Angeles County Coroner's Mortuary, Hall of Justice, Los Angeles,

and from the anatomic findings and pertinent history I ascribe the death to:

ACUTE BARBITURATE POISONING

DUE TO   INGESTION OF OVERDOSE

(final 8/27/62)

ANATOMICAL SUMMARY

EXTERNAL EXAMINATION:

1. Lavidity of face and chest with
   slight ecchymosis of the left side
   of the back and left hip.
2. Surgical scar, right upper quadrant
   of the abdomen.
3. Suprapubic surgical scar.

RESPIRATORY SYSTEM:

1. Pulmonary congestion and minimal
   edema.

LIVER AND BILIARY SYSTEM:

1. Surgical absence of gallbladder.
2. Acute passive congestion of liver.

UROGENITAL SYSTEM:

1. Congestion of kidneys.

DIGESTIVE SYSTEM:

1. Marked congestion of stomach with
   petechial mucosal hemorrhage.

The six page Autopsy Report.
(This and the next five pages).

2. Absence of appendix.

3. Congestion and purplish discoloration
    of the colon.

EXTERNAL EXAMINATION:

The unembalmed body is that of a 36-year-old
well-developed, well-nourished Caucasian
female weighing 117 pounds and measuring
65½ inches in length. The scalp is covered
with bleached blond hair. The eyes are
blue. The fixed lividity is noted in the
face, neck, chest, upper portions of arms
and the right side of the abdomen. The
faint lividity which disappears upon pressure
is noted in the back and posterior aspect
of the arms and legs. A slight ecchymotic
area is noted in the left hip and left side
of lower back. The breast shows no significant lesion. There is a horizontal 3-inch
long surgical scar in the right upper
quadrant of the abdomen. A suprapubic
surgical scar measuring 5 inches in length
is noted.

The conjunctivae are markedly congested;
however, no ecchymosis or petechiae are
noted. The nose shows no evidence of
fracture. The external auditory canals
are not remarkable. No evidence of trauma
is noted in the scalp, forehead, cheeks,
lips or chin. The neck shows no evidence
of trauma. Examination of the hands and
nails shows no defects. The lower extremities show no evidence of trauma.

BODY CAVITY:

The usual Y-shaped incision is made to
open the thoracic and abdominal cavities
The pleural and abdominal cavities contain

no excess of fluid or blood. The mediastinum
shows no shifting or widening. The diaphragm
is within normal limits. The lower edge
of the liver is within the costal margin.
The organs are in normal position and
relationship.

CARDIOVASCULAR SYSTEM:

The heart weighs 300 grams. The pericardial
cavity contains no excess of fluid. The
epicardium and pericardium are smooth and
glistening. The left ventricular wall
measures 1.1 cm. and the right 0.2 cm.
The papillary muscles are not hypertrophic.
The chordae tendineae are not thickened or
shortened. The valves have the usual number
of leaflets which are thin and pliable.
The tricuspid valve measures 10 cm., the
pulmonary valve 6.5 cm., mitral valve 9.5
cm. and aortic valve 7 cm. in circumference.
There is no septal defect. The foramen
ovale is closed.

The coronary arteries arise from their usual
location and are distributed in normal
fashion. Multiple sections of the anterior
descending branch of the left coronary artery
with a 5 mm. interval demonstrate a patent
lumen throughout. The circumflex branch
and the right coronary artery also demonstrate
a patent lumen. The pulmonary artery contains
no thrombus.

The aorta has a bright yellow smooth intima.

RESPIRATORY SYSTEM:

The right lung weighs 465 grams and the left
420 grams. Both lungs are moderately congested
with some edema. The surface is dark red
with mottling. The posterior portion of the
lungs shows severe congestion. The tracheo-
bronchial tree contains no aspirated material
or blood. Multiple sections of the lungs

show congestion and edematous fluid exuding
from the cut surface. No consolidation or
suppuration is noted. The mucosa of the
larynx is grayish white.

LIVER AND BILIARY SYSTEM:

The liver weighs 1890 grams. The surface
is dark brown and smooth. There are marked
adhesions through the omentum and abdominal
wall in the lower portion of the liver as
the gallbladder has been removed. The
common duct is widely patent. No calculus
or obstructive material is found. Multiple
sections of the liver show slight accentuation
of the lobular pattern; however, no hemorrhage
or tumor is found.

HEMIC AND LYMPHATIC SYSTEM:

The spleen weighs 190 grams. The surface
is dark red and smooth. Section shows dark
red homogeneous firm cut surface. The
malpighian bodies are not clearly identified.
There is no evidence of lymphadenopathy.
The bone marrow is dark red in color.

ENDOCRINE SYSTEM:

The adrenal glands have the usual architec-
tural cortex and medulla. The thyroid glands
are of normal size, color and consistency.

URINARY SYSTEM:

The kidneys together weigh 350 grams. Their
capsules can be stripped without difficulty.
Dissection shows a moderately congested
parenchyma. The cortical surface is smooth.
The pelves and ureters are not dilated or
stenosed. The urinary bladder contains
approximately 150 cc. of clear straw-colored
fluid. The mucosa is not altered.

GENITAL SYSTEM:

The external genitalia shows no gross
abnormality. Distribution of the pubic
hair is of female pattern. The uterus
is of the usual size. Multiple sections
of the uterus show the usual thickness of
the uterine wall without tumor nodules.
The endometrium is grayish yellow, measuring
up to 0.2 cm in thickness. No polyp or
tumor is found. The cervix is clear,
showing no nabothian cysts. The tubes are
intact. The openings of the fimbria are
patent. The right ovary demonstrates
recent corpus luteum haemorrhagicum. The
left ovary shows corpora lutea and albicantia.
A vaginal smear is taken.

DIGESTIVE SYSTEM:

The esophagus has a longitudinal folding
mucosa. The stomach is almost completely
empty. The contents is brownish mucoid
fluid. The volume is estimated to be no
more than 20 cc. No residue of the pills
is noted. A smear made from the gastric
contents and examined under the polarized
microscope shows no refractile crystals.
The mucosa shows marked congestion and
submucosal petechial hemorrhage diffusely.
The duodenum shows no ulcer. The contents
of the duodenum is also examined under
polarized microscope and shows no refractile
crystals. The remainder of the small
intestine shows no gross abnormality. The
appendix is absent. The colon shows
marked congestion and purplish discoloration.
The fecal contents is light brown and formed.
The mucosa shows no discoloration.

The pancreas has a tan lobular architecture.
Multiple sections shows a patent duct.

SKELETOMUSCULAR SYSTEM:

The clavicle, ribs, vertebrae and pelvic
bones show no fracture lines. All bones
of the extremities are examined by palpation
showing no evidence of fracture.

HEAD AND CENTRAL NERVOUS SYSTEM:

The brain weighs 1440 grams. Upon reflection
of the scalp there is no evidence of contusion
or hemorrhage. The temporal muscles are
intact. Upon removal of the dura mater the
cerebrospinal fluid is clear. The superficial vessels are slightly congested. The
convolutions of the brain are not flattened.
The contour of the brain is not distorted.
No blood is found in the epidural, subdural
or subarachnoid spaces. Multiple sections
of the brain show the usual symmetrical
ventricles and basal ganglia. Examination
of the cerebellum and brain stem shows no
gross abnormality. Following removal of
the dura mater from the base of the skull
and calvarium no skull fracture is demonstrated.

Liver temperature taken at 10:30 a. m.
registered 89° F.

SPECIMEN:

Unembalmed blood is taken for alcohol and
barbiturate examination. Liver, kidney,
stomach and contents, urine and intestine
are saved for further toxicological study.
A vaginal smear is made.

T. NOGUCHI, M. D.
DEPUTY MEDICAL EXAMINER

TN:ag:G

8

The Miner Memorandum

It was some considerable time before John Miner realised that his memorandum had 'gone missing'. At first it appeared the recipients were simply ignoring it, but then he became aware that both of the copies he sent, one to the coroner and one to the district attorney, were not where they should have been.

Miner had been sent to interview Dr Ralph Greenson at his home because Greenson's word on Marilyn's death was second only in importance to that of Dr Noguchi, the autopsist. Greenson was extremely close to Marilyn and privy to her innermost secrets and private thoughts. There is no doubt that the coroner, Dr Curphey, would strengthen his hand immeasurably by obtaining the support Greenson — and only Greenson — could give him in making a case for suicide. Dr Greenson had already voiced an opinion of suicide when Marilyn had been found dead on Sunday 5 August.

It was three days later, on Wednesday 8 August, when, by appointment, John Miner visited him to obtain a statement. Ralph Greenson had never stopped thinking about events since they had happened. No doubt he appreciated that it was John Miner who had been asked to interview him, for he knew Miner, and the respect John Miner had for him was reciprocated. Here was a man he could be comfortable with as he laid his soul bare. Miner was a man who had a background of medical knowledge and an understanding of what psychiatry was all about, and even more than that, he was a man Greenson could trust implicitly.

They talked for four hours. It was clear from the beginning that Dr Greenson was under great stress. His worry showed and he was glad to unburden himself to John Miner. He had now had ample time to reflect, and he told Miner he was certain Marilyn Monroe did not take her own life. Not only that but, while he did not offer an opinion on the possibility of her death being due to an accident, John Miner drew the conclusion that this could also be ruled out.

I talked to John Miner twice in Los Angeles for lengthy periods, and I have had much discussion with him by telephone and correspondence. He had kept a copy of the memorandum sent to the coroner and district attorney, but finding it after forty years proved to be too difficult. Moving from one house to another had finally seen it consigned to that corner — a cupboard, attic, or file — which collects all the documents we wish to retrieve. I asked him if he could reconstruct it for me and he offered to do his best. Here, to the best of his knowledge and belief, is what the memorandum contained:

To: Theodore J Curphey, MD,
Chief Medical Examiner, Coroner of Los
Angeles County, Hall of Justice,
Los Angeles, CA 90012

After I attended her autopsy, you asked me
to interview Marilyn Monroe's Psychiatrist,
Ralph Greenson, MD on the suicide issue.

Dr Greenson granted the interview on
condition that I would not ever reveal what
was said or heard during the interview, but I
could make known whatever conclusion I
reached on the suicide question.

Dr Greenson said, 'Marilyn Monroe did not
commit suicide. However, my opinion is
subject to bias, because a patient's suicide is
a catastrophe for her psychiatrist, so I will
let her own voice on a tape she recorded for
me at her home help you. It is a stream of
consciousness of her thoughts which she
was unable to say in her office sessions.'

Ted, what she said on her tapes rules out
any possibility that Marilyn Monroe either
deliberately or accidentally killed herself.
She did _not_ commit suicide.

Dated 8/8/62   John W Miner,
                Deputy District Attorney,
                Head, Medical Legal Section,
                Liaison Officer to the Coroner.

John Miner was faithful to his word never to reveal what was said and what he had heard at that meeting with Greenson until, many years after Greenson's death in 1979, Greenson's integrity came under attack, especially by James Hall, who, as we recounted in an earlier chapter, accused Greenson of murder. Miner was aware that the doctor's widow, Hildi, was distressed by what was being said, and he approached her to ask for release from his promise to her husband, so that he could draw on what he knew in the doctor's defence. She agreed, and he at first publicised only those segments which would defend Greenson's character. For instance, no-one in his right mind would, in the face of a suicide verdict, argue the case *against* suicide if he had carried out a murder. He would have had

John Miner pictured with singer Dinah Shore in 1962. Photo Matthew Smith Collection.

only to remain silent and there would be no case to answer, regardless of tittle-tattle.

John Miner has never revealed the contents of the tapes he heard, of which he had a transcript, until he gave the transcript to me for publication in this book. He had reached the conclusion it might take everything on the tapes to be known to confirm that Marilyn should not be given a place in the history of Hollywood bearing the stigma of suicide. The contents of the tapes are revealing in many respects. I have not revealed those highly intimate sequences which were clearly for her doctor's ears only, although I should point out that the tapes were not made by arrangement with Dr Greenson as part of her therapy: it was Marilyn's novel idea that she might achieve greater freedom speaking to her analyst by means of tapes made in privacy. I may say that the sequences from the transcript which I do not reveal would do no more than illustrate that the doctor's techniques were producing results.

The contents of the Miner memorandum indicate that a cover up, which we shall describe in the next chapter, did take place. In the face of what the memorandum told him, the coroner should have instantly ordered an inquest into Marilyn's death when there would at least have been a chance that all would have been revealed. But it was clear there was no intention of letting the truth of Marilyn's death come out.

9

The Media Machine

Newspapers, magazines, radio and television across the world were hungry for news about Marilyn's death. It would not be enough to make a bald announcement; the public wanted to know the details of what had happened to her; they wanted to know when, where and exactly how she had died. This was a story that would grow rather than diminish, with the autopsy, the coroner's report and the police report punctuating the developing story.

Arthur Jacobs was the man who would feed the stories to the world. Arthur, who ran his own business — the Arthur P Jacobs Company — had been signed as media consultant to Marilyn by Twentieth Century Fox, and had a powerful organisation operating out of Los Angeles and New York. Pat Newcomb worked for Arthur but was attached, mainly, to Marilyn. Marilyn had been big business for Arthur Jacobs. The requests for interviews and articles had come in steadily, and alongside them requests for Marilyn to make appearances at charity functions, award ceremonies, and the like. Pat Newcomb had been kept very busy.

Arthur Jacobs came from a wealthy family and was educated at the University of Southern

California, graduating in business studies. He served in the Second World War, and returned to Los Angeles with two special friends. The three had become runners — the lowest of the low — at the Warner Brothers Studio, and all three had managed to get fired on the same day. One of his friends was Dick Carroll, who did well in the haberdashery business in Los Angeles. The other, Harry Lewis, became famous for his Hamburger Hamlets all over the area. Arthur found his niche in the publicity business.

Apjac, as he was called, became a weaver of other people's dreams. It mattered nothing if his clients were ordinary, unexciting people. It was his job to make them appear exciting, to give them backgrounds for which they could only have wished, to bestow upon them glamour, mystery, fascination, as the case demanded. Hollywood was the town of make believe, and Arthur Jacobs was an image creator. His clients would eventually include, among others, Marlene Dietrich and Grace Kelly.

If Hollywood was a dream factory then the Arthur P Jacobs Company was a dream factory within a dream factory. His own marriage might have come straight out of the pages of a romantic storybook. One day on the set of *Monte Carlo Story*, which was starring Marlene Dietrich, he met a young actress, Natalie Trundy, and fell in love with her. Only fourteen at the time, however, Natalie was a bit young for a grown-up romance, so Arthur said to her, 'I'm going to marry you when you grow up.' And he did. They became engaged during the summer of 1962, and Arthur was with Natalie the night the crisis over Marilyn blew up.

They were listening to the music of Henry Mancini at the Hollywood Bowl when the phone call came through saying there was a problem with Marilyn. Arthur had had plans for that evening. Sipping champagne while they listened to Mancini, he had booked a table for a party to follow the Mancini concert at Chasen's, the premier restaurant in Los Angeles. The call left him no choice, however. He went to Marilyn's house immediately and, as far as we can construct, found her in a comatose condition. She was not dead, and Arthur may, at that time, have been putting together stories in his mind to explain a sudden unaccountable illness or another of her 'cry for help' overdoses. But she could not be roused and nothing her doctors could do was of any help, so it became necessary to call an ambulance. This was not the kind of action publicists took lightly. When Marilyn was rushed off to hospital, any story Arthur might have concocted was, no doubt, by then needing revision. But the revision that became necessary in the end was not the one he would expect — or welcome.

When Marilyn was brought back to her house dead, a problem of enormous proportions launched itself on the group of people who were present at the house. Apart from Arthur, the group included Peter Lawford, who likely accompanied her in the hospital dash, her doctors Ralph Greenson and Hyman Engelberg, and housekeeper Eunice Murray. It would have been Peter Lawford who expressed the concerns that would shortly engulf the small group. There were two facts that had to be reconciled. The first of these was that they had carried out all the usual procedures and had not been able to resuscitate Marilyn. It was unlikely, therefore, that she had died of an overdose. It is not unlikely that Eunice Murray contributed that she had had a late visitor, after which she had not been able to rouse her. In these circumstances there was only one conclusion to be drawn: she had been murdered.

The second fact to be taken into account was that the Attorney General had been in the house only a few hours before, and they had had a furious row. If fact one and fact two were taken together, it would appear at first sight that Robert Kennedy had been responsible for her death, and since Lawford had been with Robert Kennedy when she had, virtually, thrown them out, he knew the Attorney General was not involved in any way with her death. It was a nightmare situation for Robert Kennedy. Simply being involved in a murder investigation of any kind would create a situation in which he would be expected to resign. Assuming his innocence, involvement in an investigation into the death of Marilyn Monroe, when news of his relationship with her would be bound to leak, would undoubtedly spell the end of his career, and bring calls for the resignation of his brother, the President.

Knowing that Chief of Police William Parker was a friend of Robert Kennedy, it is almost certain he was the first person called in to help sort out the mess. Milton Rudin, Marilyn's lawyer, was also quickly brought into the discussions, probably in order to prevent him blundering in with questions that would blow the gaff. It was most likely Parker who realised the murder

Chief of Los Angeles Police Department, William Parker. Photo Matthew Smith Collection.

of Marilyn, in the circumstances described to him, pointed to a conspiracy on the part of the Kennedys' enemies to achieve exactly what at first sight appeared to have been achieved: the involvement of Robert Kennedy in a murder investigation which, by itself, would require him to resign and ultimately bring about the resignation of President Kennedy. Parker could control his police officers and the coroner's office as well, but this by itself would not prevent the news of Marilyn's death raising doubts in the minds of millions of fans who would want to know the details of how she died. He could also not prevent an army of investigators, amateur and professional, from invading Los Angeles determined to get to the bottom of the perceived mystery.

Arthur Jacobs was the consummate public relations man. He knew exactly how to feed into the hungry media machine the stories about Marilyn that would spike the guns of the curious. So effective was his operation that, combined with the full-scale cover up organised by Police Chief William Parker, the position of the Kennedys was well and truly protected and the activities of the seekers of the truth were staved off for more than 20 years. Even then it would be a very long time before the world became aware of the real background to the death of the star.

As part of her job Pat Newcomb was heavily involved in 'placing' stories about Marilyn at this time. On the face of it, this work was little different from that which she had carried out when Marilyn was alive. Pat was an astute and able member of Jacobs' staff, with all the skills of the 'spin doctor'. She had been responsible for reading the correspondence from those who wanted articles on Marilyn for publication, or who wanted to come and interview her. She knew how to present Marilyn in the best possible light, hiding her indiscretions and hyping up her achievements. But what she was doing now must have seemed hollow. Selling the story of Marilyn's death may have involved going through the same motions and might have required the same talents, but it was not the same. It would never be the same.

Arthur Jacobs' office, normally a hive of activity, quickly became a hive of quite extraordinary activity. He had soon transferred the planning of this manipulation of the world's media from Fifth Helena Drive to his office, and, as time went on, some of the details of what went on began to surface. Rupert Allan spoke of the operation as ' . . . carefully done and beautifully executed'. Photographer Lawrence Schiller was in Jacobs' office for some reason and remembers hearing Arthur discussing with Pat Newcomb 'what the telephone logs would reveal'. Natalie spoke of Arthur 'fudging the whole thing'.

Someone who represented the Kennedy family attended one meeting, and it may be conjectured that funds were made available through him to seal the lips of those whose silence was required in order to allow the media control and the ground-level cover up to succeed. By all appearances this was an important 'third dimension' to the plan. Allegations of 'hush money' being offered and other indications of 'sweeteners' are not hard to find.

Arthur Jacobs, no doubt, pleased a lot of people in his successful manipulation of the world's media in relation to Marilyn's death and the rescue of the Kennedy brothers. It may have been no coincidence that Twentieth Century Fox launched him as a producer. He was very successful, producing the film that had originally been planned for Marilyn, *What a Way to Go*, the Rex Harrison musical fantasy, *Doctor Doolittle*, and a remake of *Goodbye Mr Chips*. His most lucrative features, however, were *Planet of the Apes* and the sequels that followed. Natalie played in each of his movies except for *What a Way to Go*.

As for Pat Newcomb, after Arthur fired her, she quickly left for the Kennedy compound at Hyannis Port and then went on a world tour. Six months later she became an employee of the United States government in Washington. Much later she returned to Los Angeles and her old profession in public relations. She is still in practice, and has represented many top Hollywood stars.

10

BLANKET OF SECRECY

There is little doubt that the police knew about Marilyn's death long before Sergeant Jack Clemmons was called at 4.25 a.m. on Sunday 5 August. As we said earlier, ambulance driver Ken Hunter mentioned the presence of the police at the time he was at Marilyn's house before he declined to say any more about his activities there, and Marilyn's neighbours also saw police cars in the cul-de-sac at the same time they witnessed the ambulance being there. But without any of this we can deduce the early role Los Angeles Police Department played in the drama of Marilyn's death by what immediately happened.

It would seem it had been decided, with police approval, that any suggestion of foul play would be totally disregarded, as far as public pronouncements would be concerned. The conference of sorts, to discuss how to handle the public announcement of Marilyn's death, and to which the police were party, was held immediately after she died. Michael Selsman, a member of Arthur Jacobs' staff who was present at Jacobs' strategy meetings, told us of another important participant in the cover up planning. It is his recollection that they were instructed by the FBI or the State Department — he didn't recall which — not to mention the Kennedys in any context, whatever they did. It appears government departments in Washington were well informed on what had been going on in Los Angeles.

The small group discussing the situation with Arthur Jacobs lost no time in deciding that, in order to protect the integrity of the President and the Attorney General, Robert F Kennedy, who was too close to the death scene that night for comfort, any consideration of murder would be ruled out altogether. Plans were laid for the media campaign and, in the meantime, it was over to the Police Department and William Parker. The token investigation conducted by Sergeant Robert Byron bore witness to Parker's influence. The uncertain, changeable evidence of the principals questioned at Marilyn's house during that night was also an indication that 'something had been arranged', and the hidden evidence relating to the belated ambulance dash to the Santa Monica Hospital was another clear indication. The signs began to appear everywhere. Marilyn's 'toll charge' records for the telephone calls she had made were confiscated, apparently by FBI agents, and quickly passed on to Police Chief William Parker, no less.

Tom Reddin, William Parker's assistant, now retired, told me that, in fact, a great deal of secret investigation into Marilyn's death took place, as was evidenced by a bulky file which he knew to exist. We now know that the enquiry was carried out by John Dickie at the behest of Chief

Deputy District Attorney Manley J Bowler. The file included details of an interview with Robert Kennedy, but none of this was ever released. The file disappeared, a slim 'public' file taking its place, Tom Reddin said. It is rumoured the bulky file was taken by Chief Parker, personally, on a trip he took to Washington DC, and it was never brought back.

William Parker was highly thought of as Chief of Police. He was a decisive character who wielded great power over those under his control. What he said went, as far as his officers were concerned, and what he said was to be relied upon, as far as the public was concerned. But why would he involve himself in a cover up which, if it backfired, was sure to wreck his career? I can see two possible reasons for his actions. First, it would seem he saw a clear indication that there was a plot afoot to involve Robert Kennedy in a scandal that would sink without trace the integrity and careers of the Attorney General and his brother, the President. It would seem he was totally satisfied Robert Kennedy was not in any way involved with Marilyn's demise, and his defence for his high-handed — indeed unlawful — actions would likely be that justice, as he saw it, demanded Robert Kennedy and the President be protected from such an infamous conspiracy. Tom Reddin, who knew his boss as few others would, speaks extremely highly of him. It would appear, therefore, that if he had not been convinced of the innocence of the Kennedys he would in no way have involved himself in such an enormous deception. Neither would he have put his career on the line.

The other reason I offer, notwithstanding what has just been said, is that William Parker was an extremely ambitious man. His chief aim was to become the ultimate police chief. He had already been honoured by the country's top lawman, Robert Kennedy himself. Tom Reddin described the occasion to me. 'There he was in a room full of chiefs of police being addressed by the Attorney General. Kennedy indicated Chief Parker saying, 'And here is the finest of them all sitting in the front row,' or something to that

Tom Reddin was Police Chief William Parker's
assistant and eventually became
LAPD Chief himself.
Photo Matthew Smith Collection.

effect. Parker would have killed to get attention like that. Despite the attention he had already been given, here was the chief law enforcement officer of the United States saying that he was the best police chief in the country or in history, or whatever the grand terms were. This would indicate to me,' said Tom Reddin, not without tact, 'that he might be prone to do something that might be of assistance to the Kennedy family. Parker loved being close to those in power, and he was rumoured for some years as a possible successor to J Edgar Hoover. He loved national attention and it makes one wonder could he, perhaps, have the motivation or the inclination to get rid of that report [on Marilyn's death].' It was Sergeant Jack Clemmons, when I talked to him, who told me there was only one man who had the power and authority — the clout — to carry out such a cover up: Chief Parker. 'No one would dare challenge his orders, such was the authority he commanded,' he said.

Key publicist Arthur Jacobs was early on the scene at Marilyn's house, we know; Peter Lawford, brother-in-law of the Attorney General, seemed never to be far away. There has always been speculation, strongly denied that Pat Newcomb was soon there as well, and Milton Rudin arrived at an undisclosed time which could have been very soon after Marilyn's death. To these may be added the two doctors, who fell in with the plans. Appropriately, these five or six people represent the core of the silence that surrounded the event. Arthur Jacobs did not even discuss these matters with Natalie, his wife-to-be; Lawford had so much to say about it which was contradictory and unreliable that, effectively, he said nothing; Milton Rudin was the only person I can remember who hung up on me when I tried to question him on the telephone about Marilyn's death, and Pat Newcomb went one better; I had travelled thousands of miles to be able to speak to her personally, but when we met she, also, stonewalled. She said nothing.

Whether one or more of the cars seen outside Marilyn's house at the time the ambulance was there belonged to the police we do not know, though witnesses assumed they did. On reflection it would seem entirely possible the Chief would turn up personally in such circumstances. It was hardly something he would delegate to another or risk dealing with on the telephone. It is known that Chief Parker received a call at his home Saturday night before 11.30 p.m., re-routed through the police switchboard, and it would, therefore, not be unreasonable to believe that he met with those who were at Marilyn's house that night to agree a rigid story which would suit his purposes. He allowed himself plenty of time for this, a meeting with his own staff was not called until 7.00 a.m.

Others were soon drawn into the ring of silence, of course. The ambulance drivers, Hunter and Liebowitz, to begin with; Sergeant Marvin Iannone, who is now Chief of Beverley Hills Police Department, who agreed to talk to me when I made a transatlantic call to him, only to refuse any discussion about Marilyn when I was actually seated opposite him; and Sergeant Robert Byron, who, though now retired, still will not talk to me about his experiences. He has tried to tell me he can't even remember being there. Researcher Anthony Summers did a little better than I did. Interestingly, speaking of those who were questioned at Marilyn's house, Byron told him, 'There was a lot more they could have told us ... but we did not do what we'd normally do, and drag them into the station.' Housekeeper, Mrs Eunice Murray, may be added to the list of the silent, forming a distinct pattern, and it was not long before the coroner, Theodore Curphey, joined them.

The first — in fact the only one — to break ranks was Dr Ralph Greenson. Greenson was clearly party to what had been agreed, for it was he who reported Marilyn had committed suicide, but it appears he quickly thought better of his involvement in a cover up, and by the time he was interviewed by Deputy District Attorney John Miner, made it clear he did not believe it true that she had killed herself, or that she had accidentally killed herself. It has to be noted, however, that he did not *say* he believed she had been murdered, though there would seem to be no other alternative. But he did not come straight out and shatter any agreement for a cover up which had been reached at the house at the time of Marilyn's death. Time would prove it would have made no difference if he had, for Miner's memo disappeared, and no word of Greenson's withdrawal from supporting suicide was leaked to the press.

Even though Marilyn had gone through the motions of suicide more than once before, a number of journalists were reluctant to accept she had overdosed. The earlier instances had been recognised as the classic 'call for help', her attempts always being at times and in circumstances where she would be 'discovered' and 'saved'. And Marilyn's friends knew she was both knowledgeable and adept when it came to the management of drugs, the mixing of them and the estimation of drug toleration. It was no secret that Marilyn was on a high and doing well at the time she was supposed to have killed herself. And some of the most persistent of the journalists were very experienced at winkling out stories. One of these was Florabel Muir, crime reporter for the Hearst Corporation, who had tried to identify the woman who cried, *'Murderers! Murderers!'* outside Marilyn's house in the wee small hours.

Florabel Muir was not slow to realise that the telephone calls made by Marilyn in the period before her death might be revealing. She tried to get these details from the General Telephone Company, but learned that two men in smart suits and polished shoes had taken them, jumping into a car carrying government license plates, according to company employees. It is reasonable to believe they were FBI agents, so Muir was surprised to learn that the telephone details had quickly fallen into the hands of Chief Parker. She knew he had got details of calls Marilyn had made during the six weeks before her death: he boasted of it and waved the sheets in front of her. She wrote in her column, 'Strange pressures are being forced on the Los Angeles Police Department.' Florabel had got the right vibes, but her 'strange pressures' were, it seems, inflicted on the police by the police themselves.

New York's top-ranking celebrity reporter, Dorothy Kilgallen, told her paper that the last man to talk to Marilyn was Robert Kennedy but, at that time, she could not prove it. She wrote a piece going as far as she could without naming the Attorney General, but taking a soft approach which acknowledged Marilyn as a suicide. It was not long after this, however, Kilgallen completely changed her mind about what had happened and decided Marilyn had been murdered.

Parker did not seem to mind talking to reporters about the toll-call sheets in his possession. He told the news editor of United Press International that 'at least six phone calls were made by Marilyn to the Justice Department'. Newscaster George Putnam was also told by the Chief, 'Marilyn was trying to reach Mr Kennedy. She called the Justice Department in Washington, DC — not his private number but through the switchboard. Marilyn tried to reach Bobby Kennedy on eight different occasions the week before she died but was unsuccessful.' William Parker was well aware that he was giving nothing away, since any member of the public has the right to telephone the Justice Department. Also, by openly telling of the attempts Marilyn had made to reach Robert Kennedy he was spiking the guns of those who wanted to read something more into the situation. Researcher Anthony Summers would track down some of the missing toll sheets 20 years after Marilyn's death, but these told him little more than he already knew.

The actions of the coroner, Dr Theodore Curphey, advertised a cover up, since he could not possibly have declared Marilyn a suicide based on Thomas Noguchi's submissions, and in the light of the disappearing body samples and smears. He had, also, received a memo from John Miner telling him that Dr Greenson, who had been the one to tell the police Marilyn had committed suicide, now distinctly said he believed she had *not* committed suicide. For much of the time, the coroner's office was the hub of the cover up.

Curphey asked for the services of a newly instituted organisation which came to be called the Suicide Team. Led by a psychologist, Dr Norman L Farberow, the team included Dr Robert E Litman, a psychiatrist, and Dr Norman Tabachnik. They were to investigate Marilyn's background and circumstances. Their report ran:

Marilyn Monroe died on the night of August 4 or the early morning of August 5, 1962. Examination of the toxicology laboratory indicates that death was due to a self-administered overdose of sedative drugs. We have been asked, as consultants, to examine the life situation of the deceased and give an opinion regarding the intent of Miss Monroe when she ingested the sedative drugs which caused her death. From the data obtained, the following points are the most important and relevant:

Miss Monroe had suffered from psychiatric disturbance for a long time. She experienced several fears and frequent depressions. Mood changes were abrupt and unpredictable. Among symptoms of disorganization, sleeping disturbance was prominent, for which she had been taking sedative drugs for many years. She was thus familiar with and experienced in the use of sedative drugs and well aware of their dangers.

Recently one of the main objectives of her psychiatric treatment had been the reduction of her intake of drugs. This has been partially successful during the last two months. She was reported to be following doctor's orders in her use of the drugs; and the amount of drugs found in her room at the time of her death was not unusual.

In our investigation we have learned that Miss Monroe had expressed wishes to give up, to withdraw, and even to die. On more than one occasion in the past, when disappointed and depressed, she had made a suicide attempt using sedative drugs. On these occasions, she had called for help and had been rescued.

From the information collected about the events of the evening of August 4, it is our opinion that the same pattern was repeated except for the rescue. It has been our *practice with similar information collected in other cases in the past to recommend a certification for such deaths as probable suicide.*

Additional clues for suicide provided by the physical evidence are: (1) the high level of barbiturates and chloral hydrate in the blood which, with other evidence from the autopsy, indicates the probable ingestion of a large amount of the drugs within a short period of time; (2) the completely empty bottle of Nembutal, the prescription for which was filled the day before the ingestion of the drugs; and (3) the locked door which was unusual.

On the basis of all the information obtained it is our opinion that the case is a probable suicide.

Dr Noguchi's findings gave no support whatever that Marilyn died from the *ingestion* of the barbiturates. She most certainly had died from barbiturate poisoning, but he merely reported its presence in her bloodstream and liver and was prevented from finding out how it had got there by the disposal of the samples and smears. From what was reported, medical knowledge would have rejected the possibility that the drugs had been taken orally all at one time. It would appear, therefore, that the Suicide Team acted on the word of the coroner, Dr Curphey, in regard to this assumption. It would hardly be the other way round: Curphey would have corrected such an assertion without hesitation had the Team jumped to an erroneous conclusion of that kind. It is interesting that the Team came up with the *probable* suicide verdict. Did Curphey take it from them, or did they take it from him? The fact the Suicide Team was called in at all in such an 'open and shut' case was perhaps the most remarkable feature of all this, but then the Team's brief concerned finding out *how* the suicide had occurred and *why* the suicide had occurred; it did not include *whether* it had occurred. But there may have been an ulterior motive for its involvement . . .

I am indebted to Thomas Noguchi for pointing out that while, in other cases, ' . . . a suicide panel can help determine the truth and end controversy and confusion,' he goes on ' . . . unfortunately, it would not do so in the Monroe case, and for a special reason. The people questioned by the panel were promised confidentiality in order to encourage them to speak openly of intimate matters. And because of the confidentiality pledge, *Dr Curphey ordered that the reports of interviews and the panel's notes remain closed,* as are all such confidential reports . . . the fact that the interview notes have been kept secret . . . naturally, inspired a charge of an official cover up.' [Author's emphasis.] Curphey had been asked by journalists to say who had made statements so that they might further question those involved. The Coroner had been adamant in his reply: 'We will not expose the names of the people who gave their accounts and reports to us in confidence.' This was an extremely convenient cover for secrecy.

Had there been an inquest the people involved would have been obliged to answer questions without the option and without the protection of anonymity. But there was no inquest on Marilyn's death.

Publicist Arthur Jacobs has been described as the architect of the cover up. It would seem he arrived at the house before Marilyn died and certainly realised what had happened. He was an accomplished, top level 'spin doctor', and his suicide story was swallowed hook, line and sinker across the world at the time. How much he told his wife we do not know. She said, on the one hand, that he did not confide in her, but then, she also said he told her he, ' . . . fudged the whole thing.'

Taken together, the experiences of Sergeant Jack Clemmons, paraded as the first police officer to attend the house after the announcement of 'suicide', the curious response — or lack of response — by the officers designated to investigate the death; the disappearing samples which frustrated a complete autopsy; and the reaction of the coroner's office determined to establish the death as suicide, should alone have been sufficiently convincing that a cover up had been set in motion. Add to that the disappearing telephone toll records; the inches thick file on a secret investigation that suddenly became a slender version; the deeply suspicious silence on the part of those near to Marilyn when she died; the indications of money surfacing among people involved, and collectively it becomes indisputable that a cover up took place.

I believe Peter Lawford was well aware of what had happened to Marilyn and why. He had a great deal to say about her death, all of which supported the suicide theory. His story did not bear out however, as we shall discover, and, with his close ties to the Kennedy family, it is not difficult to see why he was anxious for a verdict of suicide. But mothers know their sons and are often very astute. Lawford's mother, Lady May Lawford, is quoted by Peter Harry Brown and Patte Barham in their book[1] as saying, 'Peter was so enamoured of the Kennedy charisma that if Jack or Bobby asked him to, he would have done anything — legal or illegal'. That, by itself, was quite stunning, but then she added 'So it was with Marilyn's death — he had a major part in the cover up.'

[1] Peter Harry Brown and Patte B Barham, *Marilyn — The Last Take*, Dutton, New York 1992

11

NOT TO BE OPENED

The respective roles played by Thomas Noguchi and John Miner in the unravelling of the cover up surrounding the death of Marilyn Monroe have been critical. Without their contributions we would still be very much in the dark, as the veil of secrecy that surrounded the events at her house in Fifth Helena Drive at Brentwood on the night of 4 August was never intended to be lifted.

Dr Noguchi would not acknowledge any part in piercing the secrets surrounding her death, but he would accept that he is a seeker for the truth, and in the honest manner in which he conducted the autopsy on Marilyn he served us well. In spite of his lack of seniority in the coroner's department, he did not hesitate to make it clear he could not complete his work because the body samples and smears had been disposed of. This would not have made him popular, but he realised he had a duty to speak up. I applaud, also, the honesty expressed in the chapter of his book[1] that dealt with the autopsy, even if, while I accept his findings, I might not agree with all his opinions.

---

[1] Thomas T Noguchi with Joseph Di Mona, *Coroner*, Simon & Schuster, New York 1983

108

Following the autopsy on Marilyn Monroe, Thomas Noguchi became known as the 'Coroner of the Stars', because he went on to perform autopsies on Janis Joplin, Sharon Tate, Natalie Wood, William Holden and John Belushi. Noguchi would also conduct the autopsy on the body of Robert Kennedy after he was gunned down in Los Angeles in 1968.

John Miner studied medicine before he opted to go into law, and after his appointment as a Deputy District Attorney of Los Angeles, founded and headed the Medical-Legal Section which specialised in the investigation and prosecution of crimes presenting complex medical problems. He was designated as liaison

John K Van de Kamp. His investigation didn't even muddy the waters.

to the County's Chief Medical Examiner-Coroner, and it was in this capacity, representing the DA, that he was present throughout the autopsy of Marilyn Monroe. At the time, Dr Noguchi did not grasp the significance of John Miner's attendance, and it was much later he admitted, 'In retrospect, I should have been alerted at once to the fact that this was a 'special case' by the presence of Deputy District Attorney John Miner . . . ' The two men got on well together, each having great respect for the other, and this is still the case today.

For 20 years the official position regarding Marilyn's death remained unchanged, then, in 1982 the impossible happened. The then-district attorney, John K Van de Kamp, under pressure from a group which included Marilyn's long-time friend Robert Slatzer, and Lionel Grandison, who had been an aide to the coroner in 1962, decided a new 'threshold' investigation should be carried out. In the intervening years, interest in how the star had died had increased rather than diminished. Miner and Noguchi, along with Slatzer and Grandison, were among those who would give evidence, and, in addition to evidence from medical experts, new statements would be taken from a variety of other people who were knowledgeable or involved in one respect or another. The investigation — or review — took three and a half months, after which a report was published. It stated:

The purpose of the threshold investigation was to determine if sufficient facts and circumstances exist to warrant the opening of a full criminal investigation as a possible homicide case. There is no Statute of Limitation applicable to Murder under California law . . .

Its findings?

. . . we conclude that there are insufficient facts to warrant opening a criminal investigation into the death of Marilyn Monroe. Although factual discrepancies exist and unanswered questions surfaced in our probe, the cumulative evidence available to us fails to support any theory of criminal conduct relating to her death . . . Documents reviewed included LAPD reports (some of which were reconstructed); Coroner's reports (including toxicological reports); FBI reports (although heavily censored); news reports and other publications.

(Author's emphases.) It would appear from this the investigation heard only what it was permitted to hear from the Police Department and the FBI.

The report on the 1982 investigation repeated the story that Eunice Murray had told the police in 1962, but it is still noted that Dr Hyman Engelberg is recorded as arriving at the scene at 3.50 a.m. on Sunday 5 August. This was accepted by the investigation in spite of the fact that Engelberg is reported to have admitted to a

111

District Attorney's investigator that he was called in between 2.30 a.m. and 3.00 a.m.. The doctor also made this admission on television.

The investigatory body had a new opportunity to question Sergeant Robert Byron about his scant enquiries into the star's death and ask him if there was more to it than had found its way into his two brief reports, which largely paraphrased what Mrs Murray and the doctors had said. The Report, however, merely refers to Byron's investigation in passing. It baldly stated, 'Sgt. Byron conducted the police investigation of the death.' If Byron was questioned at all, there is no mention of it. If he was questioned and had as little to say to the DA's investigator as he had to me, it is small wonder there was nothing to report. But if this was the case it should have merited a doubly underlined note to this effect. If it wasn't, the opportunity for enlightenment had been missed — again.

The report of the investigation soon moved on to a consideration of the autopsy and the conduct of the coroner's office. Dr Boyd G Stephens, Chief Medical Examiner-Coroner of the City and County of San Francisco, endorsed all that had happened in the autopsy and agreed with the findings. He was even permitted to render the opinion that 1982's more advanced, 'state of the art' procedures would probably not change what Dr Noguchi found in 1962. This is strange. Quite apart from the accepted opinion — it is doubtful that opinions lending support to Marilyn Monroe having been murdered would have been treated in the same way — Dr

Noguchi was present at the hearings and it is a pity he was not questioned on this important issue. In fact, when I spoke to Dr Noguchi about the autopsy some years ago, he volunteered quite the opposite of what Stephens had said. He thought newer techniques *would* have revealed more than he had been able to show with 1962 techniques.

Dr Stephens saw nothing amiss in the fact that there was no sign of the drugs or the gelatine capsules in the stomach, stating, 'These substances dissolve rapidly . . . ' Neither did he see anything unusual in the absence of refractible crystals, which Noguchi had noted. He dismissed this as 'not scientifically significant'. This is certainly not the way other distinguished pathologists saw it. Dr Cyril Wecht, Coroner of Allegheny County in Pennsylvania, and a former President of the American Academy of Forensic Sciences, told me, 'It is quite unlikely that these levels [of barbiturates] were attained following a one-time, quick ingestion of all the pills and capsules which would have been required to reach the levels found at autopsy. [This was not challenged by Stephens.] A large amount of barbiturates will *slow* gastric motility; therefore if all the drugs had been ingested at once, there would not have been enough time for her stomach to have emptied almost completely before her death.' [The author has added the emphasis].

In an attempt to dispose of the problem raised by the absence of yellow staining in the stomach and gullet, which was expected to be present if Marilyn had ingested such a large number of Nembutal capsules, the investigators enlisted the

113

help of an unnamed representative of the manufacturers of the capsules, Abbott Laboratories. No doubt to their dismay, however, the representative stated that staining from capsules *should* have been present if a volume of the capsules had been taken orally. But not to be totally defeated, it seems, the investigators grabbed at another statement made by the spokesman to the effect that he was not aware of any studies or scientific papers to support what he said. In fact, this meant precisely nothing. The absence of studies on the subject was meaningless. The implication sought by the investigators was simply not present in the statement.

Still determined to show that the absence of the yellow dye was unimportant, they next quote three autopsy surgeons, including Thomas Noguchi, who said a yellow staining was 'almost unheard of' in Nembutal deaths. Perhaps, the report speculates, the expectation of yellow staining, ' . . . may stem from confusion with the *red* dye trail associated with overdoses of seconal . . .' This flies in the face of the assertions of other experts on the subject. I asked Dr Cyril Wecht about this and he said, 'Pentobarbital [Nembutal] capsules would most likely have produced yellowish streaking in the small intestine in the proximal portion.' Another well-known medical examiner, Dr Sidney B. Weinberg, consulted by Marilyn's long-time friend Robert Slatzer, did not say it was 'almost unheard of' either. He said, 'The capsules usually have some dye in them which stains objects which they come into contact with when moist. This is often seen in the stomach and in cases where large amounts are ingested, there are focal areas of corrosion of the lining of the stomach.'

When it came to the question of whether or not an ambulance was called to Marilyn's home the night she died, the investigators acted very strangely. It appears James Hall, whose claims we discussed in an earlier chapter, offered the investigation his 'evidence' at a price. Later he changed his mind and said it could have it for nothing, but having said he would get in touch, he failed to do so. Instead of finding Hall, the investigators, somewhat remarkably, simply drew upon a newspaper account of what he had said. Not surprisingly, they dismissed his claims, but not before a lengthy consideration of the story. When it came to Ken Hunter's story, however — and it appears in his case the investigators spoke to him — they render only a brief account of what he said. The investigation makes no appraisal of his story, neither expressing an opinion in favour or against. In fact, the context in which it was quoted suggested it was being used to discredit Hall's claims, which, if this is the case, is distinctly odd. Such procedures can hardly be related to the establishment of the truth.

The subject of Chief Parker's seizure of the telephone records was raised. The Report euphemistically referred to this as the toll records being 'secured' by the Police Department, and in this they attempt to dissociate Parker from any personal involvement in the matter. 'There is no evidence that Chief Parker either did or did not ask his investigators to secure the records,' the report of the investigation blithely says. 'There was, however,' the report continues, 'a clear investigative purpose for securing the records. The records were secured approximately 14 or 15 days after the death of Miss Monroe.' If the investigators had been as efficient at locating and considering the published statements made by journalists George Putnam and Florabel Muir, as they had been with that made by James Hall, they would have known exactly what had happened to the toll records. Putnam and Muir were both in conversation with Chief Parker on the subject of the records, the contents of which he made clear he knew. Parker even showed them to Florabel Muir, whose own enquiries revealed they had been 'secured' within a few hours of Marilyn dying.

In an attempt to defuse rumours that the then-senior LAPD official, Ed Davis, made a secret trip to Washington to discuss with Robert Kennedy his relationship with Marilyn Monroe, the investigators made a telephone call to Davis, who, after becoming Chief of Police himself, had by this time become a senator. The telephone call was to ask him about what was being said. 'He flatly denied any such contact,' the report on the investigation said, and went on, 'In the absence of any evidence supporting the allegation concerning Davis' trip, we conclude that it did not occur.' As one might say, a quick phone call settled the whole issue. 'No credible evidence suggesting that another official of LAPD made a trip to Washington in connection with the Marilyn Monroe death surfaced during our enquiry,' the report concluded.

Robert Slatzer asked the investigators what had happened to a 723-page LAPD report that he had been advised contained investigative details on Marilyn's death. The 1982 investigation dismissed this saying, 'No credible evidence suggests such a report ever existed.' I had previously discussed this with Tom Reddin, who was assistant to Chief Parker in 1962, later to become Chief himself, and is now retired. Without specific knowledge, he saw the scenario in which Parker went off to Washington, taking with him the bulky Marilyn file in his briefcase with which to ingratiate himself to Robert Kennedy, as the most likely answer to the question. He said that, of a sudden, the bulky file on Marilyn suddenly became a slim file containing, perhaps, some 50 documents. To add to the interest of Tom Reddin's remarks, he was not commenting on Robert Slatzer's approach to the 1982 investigators. His opinion related to a general question from me on what had happened to the Marilyn data.

It was interesting that the matter of John Miner's missing memos was raised, no doubt by Miner himself. The investigation noted that these conveyed to the coroner and the then-district attorney the information that the outcome of the interview Miner had with Dr Ralph Greenson was that Greenson no longer supported the suicide theory. By this time Greenson was dead and no significance was placed on the doctor's stance. It would appear from the report that no investigation was held to try and establish how both copies of Miner's memo has disappeared, no implications were drawn, and, in fact, the whole episode was barely mentioned.

The matters raised by Lionel Grandison were considered by the DA's investigators. Grandison had been a deputy coroner's aide in 1962, and it is noticed the report makes a point of underlining the lowly status attached to his appointment. There were three issues — or complaints — with which Grandison was involved, all of which were important. First, he claims he was coerced into adding his signature to the death certificate for Marilyn, by the coroner, Theodore Curphey. He initially declined signing because the file was not complete, he said, and it was his job to see that all documents associated with the Coroner's Report were in the 'closing package.'

After outlining Grandison's complaint, the Report breaks off to show his background, which we might be forgiven for concluding was a means of belittling the man's attainments and his overall credentials. It might also have been said to include an attempt at character assassination, in that it drew attention to a brush he once had with the law even though it conceded its seriousness had been reduced to that of 'misdemeanour'. Having gone to all this trouble to discredit the complainant, the Report goes on to say little more than, 'if he hadn't signed the Death Certificate someone else would have,' which does not deal with the matter raised at all satisfactorily.

The second issue was one relating to bruising

and red marks Grandison claimed to have seen behind Marilyn's legs. There was no support for this claim whatever, though this did not, of course, negate his first complaint relating to the Death Certificate.

The third issue, however, was the one that rang bells through the investigation. It related to the existence of a red diary that Grandison said he listed among Marilyn's possessions when she was received

at the coroner's office, and which, with a scrawled note, he claimed, disappeared. There is certainly a chance that such a book — with a slip of paper inside — might have been picked up by the coroner's men when they were sent back — Grandison's claim — to the house for something which would give details of her relatives. It would appear the district attorney's investigators were satisfied this was a distinct possibility. Grandison claimed that when he opened the book and read some of the entries he placed it in the safe. Next day, he said, it had vanished.

Sergeant Jack Clemmons saw no red diary, however, nor for that matter, any other documents or letters, but that by itself is not significant: there is no accounting for what might have been produced in that house in those hours following Marilyn's death. We have already drawn attention (see photo caption on page 23), to the letters and scripts that were photographed beneath the bedside table in Marilyn's bedroom. Either the photograph was taken before Clemmons' arrival, or else the papers had been placed there after Clemmons' departure for the benefit of the camera, since there was no sign of such when he was there. He commented on the absence of documents of any kind, and drew attention to the inappropriate tidiness of the place. He said he realised it had been cleaned up before he arrived. From what we now know it would need to have been. The place was apparently pulled apart, with documents all over the place during the hours between Marilyn's death and Clemmons being called.

In the context of the new investigation, what is most interesting about Grandison's assertion that the diary was in the coroner's department and then disappeared is the amount of squirming that took place to discredit the claim, not just to the red diary having been there, but that it had ever existed. Hence the Report could not fail to draw attention to the fact that Robert Slatzer had confirmed seeing the red diary, said to contain, 'names of government figures and perhaps matters relating to sensitive government operations,' for it wanted to draw attention to the fact that Grandison admitted having read Slatzer's book, *The Life and Curious Death of Marilyn Monroe*, which mentions its existence.

120

It then went on to claim that Robert Slatzer was the only source alleging the existence of the diary, however. But this is not true. I interviewed a close friend of Marilyn's, film actress Jeanne Carmen, who had seen Marilyn with Robert Kennedy at her home. She tells how when Kennedy opened the book and saw what was in it he threw it across the room shouting, 'Get rid of this.' Why did the investigators not ask Jeanne?

Anxious to bury any idea that the red diary existed, the Report quotes that it had not been seen by Pat Newcomb, Eunice Murray, Doctors Greenson and Engelberg or Marilyn's 'masseuse' (presumably, in fact, her masseur, Ralph Roberts), and these were the people closest to her at her home. Diaries, however, in their very nature, are personal and usually secret things, and it should come as no surprise that those around her did not know of its existence. For the investigators to have admitted that there was such a book, however, would have opened the door to theories that would accommodate reasons for murdering Marilyn, and the DA, even in 1982, was not allowing that.

The Report concluded: 'Our threshold examination was approached with an open mind. We examined documents and witness statements without any preconceptions, bias, or prejudice. However, as the various allegations were subjected to detailed examination and as the scenario of Marilyn Monroe's death was fitted into place, we were drawn to the conclusion that the homicide hypothesis must be viewed with extreme skepticism.' I would also, very much, like to take issue with the Report on this series of statements. In the light of the account of the investigation rendered above it is astounding such a claim could be made. It appears the threshold investigation was used to shore up the deeply erroneous findings of 1962. When faced with evidence that foul play may have resulted in Marilyn's death, the investigators went out of their way to find reasons for dismissing it. When faced with embarrassing indications that a cover up had taken place they sought to apply whitewash. And when anything slipped through their net, they simply ignored what they could not explain.

John Miner believes Marilyn's body should be disinterred for a new autopsy to be carried out. When I mentioned this to Thomas Noguchi his eyes lit up and he said he would very much like to be involved with a new autopsy. He said he believed that new techniques might well reveal how those drugs were introduced into her system, so that the truth of her death would finally be known. John Miner has very positive ideas about doing a lot more stirring which he hopes will lead to a new, unfettered, investigation into Marilyn's death.

So far an inquest has never been carried out on Marilyn's death. It is worth recounting the most recent attempt to bring everything out into the open was three years after the so-called investigation reported above. And thereby hangs another — fascinating — tale.

12

DEFINITELY NOT

Following the publication of Anthony Summers' book *Goddess, The Secret Lives of Marilyn Monroe* in 1985, Marilyn's friend, the indefatigable Robert Slatzer waded in with another attempt to establish, this time, a genuine investigation into Marilyn's death. He approached Mike Antonovich, of the Los Angeles County Board of Supervisors. To his great satisfaction, that body voted unanimously to recommend that an official investigation be launched by the Grand Jury into the circumstances surrounding Marilyn's death and the mounting evidence that a cover up had taken place. It has to be said, however, that this decision may have reflected what might be called political posturing rather than an expression of genuine concern about past injustices.

The Grand Jury's Criminal Justice Committee considered the evidence and declared Coroner Curphey's 'possible suicide' verdict left doubts, while the evidence of a cover up was acknowledged. Sam Cordova, the Grand Jury foreman, who became surrounded by controversy, announced that the Justice Committee had agreed to reinvestigate

Marilyn's death. Cordova was not the man to sit back and wait for case material to come 'down from above', as it were. Cordova liked to be abreast of everything that was happening and, if possible, ahead of everything that was happening. The Grand Jury foreman liked to run his own ship, which did not suit the District Attorney.

Sam Cordova began to do all the right things when he got into investigating Marilyn's death. He started to re-examine the grey areas of the case, and made public the fact that he did not like what he was seeing and expected to challenge the 'probable suicide' verdict. This had all the makings of a headline-hitting national campaign. Meanwhile, District Attorney Ira Reiner, jealous of his authority, was unwilling to allow an upstart of a Grand Jury foreman to run such a show. Though he had no right to do so, he began taking steps to bring matters under his own control. Cordova had promised that a press conference would be held at which the Grand Jury's deliberations would be made known, and it was at this point Reiner struck. Incredibly, he stepped in and declared Cordova's announcement 'irresponsible' and 'untrue'. On the same day the press conference was scheduled, Cordova was removed from office by a Superior Court judge and replaced forthwith. This was quite unprecedented.

Predictably, the new foreman was not in favour of the investigation into Marilyn's death, and it simply did not happen. Robert Slatzer, in his book *The Marilyn Files*[1], tells that the resolution of the Los Angeles Board of Supervisors to reinvestigate Marilyn's death in 1985 was not the first time it had made such a recommendation. It had done so in 1982 when, of a sudden, District Attorney John Van de Kamp scrambled together a press conference to announce that he had already begun a new investigation the previous week. Strangely, this apparently had not been made public. It is hard to believe that it was not more likely the Democrat district attorney had jumped in to spike the guns of the Republican Board of Supervisors. History was just as likely being repeated when District Attorney Reiner saw which way the Board of Supervisors was leaning in 1985, though there was here a large helping of personality projection and status preservation on Reiner's part, for good measure.

The account given in the previous chapter of the 1982 Van de Kamp enquiry reveals a 'loaded' reinvestigation dedicated to preserving the status quo. The signal failure of all the probes and so-called probes into Marilyn's death is that those who knew the answers were not challenged to reveal what they knew under oath. It would seem clear that it has always been preferred they don't talk. The 1985 Grand Jury investigation would have had the power to exact compliance from those who had refused to tell what they

---

[1] Robert F Slatzer, *The Marilyn Files*, Spi Books New York, 1992

knew under pain of fines or jail sentences. Besides which, failure to cooperate would have involved the kind of publicity not sought by any of those who may have been subpoenad.

The 1985 Grand Jury, however, just fizzled out bearing all the marks of being dowsed by a political machine, thoroughly laced with the complications of warring personalities. When Reiner assumed command of the situation he promised that an investigation into Marilyn's death *would* be carried out, only to report very promptly afterwards that there was no need. He announced that ' . . . no evidence . . . has been brought to our attention which would support a reasonable belief or even a bare suspicion that Miss Monroe was murdered. The star's death was a matter of historical interest only'. In making this last statement District Attorney Reiner appeared to betray he did not have any grasp of the importance or desirability of establishing truth. It would seem, also, he did not rate history important enough to be accorded truth, either.

By all appearances, priorities had been established and achieved, however. The powers that be who had managed to keep control over John Van de Kamp's investigation were unwilling to let that control slip away by allowing the Board of Supervisors to raise its 'runaway' Grand Jury head. There would be no further digging into the mysteries which surrounded the star's death while he was around. Definitely not.

13

THE TESTIMONY OF MRS MURRAY

Mrs Murray told lies. Either that or her grasp on things around her was so lacking as to be unbelievable. But she was neither a weak personality, nor incapable. Marilyn's so-called housekeeper changed her story so many times she became totally unreliable to those trying to piece together the true sequence of events surrounding Marilyn's death. Yet she was a key player in the drama and could not be ignored.

Born Eunice Joerndt in 1902, she married John Murray in 1924. Some twenty-odd years later he built a hacienda-type house in Santa Monica, and they lived there for three years, until they divorced. The house was then sold to Dr Ralph Greenson and Mrs Murray moved into an apartment.

In her initial interviews with the police she said she had found Marilyn's body at about midnight, but this was clearly set to cause problems since the police were not notified until nearly four and a half hours later. Questioned subsequently, Mrs Murray revised her timescale, saying the body had been found at about 3.30 a.m., and went on to adjust her story to suit. The framework of the story was that she had visited the bathroom and had noticed a light still showing under Marilyn's bedroom door. Since the door was locked and she could not get an answer from Marilyn, she went outside and pushed the bedroom curtains open by using a poker through a small open window, and had seen Marilyn lying on the bed. She said she then telephoned Dr Greenson, who came over and gained access to the bedroom by breaking a window. Dr Greenson told her Marilyn was dead. In another version of events it had been Dr Greenson who had peered through the bedroom window rather than Mrs Murray, though how anyone could have seen past the curtains was curious in itself. The proper curtains had not been hung in the bedroom, and the makeshift curtain that had been temporarily fixed right across the window would have been difficult, if not impossible, to push aside from outside, even with a poker.

In one story Mrs Murray had been the one to telephone Dr Engelberg, and in another it had been Dr Greenson, but regardless of who had called him, Dr Engelberg was said to have arrived in time to certify death at 3.50 a.m. When I interviewed Dr Greenson's wife, Hildi, she recalled that Ralph had a call from Marilyn's house and left home just after midnight. Before this time he would not have been available, since he had taken his wife out for dinner that Saturday night. This, however, made nonsense of the revised timescale concocted by Murray, Greenson and Engelberg. To demolish the story altogether, Engelberg admitted, much later, that he had arrived at the house shortly after 2.30

a.m., and that the alarm had first been raised between 11.00 p.m. and midnight. If Engelberg knew about a panic taking place long before midnight, it may be speculated that he was called but could not be reached because he, too, was out for the evening, and that a message had been left to which he responded when he got home.

When giving evidence to Sergeant Robert Byron, Mrs Murray said Marilyn had gone to bed at 8.00 p.m. But she later contradicted herself when telling the sergeant about a telephone call which had been received from Joe DiMaggio Jr, Marilyn's stepson, whom Marilyn greatly liked and who kept in touch with her. The difficulty arose when Mrs Murray said she took the telephone in to Marilyn, *in bed, at 7.30*

Mrs Eunice Murray. How much did she really know?
Photo Robert F Slatzer Collection

p.m. Remarkably, Sergeant Byron noted both statements without attempting to reconcile them. Even more remarkably, his superiors did not challenge the discrepancy. Mrs Murray changed this again when she wrote her book, *Marilyn: The Last Months*, in which she now said she *called* Marilyn to take the call in the third, empty, bedroom. As was noted earlier, Mrs Murray said she was alerted by seeing a light showing under Marilyn's bedroom door. Had Byron looked around, he might have spotted that the thick pile carpet left no crack for Mrs Murray to see a light under the bedroom door, and, in any case, the housekeeper would not have needed to pass the door to visit the bathroom. In her book, which she wrote 13 years after Marilyn's death, Mrs Murray contradicts herself on this point also, explaining that 'questioners jumped to the conclusion that I had seen the light under the door. In such a state of shock, I would not have stopped to think of that as important . . . I knew that the new white wool carpet filled the space under the door . . . This I remembered later, but not until after I had agreed that I had seen a light under the door.' While Byron's investigation was half-hearted and inadequate, it is interesting to find indications that his superiors were not concerned at this. And Mrs Murray flitting from one version of things to another only served to expose her testimony as a pack of lies.

Sixty-year-old Eunice Murray began working for Marilyn Monroe before Christmas, 1961, at about the time Dr Greenson had suggested the star began looking for a house to buy. Mrs Murray helped Marilyn to house-hunt and also helped her choose furnishings when she finally decided upon the house she wanted. The house was a hacienda type, reminiscent of Greenson's house which Marilyn liked. Marilyn hired Mrs Murray's son-in-law, Norman Jeffries, as a handyman, to help sort out the shortcomings in her new house.

Mrs Murray, a mature lady with psychiatric nursing experience, was referred to as Marilyn's housekeeper. But, appointed at a time when Marilyn was having difficulty getting the services of a nurse because of her treatment of them, it was obvious she was to be more than a mere housekeeper. She had been recommended to Marilyn by Ralph Greenson, as 'companion and decorator', but the implications were that she kept a watching brief on Marilyn and regarded Greenson as her real boss. She answered to him, keeping him informed of her charge's movements. Mrs Murray told a reporter for the *Los Angeles Herald-Examiner*, 'Dr Greenson gave me certain instructions about Marilyn, but I can't say what they were.' Typically, she later denied she had said this. She also claimed that she had very little contact with Dr Greenson.

Marilyn knew nothing of this, but it seemed that she had accepted Mrs Murray was not to be taken to task for shortcomings when it came to carrying out a housekeeper's duties. An instance came to light when the star was being interviewed at her home by Richard Merriman, who wrote for *Life* magazine. When it got late,

Marilyn offered him food, asking him if he would like a nice steak. She went to the refrigerator and found there was neither steak nor food of any kind in the house she could offer her guest. If Mrs Murray was really intended to be a housekeeper, her performance, it seemed, left a great deal to be desired. Marilyn, however, was not reported as being fazed by this. It seems she just accepted it and, embarrassingly, her guest was obliged to, also.

Mrs Murray spoke of a conversation she claimed she had had with the star on the very day she died, in which Marilyn asked her if there was any oxygen in the house, lending support to the idea that Marilyn had planned another 'suicide' episode which had this time gone wrong. Such a question from Marilyn would have been extremely odd; the idea that anyone would enquire about oxygen in the same manner as asking if there was any fruit in the pantry. People did not keep oxygen about the house in the normal way, and if for any reason any had been bought, Marilyn would surely have known about it. Mrs Murray was eventually to say it was some time after the star's death she realised the connection between the oxygen enquiry and attempted suicide.

But this was not Mrs Murray's only hint at 'accidental suicide.' She told neighbour Abe Landau she thought Marilyn had taken the capsules and dropped off, only to wake and, having forgotten she had taken the first lot, took more and died from the accidental overdose. She embroidered the story further in her book: in this version she speculates she might have taken a capsule and gone to sleep, been roused by the telephone ringing, taken another capsule to get back to sleep, and finding this did not work, reached for another, and so on until she was overwhelmed. Could she really mean that by this means she had 'accidentally' taken more than forty capsules? This lends more insight into Mrs Murray and her motives rather than shedding light on what really happened. She had her agenda, and one thing is certain: the lady knew a lot more than she ever told.

When it came to her planned and rehearsed version of events the night Marilyn died, by the time she wrote her book Mrs Murray was left with little of what she had originally claimed in her story to the police. She now said it was some 'sixth sense' which had warned her, and 'impelled' her to open the hall door, when she saw the telephone wire snaking under Marilyn's door. Whatever she said, Mrs Murray appeared to have motive, and she dropped her guard only twice. The first time was in 1982, when she was being interviewed by researcher Justin Clayton. She spoke of having 'found Marilyn's door ajar' then, realising what she had said, attempted to erase her comment, reverting to the rehearsed 'locked door' story, but Clayton had taken it all in. In this interview she also slipped back to her earlier timescale for the discovery of the body: she spoke of finding the body 'about midnight'.

The admission that when Mrs Murray went to the bedroom she found the door ajar warrants very close examination. If the door was *normally*

133

locked at night because Marilyn feared prowlers, why was it open now? Had it been locked earlier? There were many questions which might have been answered if Mrs Murray had provided the vital information that the bedroom door was open when she approached it. In fact, Marilyn's masseur and close friend, Ralph Roberts, said the door was never locked. He was in a position to know this, also, for he often gave Marilyn massages late in the evening when she was settling down for sleep. Cherie Redmond, who was Marilyn's business secretary when she died, commented to Hedda Rosten, who was doing secretarial work for Marilyn in New York, that she couldn't find a lock in the house which worked.

Furthermore, there were important 'knock on' consequences to this new 'open door' version of things. It hacked at the roots of the broken window story, for instance, and Dr Greenson climbing in to find Marilyn's body. Who really broke the window? And why? These were important questions in relation to facts hitherto unchallenged.

The second occasion Mrs Murray spoke spontaneously was after the recording session for the BBC in 1985, when she admitted that an ambulance — with doctor — had, in fact, arrived at the house. And for good measure, while she felt talkative she settled, once and for all, that Robert Kennedy had called at the house the day Marilyn died. In her book, Mrs Murray staunchly denied there was 'romantic interest' between them. We shall return to this important statement later, however. Then Mrs Murray made an admission which turned the ground she covered in her original statements to the police in 1962 into quicksand, saying, 'I told whatever I thought was . . . good to tell.' Mrs Murray then regretted being loose-tongued, and after this she joined the ranks of the silent once more.

Marilyn did not get on with Eunice Murray. She put up with her because Ralph Greenson wanted her to. This did not mean there were not eruptions in the relationship, however. On one occasion, when Ralph Greenson was holidaying abroad during the making of *Something's Got to Give*, Marilyn fired her. On another occasion it was Mrs Murray who packed her bags and was

Paula Strasberg, 'Black Bart' to those on the set because of always dressing in black. Marilyn fired her.
Photo Robert F Slatzer Collection

on the point of leaving. But one way or another, the 'housekeeper' survived, and she made no mention of these events in her 1975 book. Eunice appeared to be an important feature of Greenson's strategy for treating the star, who became his main patient, his main concern. Some would say she was his obsession. While still away on his five-week holiday, he contacted Marilyn and told her to double Mrs Murray's salary to $200 per week. We do not know why, but it would not be a wild guess that it had something to do with getting Eunice to return, Marilyn having fired her.

In the week before she died, Marilyn had made some far-reaching changes as part of her new deal with the studio, and she planned more. Her acting coach, Paula Strasberg, wife of Lee Strasberg — called by studio crews 'Black Bart', because she dressed all in black — was upsetting the studio by turning up for every day's shooting and interfering with what was happening on the set. Marilyn fired her, giving her a one-way ticket to New York. It has been suggested that the appointment Marilyn had with her lawyer on the Monday after she died was to make changes to her will and included cutting out the Strasbergs. Since this didn't happen Lee was the prime beneficiary.

Another change demanded involved Ralph Greenson, who, with Marilyn's new lawyer, Mickey Rudin — interestingly, Greenson's brother in law — had assumed the role of negotiator with the studio. It was demanded this be stopped and Marilyn agreed. But Marilyn, having fulfilled Fox's demands, was making a clean sweep, and now planned some further revisions in her private affairs.

Next to go would be Mrs Murray. And she meant it this time. Marilyn had now tumbled to the fact that her so-called housekeeper was little more than a spy, and she was embarrassed. Her masseur, Ralph Roberts, to whom she confided, said, 'Marilyn caught on just before she died and felt very betrayed.' Since Dr. Greenson was in every way involved with Mrs Murray's appointment, her problem was how to get rid of her without upsetting her psychiatrist, who was now booted out by the studio. In a later chapter we will hear from Marilyn herself — via her tape recordings — on how she planned to deal with this situation.

Marilyn's friends were not surprised at her decision to make changes. Their only surprise was that she had not done it before. She was under pressure from those who were there to *relieve* her of pressure. She was seeing Ralph Greenson as much as twice a day, which was not only costly; it was restrictive. As we have said, by this time the doctor was not only treating her as a psychiatrist, he was involving himself in her work arrangements, at times making guarantees to get her to the set, ready for work. She was determined to make a new start, but she relied on Greenson and she would have to think out any revisions to his role carefully. Peter Levathes, a studio executive, said, 'Marilyn couldn't walk across a room without advice and counsel and people with vested interest.'

14

The Listeners

Jimmy Hoffa wanted to nail Robert Kennedy. The Attorney General had declared war on the mafia hoodlum who had taken control of the Teamsters' Union, and the union boss was planning to get first strike in. Hoffa saw Robert Kennedy as 'a man who had no principles'. Kennedy declared Hoffa and his Teamsters' empire to be 'a conspiracy of evil'. Hoffa, in his attempts to keep tabs on what was happening to the Kennedy brothers when they came west, had Hollywood private eye Fred Otash bug Peter Lawford's house. Lawford was married to Patricia Kennedy, sister of Jack and Robert, who became frequent visitors to the Lawford's splendid mansion, located at the beachfront at Santa Monica. It was small wonder the house, which had been built for MGM boss Louis B Mayer, was called the West Coast White House.

The bugs at Lawford's home first served to monitor the relationship between Marilyn and Jack Kennedy, providing embarrassing data of the kind Hoffa was seeking. Jack Kennedy appeared to be naively unaware that he was under surveillance and he was, therefore, relaxed and off his guard. It came as a huge bonus some time afterwards that the overworked bugs quickly drew to the attention of the listeners that as that relationship seemed to peter out another began. This time it was Robert Kennedy who was becoming involved with Marilyn and, with the secrets of the house being yielded via the bugs, Hoffa knew when the chance of blackmail was on offer.

He engaged Fred Otash again, this time to bug Marilyn's apartment, and when she moved into

Bernard Spindel, ace wire tapper. He listened in at Marilyn's house on Jimmy Hoffa's behalf. Here he demonstrates to Senator Malcolm S Forbes
Photo AP Wide World

her new house he had that bugged as well, her rooms — even the bathroom — as well as the phones. This time the 'product' of the taps was then to be recorded on tape, and this is where surveillance expert Bernard Spindel came in. Bernard Spindel had developed his skills when he served in the US Army Signal Corps during the war. Using the newest techniques in electronic surveillance, he was assigned to the intelligence agencies and honed his talent for listening to the enemy to distinguished levels. When the war ended he used the techniques he had developed as a private detective and worked on divorce cases and fraud probes. He registered a detective agency in his wife's maiden name — the B. R. Fox Company — which complied with the requirements of the law, but his activities carrying out bugging or debugging operations involved him sailing perilously close to the judicial wind.

For someone dedicated to a profession that demanded he spent a large part of his time working on the wrong side of the law, it must have been somewhat tongue in cheek for him to contribute lectures to the New York City Anti-Crime Committee. But then, as far as his work putting him on the wrong side of the law was concerned, Spindel, in a book he wrote in 1968 called *The Ominous Ear*, explained that 'When a citizen taps a phone it's called wiretapping. For the FBI it's labelled monitoring, when the phone company is listening in, they interpret the act as just observing.' To Spindel it appears to be all the same thing. In his book he tells how new age electronics have been acquired and used by those who want to achieve character assassination, the invasion of privacy and legal coercion, and he goes on to include on his list those who are determined to acquire political power and those who are simply out and out blackmailers. It is noted that, not surprisingly, Spindel avoided considerations of the moral and legal aspects of electronic eavesdropping when he wrote his book.

Jimmy Hoffa was quick to recognise the potential in the abilities of the ace wire-tapper. He acquired Spindel's services, and found plenty of work for him to do. Hoffa was linked to Sam Giancana and the notorious Chicago syndicate, and the two mafiosi shared the information obtained by Bernard Spindel. He gave Spindel the job of locating and removing the listening devices that others had secreted in his offices while at the same time planting fresh bugs on his premises for reasons best known to himself. Perhaps the most daring example of their enterprising phone tapping was that in which they monitored Robert Kennedy's Justice Department lines. Kennedy knew all about Spindel and tried making overtures to him to get him to change sides. In spite of a one-to-one meeting in which he tried to persuade the master wire-tapper to join him, Spindel refused and thereby advertised his hostility towards the Attorney General.

When Robert Kennedy began his relationship with Marilyn the recording machines were busier than ever, and large volumes of tape were consumed in the operation. An often quoted soundbite from the miles of tape recorded, in which a voice purportedly recorded the night Marilyn died was heard to say, 'What shall we do with the body now?' was later amended to 'What shall we do with her dead body?' This was, on the face of it, pretty damning when linked to a claim that Robert Kennedy was in her house at the time. Even more damning was the other snippet from the tapes, purported to be from an incoming telephone call from San Francisco (the operator announced where long-distance calls were coming from in those days) late on the night Marilyn died, in which a man's voice, supposedly Kennedy's, asked, 'Is she dead?' which was later amended to, 'Is she dead yet?'

It has to be said at once that in both instances the authenticity of the recordings is automatically brought into doubt by the variations — additions — quoted, which could only be to underline the meaning of what was being said. In turn, it was clear the purported recordings were in the hands of people bent on causing mischief with them by manipulating what was there.

In the case of the first of these soundbites, in which it seems we are being asked to accept we are listening to the voices of the perpetrators of Marilyn's murder, it would have been at least believable that someone was making the comment looking at Marilyn's drugged body before she was discovered to be in the coma from which she never recovered, but the 'dead body' takes it beyond belief. It is most likely she actually died in the ambulance that rushed her to

142

Attorney General Robert F Kennedy.
Photo Courtesy of John F Kennedy Library

hospital, and it was most unlikely the murderers would still be around to make such a comment after she was brought back to her home. This 'snippet' did not sit comfortably with other facts that later came to light.

In the case of the so-called 'Is she dead (yet)?' example, the accepted implication is that the caller is Attorney General Robert Kennedy who has 'escaped' to San Francisco while those he left behind to kill Marilyn get on with the job. The supposed purpose of his call was to raise a 'toll' entry to support the claim that he was far away from Los Angeles when she actually died. Supposing, for one moment, the voice did belong to Robert Kennedy, it is interesting to see how greatly the addition of 'yet' affects the meaning of the question. 'Is she dead?' might well be the concerned question of someone who has just been informed she has been found in a deadly coma, but by adding 'yet', the question becomes positively sinister. Whoever is asking this question sounds as though he can't wait for her to die.

Whatever Bernard Spindel recorded here becomes highly suspect in view of the additions made to the original quotations. In the case of the 'Is she dead (yet)?' example, unless the voice heard could be identified beyond question as belonging to Robert Kennedy, Spindel has nothing, and the prospect of such from a bug transmitter would be a very tall order. It might be added that, if Kennedy had been involved in Marilyn's death — which I do not believe — and had made his 'escape' to San Francisco, he would have been crazy to ring Marilyn's house. He could have telephoned anybody anywhere to raise a 'toll' entry to establish where he was. In the case of the 'What shall we do with the (dead) body?' example, there is no suggestion the voice on the tape is that of Robert Kennedy. At best, it tells us only that someone was so anxious for us to believe the owner of the voice was looking at Marilyn's corpse that the word 'dead' was added just to make sure.

Both of these highly publicised examples of what Spindel held on his tapes, especially with

144

the additions made to them, serve to illustrate well the innate weaknesses in relying upon tape recordings as evidence. To begin with there is nothing in the recordings themselves that will identify when they were made or where they were made, and this by itself can be a fatal flaw. Fragments of sounds in the hands of a master like Bernard Spindel could be made to represent just about anything he cared to make it. The editing processes, which, in the hands of amateurs can totally destroy authenticity, were not a problem to the expert Spindel. Background noises could be added to order, and the sequence of the recordings could be interchanged to suit the purposes of the recordist.

Even in this electronically sophisticated age the poor definition of recordings derived from transmissions from bugs and taps is well known. 'Mush' can be horrendous from both sources, and in the case of transmissions from bugs the signal is likely to wax and wane according to the proximity of the voice to the bug. These problems were much greater in 1962. Then, when all is said and done, if someone has to explain what the listener is hearing there is, obviously, a distinct limit to the value of any sound recording. Bumps and what might be scuffles are just that and no more, and opinions rendered on what they represent are just that and no more. The proverbial biscuit must go to the claim that Spindel recorded the sound of a body being placed on a bed. This defies belief. It goes without saying that this sequence is one of those that requires someone to explain what it is.

The extract contained what was described as, ' . . . thumping, bumping noises, then muffled, calming sounds. It sounded as though she was being put on a bed.' What we are being told about here, in fact, adds up to little more than a description of a few indeterminate noises, and at least the person describing is not tempted to place too positive an interpretation on what he claims to have heard. This can hardly be said for whoever provided the hard and fast — and, indeed, brash — example quoted by Milo Speriglio, in his book, *Marilyn Monroe: Murder Cover-up:* 'Marilyn was slapped around. You could actually hear her being slapped, even hear her body fall to the floor. You could hear her hit the deck, all the sounds that took place in her house that night . . . ' The latter must rank as something of another classic, and by this time we must be aware that the reported contents of the fragments of the tapes Spindel allowed to be heard by selected individuals would vary according to who and what the selected individuals were, bearing in mind that interpretations made by any one of us are likely to be affected by our individual biases, points of view and dispositions.

Not many people claim to have heard extracts from Spindel's tapes, and no one has claimed to have listened to them all. This is likely because continuous recording produces, in the main, nothing. The blank sequences where nothing is happening, totalling hours and hours, obviously forms by far the greatest part of the sum. The sounds recorded would then be assembled on smaller tapes, having, of necessity, gone through an editing process. Taken altogether, there were very few people who claimed to have heard extracts from the tapes, probably just enough to establish they existed. It would be easy to be deceived into thinking that many people listened to bits of the tapes because of the various quotations made in any number of books which discuss this aspect of Marilyn's death. Not so. Comparisons will reveal it is the same very few examples that are being repeated over and over.

Nevertheless, I believe Spindel did make recordings from sounds emanating from the homes of Peter and Pat Lawford and Marilyn Monroe. I also believe he overheard the voices of Robert Kennedy and Marilyn Monroe, but I think the value of what he recorded — from his point of view — was well below what was claimed. I accept he established that a relationship existed between Marilyn and the Attorney General, but, as hard as he tried, he fell far short of establishing that Robert Kennedy had anything to do with her death. The examples discussed above, which were added to for extra effect, represented Spindel shooting himself in the foot. They proved nothing and tended to discredit his other 'produce'.

During that Saturday, Marilyn's last day of life, Robert Kennedy would pay her two visits, even though he does not appear to have been invited nor to be welcome. Spindel's recordings of the first meeting, in the afternoon, were said to feature first love making and then a fearful row. An 'interpreter' told us, and we should bear in mind we are getting a second-hand version, that 'Their voices grew louder and louder. They were arguing about something that had been promised by Robert Kennedy. Marilyn was demanding an explanation as to why Kennedy was not going to marry her. As they argued their voices got shriller. If I had not recognised RFK's voice already, I am not sure that I would have known it was him at this point. He was screeching, high pitched like an old lady . . . '

Robert Kennedy was seeking something which he could not find: 'Where is it? Where the — is it?' In the context of his brother's affair with Marilyn, we would probably not be far out in speculating he was looking for a file of letters, photographs and other documents which Marilyn had promised to hand over to Jack Kennedy. He did not get them. A door slammed ending the sequence of recording abruptly. It sounded as though Marilyn had thrown them out. When the tape resumes we are presumably hearing what went on during the later visit of Robert Kennedy to Marilyn's house during the evening. This time Peter Lawford was with them. They were still hunting for whatever it was Kennedy wanted, and it seemed he wanted it very badly. 'We have to know. It's important to the family. You can make any arrangements you want, but we must find it.' This is direct speech being reported now, and it seems more and more likely it is a file of documents he wants. Marilyn had promised Jack Kennedy, as her part of a deal relating to the establishment of a trust for her mother, that she would hand them over to him.

There was a photograph showing Jack Kennedy — President Kennedy by this time — in the company of mobster Sam Giancana which Robert Kennedy particularly wanted to obtain. Next in the tape came the sound of tempers fraying and Marilyn ordering them out of the house. Robert Kennedy was well known for barking out commands to those around him. Perhaps he had met his match. As another piece of speculation, perhaps Jack Kennedy would have obtained his documents without any trouble if his brother had approached her in a more gentle fashion. Marilyn was rather like that.

Over a period lasting for some months, everything Marilyn did or said in her home was likely to be overheard by Hoffa and Giancana, both anxious to obtain ammunition to blackmail Robert Kennedy. This was incredible enough, but, even more incredibly, they were not the only ones whose ears were in her house. J Edgar Hoover, director of the FBI, had his agents wire out the house, ostensibly because he thought the liaison between the Attorney General and Marilyn might involve breaches in national security.

The FBI had raised what was known as a 105 file on Marilyn in view of the left-wing friends she cultivated. For this reason, Hoover was entitled to conduct surveillance on the star because of 'foreign counter-intelligence matters', in the light of which he could argue her liaison with the Attorney General was of considerable concern. But it would suit the cunning FBI boss to listen in to what was going on so that he could collect more 'dirt' to use against Robert Kennedy and his brother, the President, whose affair with Marilyn was also well known to him. The brothers were already featured in his infamous files and this would strengthen the hold he already had on them. In this Hoover was no better than the pair of hoodlums Bernard Spindel was working for. And the picture is still not yet complete; the CIA also had the house bugged. Their excuse was much the same as Hoover's, that the Attorney General's activities constituted a security risk.

If it seems strange that the CIA — whose mandate did not include the guardianship of internal national security within the borders of the United States — were involved, that was the way things were in 1962. The CIA were going their own way and doing their own thing. They ignored those who were set in authority over them when it suited them — particularly the President — and, at times, followed policies that distinctly ran counter to those of the government. For them to involve themselves in internal affairs was nothing new. The President was well aware of what was going on and had it on his agenda to sort out at the time he was assassinated. He was furious with the wayward intelligence agency and had, in 1961, declared to Senator Mike Mansfield that he would tear the CIA ' . . . into a thousand pieces and scatter it to the winds'. It is a matter for the record, however, that like Hoover, there were those in the CIA who had their own agenda when it came to the Kennedys.

J Edgar Hoover knew that the only things preventing his dismissal by the President, who did not like him, were the secret files he kept. The Kennedys were not the only ones whose secrets he knew and recorded. He had many dossiers on senators, representatives, Democrats and Republicans, and powerful people of all descriptions inside and outside government. But his files on the Kennedy brothers were his ace cards in his fight to maintain his position. It is claimed he coerced Jack Kennedy into making his friend, Lyndon Johnson, whom JFK did not like, his running mate in the presidential election, a move that surprised many at the time.

Hoover, on the other hand, was not invulnerable himself, a practising homosexual in a homophobic age and a law unto himself, and Jack Kennedy kept a file on the Director as a means of defence. There is a story that one day, however, the President, having decided that enough was enough, invited him to lunch at the White House, just Hoover, Robert Kennedy and himself, so that he could 'invite' his resignation. When the occasion arrived they started the meal amicably enough, but while they were eating the President reached into his inside pocket and withdrew an envelope, which he placed on the table beside the Director. Hoover continued eating but responded by reaching into *his* inside pocket also and taking out an envelope, larger than the other, which he laid by the President's place. The President opened the large envelope and he and his brother read the contents. The Attorney General made a bee-line for the bathroom where he vomited, while the President stopped eating and ate no more. Hoover continued eating and had dessert, also, the only one remaining at the table. There was no more talk of his retirement.

The interest that factions within the CIA had in the Kennedys was entirely different from that of Hoover. Their interest stemmed from the intense hatred for the brothers harboured by Agency veterans of the Bay of Pigs debacle the year before, which is examined in more detail in a later chapter.

Such were the influences at work behind the affair Robert Kennedy was conducting with Marilyn. The Attorney General was married and had a family: indeed, he had been named Father of the Year. He had no reputation as a womaniser, and it would seem Marilyn was something of an exception. But it would appear that those who listened in at Marilyn's house achieved what they wanted to achieve, and this resulted in her death.

Bernard Spindel claimed he had evidence of the affair between Robert Kennedy and Marilyn on tape, and, quite apart from the fact that certain individuals claimed to have listened to extracts, support came from other quarters that this was the case. I spoke to Washington journalist Ralph de Toledano, who told me he had received a commission from a wealthy businessman in the automobile industry to obtain tapes made from bugs in Marilyn's house, presumably Spindel's tapes. This was early in 1968, and the businessman represented a 'bi-partisan' anti-Kennedy group, willing to pay whatever it cost for the power it would give them over the Kennedys. De Toledano said he located the tapes and was in the process of negotiating the price when the news broke that Robert Kennedy had been murdered. The purchase, therefore, was never made.

Probably the most compelling evidence that the tapes were made came from law-enforcement officers, however. In December of 1966 a dawn raid was made by police officers on the upstate-New York home of Bernard Spindel. The charge was that he had 'feloniously, wrongfully, unlawfully, and knowingly concealed and withheld and aided in concealing and withholding certain property belonging to the New York Telephone Company.' But what had this to do with the question, 'Where's the Marilyn Monroe — Kennedy tapes?' baldly asked by one agent at the scene? In the turmoil created by the raid, Spindel's wife Barbara had to be rushed to hospital having suffered a serious heart attack. Spindel was arrested and the officers ransacked the house seeking out reels of tapes that they confiscated along with his recording equipment. Unbeknown to the dawn raiders, Spindel had bugged his own house and had a recording of the entire raid, which lasted for nine hours. On the tape he heard one man innocently asking, 'What do Marilyn Monroe tapes have to do with Bobby Kennedy?' Those who had sent him knew the answer to this question.

A long legal battle ensued. Spindel, having produced receipts for the disputed equipment, filed suit for recovery of the tapes saying they contained evidence relating to Marilyn's death. He never got them. The authorities admitted years later they had been 'lost or destroyed.' It is doubtful that Spindel's law suit was for any other reason than to try and convince the law he had made no copies of the tapes. It would have been remarkable if he had not, however. All professional sound-recording engineers follow out a policy of copying to offset the risk of the accidental erasure of valuable material, and there is no doubt Spindel was a professional. Spindel's assistant, Earl Jaycox, interviewed by author Anthony Summers, admitted he had been passed some copies of the tapes, while it is believed Spindel's wife also stored a copy. There is little doubt the raid had been inspired by Robert Kennedy as a precaution against the tapes being used by his enemies as he embarked upon his move to reach the White House. 'This was a fishing expedition,' said Spindel. 'They wanted to find out exactly what we have . . . '

The fact that a few people had been permitted to hear fragments of the tapes, though no one seems to claim to have heard them right through and this could have been a clever move, for by itself it tended to raise expectations for what might be on the parts of the tapes not permitted to be heard by anyone. They were said to be 'dynamite,' but what did they actually say, and what made it so essential for the Kennedys to acquire them? And the converse question may be added also: If they were so hot, why did Hoffa and Giancana not use them? The answer, however, may have been simpler than anyone thought.

As we know, Marilyn made tapes of herself, the transcripts of which we feature in the pages of this book. But they were not the only tapes she made. An illuminating story concerning some of these tapes appeared in the book *Marilyn: The Last Take*, which was written by Peter Harry Brown and Patte B Barham. Mickey Song, a hairdresser, was cutting Robert Kennedy's hair when, in conversation, Kennedy said to him, 'I want to thank you for always thinking of the family.' Song had no idea what the Attorney General was talking about and asked him what he meant. 'Remember the night Marilyn called you to her house and pumped you for information about the family?' Now Song remembered the occasion. He had complied with Marilyn's request for him to call on her, believing she wanted her hair done, but this was not so. She had a lot of champagne flowing and a lot of questions mingling with it which Song found embarrassing. Said Kennedy, 'You didn't know it but Marilyn taped you and then made notes from the recording. Don't worry about it. I just want you to know that the whole family thanks you.'

It was clear to the astounded Song that the Attorney General had listened to the tapes; that they were in his possession. But since this was just a few days after Marilyn died, how had he acquired them, and how had he acquired them so quickly? It became obvious that Peter Lawford, drunk as it was claimed when he was called to Marilyn's house the night of her death, was not too drunk to take advantage of a situation where he could gather up Marilyn's tapes and notebooks and other possessions he thought might link the Kennedys to her. Robert Kennedy probably also had the notebook into which she transcribed the tape she had made of Song.

Embarrassingly, private eye Fred Otash, who bugged Marilyn's house for Jimmy Hoffa, was asked by Marilyn to tap her own phones for herself. There is an obvious implication that she intended recording the product of the taps. In her unpredictable relationship with Robert Kennedy it may well have been she was looking for a measure of protection, as she saw it. Or else it could have been something much more mundane, like keeping tabs on what Mrs Murray was reporting to Ralph Greenson. It is likely, also, that these tapes were taken by Peter Lawford and passed to Robert Kennedy.

The postscript to this story of bugs and taps and recording equipment came some years after Marilyn had died. The person who then owned her house in Fifth Helena Drive had trouble with the roof, which was leaking. A roofing man was hired and found it necessary to gain access to the space above the ceiling to effect his repair. There he found an assortment of wires and electronic devices which, because of his army experience, he recognised as surveillance equipment. Whilst Marilyn in her time in the house may not have had trouble with her roof letting in water, it might be said she was plagued by rats in the attic.

15

DALLIANCES

Marilyn probably met Jack Kennedy as early as 1951, the introduction being made by Charles Feldman, her agent at that time, at a party he gave in Los Angeles. Although they did not immediately strike up a romantic relationship, she had stars in her eyes from their very first meeting. Marilyn married baseball legend Joe DiMaggio in 1952, and JFK came into the picture shortly after that, while she was still married to DiMaggio. The handsome young politician was still relatively unknown on the Pacific seaboard at that time, and at first there was no need to go to great lengths to conceal that they were meeting. As time went on, however, they became more cautious, particularly when they met in New York. It is not certain which of the Kennedy brothers she met first, but there were certainly no romantic entanglements with Robert Kennedy until long after the time the relationship with Jack had been reported. It was of Jack she said, 'I wish he hadn't married Jackie. I'd like to be his wife.'

News of the affair never reached the newspapers, but this did not mean that astute pressmen were not aware of the liaison. In the fifties and sixties it was difficult for reporters to get such items into the columns of their newspapers. This was partly because editors usually let the country's leaders live their lives in privacy. But perhaps there was also another reason. Editors did not want irate publishers to answer to, nor their jobs put in jeopardy. Publishers did not want to be dropped on suddenly by the IRS, demanding to carry out searching probes. Neither did they want to inspire unwanted interest from other government departments. Unless there was cast-iron evidence of the kind that is very hard to obtain, scandal involving political high-fliers could stir up hornets' nests, with the stirrers — even with the best of intentions — getting stung.

In the early stages of their affair, Marilyn and JFK booked rooms in relatively obscure hotels in Los Angeles, but sometimes they would meet at the Lawford's house at Santa Monica. Stories were told of wild parties on the beach with strict security to keep away prying eyes. As time went by Jack would stay at the Beverley Hills Hotel, and Marilyn would be taken there by Secret Service men. In New York it would be the Carlyle Hotel, in which the Kennedys had a suite overlooking Manhattan. In the summer of 1961 she was known to have been secretly smuggled into the hotel when Jack Kennedy was there. The Carlyle had a secret exit through neighbouring premises to the street. Once they were said to have flown off together in the President's private aircraft, the *Caroline*, and other, discreet, meetings took place in which Marilyn, having disguised her appearance with a wig, carried a secretary's notepad. Journalists had ample evidence of the relationship between Jack Kennedy and Marilyn, and what she has to say in her secret tapes leaves no doubt, though while the tapes confirm the relationship, they do not reveal how long the affair had lasted, neither how frequently they met. It appears that later in 1961, as he settled into his presidency, pressure was exerted upon Kennedy from those near him — and possibly including the family, too — that his relationship with Marilyn had to end.

The President and his brother had planned to stay at the home of Frank Sinatra when they next went to Los Angeles. The President's visit, the honour of which Sinatra no doubt thought he had earned by his staunch support of JFK, had been set up by the dutiful Peter Lawford, but then something in the nature of a brick was hurled into the singer's tranquil pool. At the last minute they cancelled their plans to stay with Sinatra and arranged instead to stay with Bing Crosby, who lived not far from Frank Sinatra's Palm Springs home. 'How could anyone blame the President? explained Lawford. 'It was virtually a case of the President going to sleep in the same bed that Giancana vacated only three weeks before.' Whether the President in fact really cared is not known, but it seems it had caught brother Robert on the raw; he threatened to resign if the arrangements to stay with Sinatra went ahead. After all, mobster Giancana was very high on the Attorney General's 'hit' list, and his anti-organised crime campaign was at that time having unprecedented success in putting

160

Robert F Kennedy talks to his brother the President
Photo Courtesy John F Kennedy Library

Mafiosi behind bars.

Sinatra was extremely offended and broke off relations with Peter Lawford. It was bad enough that the honour was not paid, but to accept hospitality at the home of his arch-rival, Crosby, was unthinkable. But then, as Marilyn well knew, Jack could not be seen with Sinatra, with his Mafia connections, any more.

The most public meeting Marilyn would ever have with Jack Kennedy came at the glitzy gathering of the stars in which she sang, 'Happy birthday, Mister President . . . ' in her most alluring, breathy voice at the party held at Madison Square Garden to celebrate his forty-fifth birthday. Her revealing dress — created by Jean-Louis — was spectacular, to say the least. Was she sewn into it — or poured into it? It was 19 May 1962, less than three months before she died. Marilyn had had a bad attack of nerves that night it seems. Robert Mitchum told me about it when I talked to him not long before he died. He said she had gone up to see him in his hotel room earlier on the birthday night and had said she was crying off. Mitchum persuaded her to go through with it, and eventually escorted her down to the foyer where she soon disappeared into a group of Secret Service agents waiting down there. She went, but by the time she got on to the stage she was said to be drunk.

JFK had had a spat with his wife about including Marilyn in his birthday party plans, the outcome of which was that Jackie pointedly refused to attend the celebration. Eventually there would be talk of divorce. As rumour would have it, the marriage would only be held together by the intervention of father Joe, and a million-dollar sweetener for Jackie.

Early in 1962, Jack Kennedy had sent his brother to Los Angeles ostensibly to explain to Marilyn that, under the circumstances, he could no longer see her, and, frankly, to ease the tension he was under. By all appearances, however, Robert was smitten by Marilyn when they met at the Lawford's mansion. Certainly what followed gave the impression of being a steamy affair. Robert was not as discreet as he might have been when he met Marilyn, and there were occasions when they were seen together by others. Marilyn's one time neighbour, starlet Jeanne Carmen, told me she had been at Marilyn's apartment — before she had moved into her house — when, because of Marilyn being caught in her tub when the doorbell rang, she answered and came face to face with her caller, Robert Kennedy. News of this eventually found its way back to Ethel, Robert's wife. It took time, but when it got there she was, understandably, livid.

But Robert persisted in seeing Marilyn. Marilyn, apparently, gave no thought to Ethel or the family of children caught in the crossfire of this affair. But then, it appears, neither did Robert Kennedy, which raises the question of whether there was not another, secret, agenda in the role Robert played in the Marilyn stakes. The affair went on. It had been going on for some six months when, of a sudden, it stopped. Marilyn could no longer reach the Attorney General. He cut her off: dead. It is commonly thought that it was because of this she pined, became emotionally distressed, and, a few days later, took her own life. Nothing could be further from the truth.

There seemed to be plenty of hearsay evidence that Marilyn became pregnant while the Robert Kennedy affair was in full swing. Milo Speriglio made no bones about it. Speriglio, a Van Nuys private detective who wrote a book, *Crypt 33, The Saga of Marilyn Monroe: the Final Word*, with Adela Gregory in 1993 — and whom I met while I carried out my own research — had distinct ideas about this situation. He wrote she took her plight to Robert Kennedy, believing she could persuade him to divorce Ethel and marry her. This caused uproar in the Kennedy camp, according to Speriglio, for if Marilyn produced an infant there would be no doubt in the eyes of the public that Jack Kennedy was the father because of the exposure Marilyn's appearance at the Madison Square Garden birthday party obtained. At best there would be speculation over which brother was the father and, either way, this would spell the immediate end of the Kennedys' political careers.

The President would have had to resign amid horrific scandal, the Attorney General would go, and the family would be, effectively, barred from public office. Speriglio claimed they looked to Robert to exert pressure on Marilyn to have an abortion, but this was not easy. No doubt Marilyn saw she was in a position of strength: she could *insist* Robert Kennedy divorced Ethel. She was, after all, calling the shots, she thought.

164

But according to Speriglio, this was not so, and she was finally put on the spot by the Attorney General, who turned the tables on her. The way Speriglio read the situation was that Robert Kennedy threatened her that if there was no abortion, there would be no kind of relationship with him. Marilyn was heard to say she believed Robert *would* divorce Ethel and marry her in the course of time.

Marilyn, Speriglio said, had the abortion, though he claimed it was carried out locally at the Cedars of Lebanon Hospital, while private eye Fred Otash, who said he had gleaned that Marilyn was pregnant from the tapes made by Bernard Spindel, thought, probably more accurately, that she went to Mexico. Abortion was illegal in the United States at this time. Speriglio and Otash are not the only people to have made these claims. The Fox studio seemed to be humming with rumours.

Finally, however, it must be said that it may be none of this is true, though the coincidence of Robert Kennedy dropping Marilyn like a hot potato at this time would certainly lend credence to the story, whether it was an abortion or a miscarriage. It is not surprising that among those who believe it to be the truth there are many who see it as an overpowering reason for the Kennedys to silence Marilyn once and for all by killing her. But again, they would be wrong. This would be a 'straight line' scenario that did not admit the other, desperate, influences at work in the shadows behind the whole sequence of events.

16

TOO MANY QUESTIONS

Any investigation into the death of Marilyn Monroe is sure to produce a multiplicity of questions. To the investigator the objective is to find answers, and this can be extremely frustrating when, as fast as answers are found they in turn create new questions.

An example may be found in examining the role played by Robert Kennedy in the Marilyn story. His relationship with Marilyn, which is now finally confirmed in the Marilyn Tapes, was first speculated upon by Frank A Capell, in his book *The Strange Death of Marilyn Monroe*, which came out very soon after Marilyn's death, and in the thinly veiled reference to 'the Easterner' by Fred Guiles in a series of articles for a women's magazine, which were eventually published in 1969 as *Norma Jean: The Life of Marilyn Monroe*. As time went on there was greater acceptance that Robert Kennedy had been involved in an affair with Marilyn which began some months before she died. News of Jack Kennedy's relationship with Marilyn surfaced also, and the question of how and why Robert came into the picture was answered in the assumption he was sent by Jack — who was by then President of the United States — to put an end to his relationship with Marilyn which had become untenable.

This was likely true, but why Robert Kennedy should immediately become embroiled in a smouldering affair upon meeting Marilyn raised new questions. The answer offered has always been that he simply fell head over heels for her, and this has been generally accepted. This is a simplistic answer, and I must say simplistic answers are often the best. In this case, however, careful scrutiny of what is known of their relationship raises the question of whether Robert had another, secret motive in starting an apparently passionate affair with the star. A starting point in finding the answer to this might be that Robert Kennedy was not in any way renowned for infidelity. He was happily married and had been named 'Father of the Year'. Some authors have ascribed occasional 'indiscretions' to him, though the number of these accusations, generally, is outweighed by the writers who speak highly of his moral character. What, then, was he really doing when he began a 'fling' with Marilyn?

From differing sources we have gleaned there were two pertinent influences. The first was that Jack Kennedy was quite indiscreet when he spent time with Marilyn and she learnt from him a great deal he later regretted telling her. It is speculated, for instance, one such indiscretion was telling her he was first wed to Durie Malcolm, in a marriage that was quickly terminated by his father. This led to the second, highly pertinent influence; that, during the

167

period of their involvement, she came into possession of certain 'documents' — presumably letters, notes and photographs — that Jack was anxious to recover. It is believed he was especially anxious to recover a photograph which featured him in company with mobster, Sam Giancana. The recovery of Marilyn's 'file' now attached a purpose to the question of Robert's so-called 'steamy' affair.

If the fragments of Spindel's recordings relating to the last two visits paid by Robert Kennedy to Marilyn's house — which we considered in a previous chapter — may be relied upon, there was no doubt the recovery of '*it*', which he was desperate to obtain, was more vital to Robert Kennedy than anything else on that last day of her life. 'It's important to the family. You can make any arrangement you want . . . ' he is quoted as screaming at her. But Marilyn was clearly not into selling whatever it was Robert Kennedy was seeking. JFK biographer, Thomas C Reeves, wrote, 'Bobby always spoke in commands and would use any means to get what he wanted.' This time he failed. Marilyn was flaming mad and she dug in her heels.

Looking at the events of the last few weeks of Marilyn's life, there are indications that Robert Kennedy's agenda consisted of severing the links between Marilyn and his brother and recovering the documents Jack wanted. Perhaps he saw a 'love affair' as the way to achieve both of these objectives. Perhaps there was no passion on his side. If this is so he certainly deceived Marilyn. Marilyn fell hook, line and sinker. She was

President John F Kennedy. News of his affair with Marilyn leaked.
Photo Courtesy John F Kennedy Library

convinced Robert Kennedy would divorce his wife and marry her, against all the advice given her by her friends, who could see a great deal more clearly than she how impossible that was.

Robert may have achieved the first of his objectives, but in the second he failed abysmally. He was unlikely to recover the documents Jack wanted in circumstances where he had simply dumped Marilyn. The story of her pregnancy constituted more than a rumour. A number of those close to her knew about it, and the coincidence of Robert Kennedy dumping her at that particular time seemed to fit the scenario. To the world at large, a claim by Marilyn that the child was Robert's would not stop speculation that the President might be the father. After all, the spectacular appearance Marilyn had made at his birthday party at Madison Square Garden only weeks prior was riveted into the memories of people across the country. In either case the House of Camelot would not have survived scandal of this sort. All the stories of Jack's womanising would then likely have surfaced as editors went seeking the many stories that they had spiked.

When the crisis was averted Marilyn expected to receive Robert's attentions once more but things would never again be the same. He cut her off dead. As time progressed Marilyn came to her senses at last and, as her tapes reveal, it was she who finally opted out. This did not stop her expecting Robert being civil enough to say a friendly goodbye, however, and when it was not forthcoming, and all he could think of was his brother's precious documents when they finally met, he experienced a venom which unceremoniously saw him off the premises, a Kennedy or not.

Against this background it is not difficult to see why some find it easy to believe the Kennedy brothers were responsible for Marilyn's death. A superficial case is easily made. The surface has only to be scratched, however, to find this entirely false. Besides, the notion creates more problems than it resolves. Before a million new questions are let loose, we can say we have looked at this possibility and it is clear the Kennedys were not involved. This was wrong for a whole variety of reasons. The chief of these is that killing Marilyn — or having her killed — would have totally exposed the entire Kennedy family to ruination, and that is quite apart from the rigours of law. Besides, Chief Parker valued his reputation and integrity more than to participate in the protection of a guilty man. Parker would be quite satisfied there was no Kennedy involvement before embarking on his audacious cover up. Interestingly, however, those who thought the Kennedys were behind the murder of Marilyn were thinking exactly the way her killers wanted them to think.

* * *

The quiet investigation into Marilyn's death produced a file which we know was quite thick. The file, until it disappeared, raised questions about its content and who was given access to it.

Mayor of Los Angeles, Sam Yorty, was not above creating questions or providing hard and fast answers. To a number of people he confirmed, for instance, that Robert Kennedy was known to be in Los Angeles the day Marilyn died at a time when there was real doubt about his whereabouts, and considerable reluctance to allow his name to be linked to that of Marilyn. Yorty and Police Chief William Parker were good friends, and it would have been expected that Yorty — Parker's boss — might have been one of those privileged to examine the voluminous file before it disappeared. This is an unresolved question, some researchers believing he saw the file and others believing he did not. There is no doubt, however, that when Chief Parker died, Sam Yorty contacted the Police Department asking them to send him the Marilyn file. They sent word back, 'It isn't here,' and the Mayor was left to wonder what was going on.

As time progressed Mayor Yorty, a known power broker in his day, was upset to discover they had had a file — of sorts — all along. He was upset because these were people he ranked as his friends who had, effectively, refused to comply with his request. Yorty was an astute man, and he clearly knew — or guessed — some of the answers, at least, to the questions the Marilyn file raised. Of the cover up he is quoted as saying, 'Lawford took care of what he could,' which suggested he had inside information. When he spoke of the Police Department's unwillingness to send him the file he said, 'They must have had a secret they didn't want to come out.' That was putting it mildly.

Police Chief William Parker's actions at the time of Marilyn's death raised some interesting questions. Why, for instance, did he not put Thad Brown, his Chief of Detectives and Deputy Police Chief on the case? It was Brown who, soon after the news of Marilyn's death broke, told Parker that he knew Robert Kennedy was in Los Angeles on the day she died. After that the case was put in the hands of Captain James Hamilton, who was Head of the Intelligence Division. Hamilton and Parker played their cards close to their chests. Even Hamilton's own staff was aware of the secrecy involved in this enquiry. Thad Brown, a man who earned enormous respect for his devotion to duty, must soon have understood what was happening, for he began poking about, putting together a file of his own which grew in volume. This 'archive' was stored in his garage. Tom Reddin, Deputy to Parker and who succeeded him upon his death, told me Thad's son found it after his death. The whereabouts of this file is now unknown.

Tom Reddin told me he was given sight of the 'Marilyn file' which survived. It had something like fifty — some say many fewer — sheets in it, and the contents were described as inconsequential. More recently the Police Department have said that the reports have now been destroyed.

Whether or not FBI Director, J Edgar Hoover, saw the original Marilyn file is a matter for conjecture. On balance it is unlikely, though this does not mean his agents did not report back on material going into it. In the long run it did not matter to him. Later in the month Marilyn died, the FBI produced a report on 'rumors of an affair between Mr Kennedy and film actress Marilyn Monroe,' to which Robert Kennedy made a bland reply. He said he had met her but these, 'allegations have a way of growing beyond any semblance of truth.' The rumours were enough to allow Hoover to achieve his aim. He had the power to maintain his position with what his secret file on John F Kennedy contained. There is little speculation in believing that by then he had what he needed to maintain his position — his insurance — if Robert Kennedy should attain the Presidency, as it was commonly believed he one day would.

The power and role of J Edgar Hoover should not be underestimated. It was only one year after Marilyn died that President Kennedy was assassinated in Dallas, Texas. The night before Kennedy was murdered Dallas oil baron, Clint Murchison, threw a party which was attended by many notables, including President-to-be Richard Nixon and President-to-be Lyndon B Johnson. Johnson made the trip from nearby Fort Worth to attend the party, leaving the President and his entourage resting in nearby Fort Worth before their planned visit to Dallas. It was also said that J Edgar Hoover, who was known to be in the vicinity, attended, and an eye-witness spoke of a private meeting taking place between these men after which Johnson left. The eye-witness claimed Johnson afterwards revealed he knew what was planned to happen when Kennedy reached Dallas.

An FBI employee has since claimed that a report put out by Hoover some days before the assassination revealed he had been informed about a plan to kill the President in Dallas on November 22. If the story of the events at the Murchison party are true and the claim of William S Walters, the employee who worked at the FBI New Orleans office, is also correct, treason took place in the Murchison home that night. Whatever the case, J Edgar Hoover represented a power to be reckoned with, a power neither friendly to the President nor the Attorney General.

The files on John F Kennedy and Robert Kennedy presumably survived until Hoover died, when there was wholesale clearance in his department. After Marilyn died the Director is said to have sent item after item of 'data' relating to her death to the Attorney General, as if reinforcing his position. But Robert Kennedy's involvement with Marilyn would remain a secret for many years afterwards; Robert Kennedy was brutally gunned down at the Ambassador Hotel in Los Angeles in 1968, and it was a further seven years before open claims of his involvement with Marilyn surfaced. The most notable story was by Anthony Scaduto in *Oui* magazine. Against the tide of popular acceptance of the suicide story, Scaduto's 1975 article claimed Marilyn was murdered and that it had been suppressed to protect the Kennedys.

It is commonly said that truth will out. It has to be said that the truth about Marilyn's death has taken a long time to come out, but in spite of the remarkable blanket of secrecy thrown over the whole affair by Police Chief William Parker, aided and abetted by the Arthur Jacobs publicity machine and buttressed by the action of the Coroner's office, we have finally stripped down most of the lies and eradicated the greater part of the disinformation. The disappearing police file added difficulty to difficulty, of course, and the lack of willingness to speak on the part of some who could have helped decidedly slowed us down. We can now, however, piece together a great deal of what happened in Marilyn's last days and reveal a pattern indicating the truth.

17

THE LAST DAYS

Robert Kennedy had been engaged in a relationship with Marilyn for about six months. This, indeed, achieved the first thing he had set out to do; to get Marilyn off his brother's back. But it gave the appearance of smouldering into a highly passionate affair in which Peter Lawford did the fixing up of meetings and Robert did the chasing. She eventually came to believe Robert Kennedy would divorce his wife and marry her, and when he became president after Jack, a popular notion at the time, she would be the First Lady.

If the story of her pregnancy was true, she held a terrifying trump card over both Jack and Robert until she was persuaded to have the abortion or miscarried, whichever was the case. It would not be surprising if this was what signalled the end of the affair, but for whatever reason, Robert quickly turned off his passion — if it ever was passion — only days before Marilyn died. Marilyn tried and tried to get in touch with him, but entirely without success, both through the direct number that Robert had given her and through the Justice Department switchboard. He refused to accept her calls. Robert Slatzer told her it was on the news the

Attorney General was flying out to address a Bar Association meeting in San Francisco, so she set about finding out where he would be staying.

She tried getting in touch with Peter Lawford, but he had gone to earth when the relationship had taken a dive. She eventually found him and obtained his wife Pat's number at Hyannis Port so she could ask her how to contact Robert. Whether from Pat, with whom she was very friendly, or someone else, she discovered he would be staying at the St Francis Hotel in San Francisco, and she began ringing there, but again she was unsuccessful. She even tried ringing his home number in Virginia, which was said to have enraged him. The Attorney General had brought Ethel and four of his children with him and had left them with an attorney friend, John Bates, who had a ranch near San Francisco, while he went to give his address. He registered at the St Francis and it seems he was at the hotel when Marilyn rang, but he would not accept her calls.

Marilyn was hurt. She knew the affair was over and all she expected of him was that he would say goodbye. Perhaps on Robert's part, however, the break had been premature, for it seems he had not collected the documents Jack wanted from Marilyn. From some source it appears Marilyn heard that Robert was intending to call at Los Angeles, and she felt sure he would be coming to see her, if only to say goodbye. On the night he was due into Los Angeles, Friday 3 August, the night before she died, she had an expensive meal sent to her house; Briggs Delicatessen delivered various dishes, hors d'oeuvres and champagne, but Kennedy did not show up for it. But then she had a call from Peter Lawford, who persuaded her with some difficulty to dine with him at a local restaurant.

Lawford took her to the fashionable La Scala, and when they arrived Robert Kennedy was already there, at a rear table, waiting for her. Jean Leon, the French *maître d'* of the restaurant, appeared at first to put off enquirers by telling them he had delivered food to Marilyn's house that night, a claim which did not sit well, since Briggs, whose claim was backed up by a large bill, also claimed to have supplied a meal. But Leon told the reliable Rupert Allan, a member of Arthur Jacobs' publicity team, how Marilyn and Robert Kennedy had, in fact, eaten at La Scala, and he had seen them arguing. We cannot know for sure what transpired but we can speculate with some confidence that Kennedy's top priority was to unhitch from the star, while finding a way to persuade her to hand over the documents and keep silent. A sequel to the La Scala delivered-food story surfaced later, presumably again emanating from Jean Leon, that the food he supplied to the house was ordered, not for Friday but Saturday night. That would fit well with what we know of her arrangements for Saturday. Marilyn had invited Ralph Roberts, her masseur, for a meal on the terrace that night.

People were talking, and both Marilyn and Robert knew that. Top national broadcaster and journalist Dorothy Kilgallen had written a teasing article which had appeared that very day

Attorney General Robert F Kennedy.
He and Marilyn rowed.
Photo courtesy National Archives.

in which she talked of Marilyn, ' . . . cooking in
the sex appeal department. She has appeared
vastly alluring to a handsome gentleman. A
handsome gentleman who has a bigger name
than Joe DiMaggio in his heyday — so don't
write her off.' Closer to home, Ralph Roberts,
while massaging Marilyn, had surprised her by
telling how all Hollywood was talking about her
and Bobby Kennedy.

However fast — or slow — the news was in reaching Robert's wife, Ethel, the other members of the Kennedy family knew about his relationship with Marilyn, though they would be likely to if he had flown out to Los Angeles at the behest of his brother. While Ethel might not take the same view, the others were likely to place the relationship under the heading of 'essential business'. This suggestion may have been supported by a note sent by Jean Kennedy to Marilyn that was found among her effects and surfaced some years after she died. It ran,

Dear Marilyn,

Mother asked me to write and thank you for your sweet note to Daddy — he really enjoyed it and you were very cute to send it. Understand that you and Bobby are the new item!

We all think you should come with him when he comes back east.

Love,
Jean Smith

The note existed and was genuine — we reproduce a photograph of the real thing on the next page — but it would appear to be highly mischievous. It was not until 1994, when the letter was auctioned, that Jean Kennedy finally admitted she had written it. She poured scorn on the idea of it being taken at face value, however. She said it was a joke. In the light of what we have discovered about the President despatching Robert to tidy up after him, I believe this, though

I think any humour in what it said was heavily laced with sarcasm. There was no way Marilyn would have been acceptable to the Kennedy family, most particularly mother Rose, and any genuine indication of recognition from any member of the family would have alienated both Jackie and Ethel.

But probably the most worrying thing to the Attorney General was a report that reached him

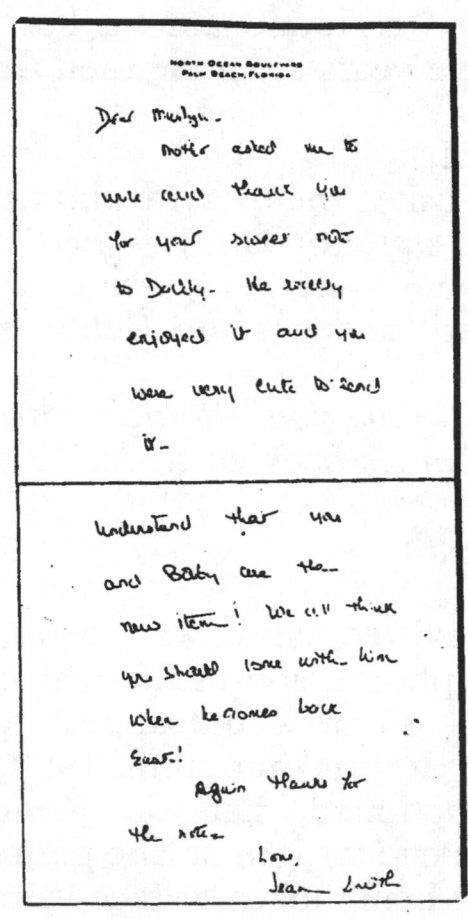

Facsimile of the letter Jean Kennedy Smith sent to Marilyn.

through Justice Department staff after he had arrived in San Francisco. He was told, baldly, 'You'd better get your ass down to LA because she's out of control.' Marilyn had let it be known to one or two people she intended calling a press conference three days later, on Monday, at 11.00 a.m. when she would 'blow the lid off the whole damn thing'. It is doubtful she would have done such a thing, but the threat certainly caused alarm in high places. It came to light long afterwards that it had been documented by the CIA and that it had attracted the attention of their top man, director James Angleton.

Even had she been serious and gone through with it, however, it is doubtful the press would give credence to whatever Marilyn said. Many journalists would not have touched it, while others would have had it spiked by their editors, leaving a few who might have got a quarter column deep inside the paper. But neither Jack nor Robert Kennedy could take this risk. Besides, it appeared she still had in her possession the file containing the letters, photograph and other documents that Jack Kennedy desperately wanted with which to make himself fireproof. We might speculate that Robert Kennedy's attitude attracted from Marilyn no more than a half promise to be at the Lawford's dinner party Saturday night.

Whatever the case, Pat Newcomb confirms that later on Friday night, presumably after the La Scala episode, they went out together for a drink, and Marilyn was said to have become the worse for drink before she went home. Peter

Lawford stayed on with them and they went on to another restaurant on Sunset Boulevard. Dress designer Billy Travilla saw them all there but was cut when he said hello to Marilyn, who, it seems, was too drunk to recognise him. Pat Newcomb had not been well lately — she had been suffering from bronchial trouble — and when they wound up their drinking session and made to go home, Marilyn invited her to stay over.

Saturday morning saw Marilyn grizzly, since she had had a very bad night and was irritated by the fact that Pat had slept well. Apart from having had too much to drink the night before, the main cause of her sleeplessness had been a series of phone calls which added up to telling her to 'leave Bobby alone, you tramp.' She had neglected to put her telephone outside the bedroom door Friday night. She did not believe the calls were from Ethel Kennedy herself, she told her friend Jeanne Carmen in an early morning phone call, but she believed Ethel had arranged for them to be made. Word had travelled.

We know of at least four other telephone calls Marilyn made that morning, and it was while she was on the phone, at ten o'clock, Mrs Murray arrived. One of her calls was to her friend, Arthur James, whom she was unable to reach, but she got through to her ex-husband's father, Isadore Miller, of whom she was very fond. Another call was to her masseur, Ralph Roberts, when they discussed meeting up that evening for a barbecue on the terrace, and the fourth was to her journalist friend, Sidney Skolsky. She chatted to Skolsky about his family, and while they were talking she told him she was seeing Robert Kennedy at the Lawford's house that night. Skolsky was apprehensive of the way Marilyn was bandying the names of the Kennedys about, and wanted someone to listen in to what was being said. He asked his daughter to do this, and she heard the conversation between Marilyn and her father that morning.

The events of the previous evening had done nothing to cheer her. If she had adopted the attitude that she *might* drop in Saturday night to the dinner party if she *felt* like it — and it certainly would make sense — it would explain a

The Lawford's house on the beach at Santa Monica.
Photo Robert F Slatzer Collection

185

lot. Perhaps when she got tipsy she was not so much drowning her sorrows, but letting off steam. But she had no way of knowing that the events of Saturday afternoon would change everything relating to Robert Kennedy irrevocably.

It would appear that Robert Kennedy, after his row with Marilyn, had not stayed at the Beverley Hills Hotel, into which he had been booked. It seems he went further afield, possibly back to the Bates' ranch or to the St Francis Hotel at San Francisco. At any rate, it was reported to Police Chief William Parker that he arrived at Los Angeles again on Saturday morning. He came into Los Angeles airport, where he made his way by helicopter to the Fox studio, to a car waiting for him. Peter Lawford was with him, and they made their way to Lawford's house on the beach road at Santa Monica, where his neighbour spotted them.

During the course of that Saturday morning, plants that Marilyn had ordered on Friday from a local nursery were delivered to Fifth Helena Drive, and a package was delivered which contained a soft toy tiger. Marilyn's hairdresser, Agnes Flanagan, who looked after the washing and styling of her hair, was there when it was delivered, and she took notice that it — or perhaps some note that came with it — seemed to depress the star. Agnes finished her work, and she quietly left without troubling her. The meaning of the tiger and the contents of the note, if there was one, are unknown, but it is not unlikely the package was sent by Robert

Kennedy. If the meeting of Friday night was a hastily called crisis meeting, and it appeared to be so, perhaps this was a communication he had planned for her to receive and had been unable to recover before it was delivered. It is just possible it was a put-off that should have been delivered the day before, when she had gone to a lot of trouble with the meal, but that alone would hardly have depressed her. It might have carried a very different message, however. If the furious nocturnal phone calls were the consequence of Ethel Kennedy having just become aware of what had been going on, it would not be surprising if a note with the tiger indicated Robert had had a solemn warning and a threat of divorce from his wife, and that was the reason for his absence from the Friday night meal she had arranged at her home. If Ethel divorced him it would put paid to his political career and his presidential ambitions. Such a note would crush any remaining affection Marilyn had for him, and would bring into sharp perspective that he had never intended divorcing Ethel to marry her, as he had apparently promised. If she had just bumped this far down to earth it is small wonder if she showed it.

It now seemed Robert was moving swiftly and with purpose, determined to conclude the business once and for all. He was sighted visiting her house during the afternoon, it would seem without an arrangement having been made or an invitation extended. Robert probably intended this to be a business meeting, when his intention was to obtain the documents Jack Kennedy needed, with any goodbye taking a lower priority. Peter Lawford was with him and, on arrival, took a drink out to the pool while Robert and Marilyn talked. Fred Otash, the private detective who claimed to have heard some of the tapes of what went on made by Bernard Spindel from bugs in Marilyn's home, told of them making love during this meeting, and then having a violent row. What she said added up to complaints she was 'passed around like a piece of meat'. She knew that any ideas of Robert Kennedy marrying her were now well and truly over. 'You've lied to me. Get out of here. Leave me alone.' The Attorney General had no option but to leave. If the acquisition of documents was his top priority he did not get them. The tapes reveal him purportedly shouting again and again, '*Where is it?*' This might have been a photograph we know his brother Jack was anxious to get hold of or, more likely, a file containing the photograph and other papers he wanted.

Kennedy tried to persuade Marilyn to see him at the Lawford's dinner party that night, but she gave him short shrift. 'Stop bothering me' was the reply he got. Fred Otash quoted Peter Lawford as saying Marilyn had tried to reach President Kennedy by phone to tell him to call Bobby off. Otash said,

According to Lawford, he had called her and she had said to him that she was passed around like a piece of meat. She had had it.

She didn't want Bobby to use her any more. She called the White House and there was no response from the President. She was told he was in Hyannis Port and she didn't connect with him. She kept trying to get him. He [Lawford] had tried to reason with her to quiet down and come to the beach house and relax. She said, 'No. I'm tired. There's nothing more for me to respond to. Just do me a favour. Tell the President I tried to get him. Tell him goodbye for me. I think my purpose has been served.'

There were a number of telephone calls that day that help to explain what was happening to Marilyn and, of even greater importance, what was not happening to her. Sometime during the afternoon she made a second call to her friend Jeanne Carmen. She had first rung her at six o'clock that morning when she couldn't sleep, and had told her about the 'leave Bobby alone' calls which had started the night before and which had gone on until 5.30 a.m. In her afternoon call she was asking Jeanne to come over and see her. Jeanne reminded Marilyn it was her birthday and thanked her for her gift of gold-coloured golf clubs (Jeanne was a professional when it came to trick golf shots which earned her both fame and popularity) but she said she couldn't come as she had birthday dates to keep. Besides, she and Marilyn already had plans to meet up on the golf course the next day, Sunday.

It was during the afternoon also that,

Jeanne Carmen
Photo Matthew Smith Collection

according to Mrs Murray, Marilyn asked if there was any oxygen in the house. As we said earlier, people do not expect their housekeepers to have put in a cylinder of oxygen on the off chance that it will be useful for something. Far more realistically this is Mrs Murray retrospectively supplying clues to support the belief her employer was planning suicide, totally uncorroborated by the other facts we have. By 4.30 p.m. Mrs Murray thought Marilyn was feeling low, she said, and she telephoned Dr Greenson and asked him to come over to see her. There was nothing unusual in this; he saw Marilyn frequently, perhaps once a day, sometimes twice, or even more. What was rather more remarkable, in view of her oxygen story and other hints at suicide, was that Mrs Murray later told Robert Slatzer 'She was full of life and eager to follow through and do things quickly and spontaneously, and her ideas were good,' when she spoke of the days before her death. This was more likely the truth.

It was at about 5.00 p.m. Peter Lawford telephoned to ask Marilyn again to join them for dinner. Robert wanted to see her, he said. Marilyn by then had no intention of going and said so. And she certainly did not want to see Robert Kennedy — ever — after their stormy afternoon session. Ralph Greenson arrived at her house shortly after 5.00 p.m., and Pat Newcomb, who had, apparently, been around all day, left at about half past six. Until she left they were sunbathing and looking at scripts. 'Marilyn was in a good mood, a happy mood,' said Pat, and Dr Greenson, it seems, did not find she had a problem. It was likely at this meeting Marilyn handed over to Dr Greenson the tapes she had recorded, the transcripts of which are featured in this book.

As Pat left, Marilyn called, 'I'll see you tomorrow. Toodle-loo.' About this time there was a telephone call from masseur Ralph Roberts, with whom Marilyn had made a

191

half-arrangement to have dinner — a barbecue — that evening. Greenson, who did not like Roberts, answered the phone and flatly told him she was not in, leaving the masseur bewildered. Dr Greenson stayed for about two hours, after which he left to take his wife out to dinner. Before he left, Mrs Murray asked if he would like her to stay over that night, but Greenson said he did not think it would be necessary. But strangely, Mrs Murray decided she would stay over anyway, though she never explained why.

But Robert Kennedy had unfinished business with Marilyn, and he returned to her house again that evening, again uninvited, perhaps in the region of 6.45 p.m. Lawford was probably with Kennedy again, and another man was with them also. As they walked from the car, women at a card party in a neighbour's house saw them. One woman said, 'Look, girls, there he is again.' At the second visit, it appeared Kennedy had stopped trying to negotiate for the file of documents; he just wanted to find where it was and take it with or without her permission. Spindel's tapes are said to have recorded Robert Kennedy saying, 'We have to know. It's important to the family. We can make any arrangements you want, but we must find it.'

Noises suggested further searching. Lawford was heard telling Kennedy to, 'Calm down', while Marilyn screamed at them to get out of the house. The tape then appeared to have recorded the sound of a bump or bumps, as though Marilyn had fallen down, followed by calming noises. Spindel, who was ever trying to get blackmail material for Jimmy Hoffa, says he believes someone in the Kennedy party killed her and that they were there when she died. But while much of the quoted excerpts from the tapes were believable, the murder claim was neither supported by the tapes nor other known facts. It is worth repeating that one extract was said to contain the words, 'What do we do with the body now?' which, in another version, became, 'What do we do with her *dead* body?' as though to drive the point home and leave nothing to the imagination. The small addition may be the indication that the contents of the extract were an invention. It would certainly conflict with other evidence we have that Marilyn was alive until much later than this.

It has to be remembered that audio recordists are known the world over for 'telling stories with sounds'. Careful editing, placing words out of sequence and transferring sounds from one tape to another can create all manner of situations that purport to be what they are not. As we have said, in one recording, the person explaining the content of the tape talks of the sound of someone being placed on a bed, which is quite absurd. It would defeat the capability of the most skilled sound recordist — even Bernard Spindel — to produce a sound that was identifiably that of someone being placed on a modern bed. These were not the beds of bygone days when the springs could be heard bending. Of course a commentary *added* for the listener might *suggest* what was being heard. And this serves to remind us that when a sound recording requires an explanation of what the listener is hearing, it advertises the sound is not explicit. It is not reliable for what it is supposed to be if it depends on an explanation for what is happening which might well come from a thoroughly biased party — such as Bernard Spindel.

The evidence for Marilyn being alive until about midnight or even later is much more reliable than Bernard Spindel's tapes, which require explanation. One such piece of evidence came from Marilyn's friend Jeanne Carmen. She told me when I interviewed her she'd had a third call from Marilyn as late as about ten o'clock, still asking Jeanne to go across and see her. Jeanne begged off since after celebrating her birthday she was tired. She would see her Sunday. Jeanne said Marilyn sounded a bit uptight and nervous, but otherwise normal. She gave no cause for any kind of alarm.

In fact, Robert Kennedy and the people who were with him would appear to have left by 7.30 p.m., and Marilyn was far from devastated as a consequence of the visit. She received a telephone call from Joe DiMaggio's son, Joe, at that time and was in no way distressed when she spoke to him. She got on well with Joe Jr and he with her, and made it clear she was delighted to get his call. He was ringing to tell her he had broken off his engagement, which he knew would please her. Marilyn had been concerned because she thought he was about to make a mistake by marrying the wrong girl. Mrs Murray caught a moment of the conversation at Marilyn's end and said she heard her laughing.

'Oh, that's wonderful,' she heard Marilyn say. Joe Jr recalls her being 'gay, happy and alert' when he spoke to her. 'If anything was amiss I wasn't aware of it.'

Peter Lawford claimed he telephoned Marilyn to invite her over to dinner at about 7.30 p.m. This was quite impossible, since she was speaking to young Joe DiMaggio, and that was verified. What Peter Lawford claimed was said in the phone call he made was both dramatic and inventive. Lawford said Marilyn's speech was thick and slurred and he had difficulty catching what she said. He said he tried to rouse her by shouting her name. Deborah Gould, whom Lawford later married, said he told her about the call. Marilyn had said it would be best for everyone if she died. Peter told Gould she said she was going to kill herself. She recounted how Lawford told her he said, 'Nonsense, Marilyn, pull yourself together . . . ' and later, callously, 'whatever you do, don't leave any notes behind.' There was another version of this call, however. In this Marilyn is purported to have said, 'Say goodbye to Pat, say goodbye to the President, and say goodbye to yourself, because you're a nice guy.' Lawford said her voice trailed away and then there were no further noises so he hung up and re-dialled her number, but got a busy signal.

Lawford had only one concern, and that was covering the backs of the Kennedys without regard for anyone or anything else, and in this he was completely successful. It is highly unlikely there ever was a second telephone call, or that

Marilyn said any of the things she was reported as saying. In fact, it would be easy to doubt there was even a first phone call at 5.00 p.m., but the fact he gave an account of its contents to his private eye, Fred Otash, would lend credence to it having taken place. Even then, of course, it has to be questioned whether Otash got a straight tale. Otash said Lawford told him, 'She said she felt sleepy and was going to bed. She did sound sleepy, but I've talked to her a hundred times before and she sounded no different. Thinking she was lonely, I asked her to have dinner with me and some friends. But Marilyn decided not to come along.' Everything being considered, this is probably what really did transpire in the call. A very different tale from the one he told later, and far more likely the truth. He afterwards saw the potential for Marilyn having said a lot of other things that would support that she was low, falling into despondency, and had suicide on her mind.

Lawford well knew that the suicide theory undermined any notions that the Kennedys were involved in Marilyn's death. It seems clear he wove a fabric of lies into his supposed telephone call, or calls, to support that Marilyn had taken her own life. The only report of Marilyn speaking in a slurred voice was much later that evening — at 9.45 p.m. — speaking to Ralph Roberts' answering service, when she had probably been dropping off to sleep. She made yet another call to Jeanne Carmen after that, however, when she was wide awake and there was no suggestion of slurring.

196

In view of the evidence that Marilyn was happily chatting to Joe DiMaggio Jr when Lawford was supposed to have made his second call and found Marilyn 'suicidal', Deborah Gould revised the timing for this and said it was probably about ten o'clock. It was about ten o'clock, however, according to Jeanne Carmen, Marilyn telephoned her and was not remotely in the suicidal mood described by Ms Gould. There is another head-on clash which makes it appear that Deborah Gould's second attempt at timing the call was 'out of the frying pan into the fire.' Peter Lawford knew what happened to Marilyn. He was, it appears, in and out of her house all night the night she died. But there is more to the story, which we will discover later.

At about 7.45 p.m. she rang Dr Greenson and caught him before he left for dinner. Whatever she said conveyed to him she had not let Robert Kennedy's visit get to her. She had quickly recovered. When Dr Greenson later spoke of this call he said she assured him she was feeling much better. She was feeling 'more cheerful' than she had felt earlier in the day, and he felt it would be unlikely that any problems would arise while he was out for dinner. It was about eight o'clock when she told Mrs Murray she was going to bed. She took her telephone into the bedroom and was known to have made four calls. The first, at about nine o'clock, was to Henry Rosenfeld, a New York dress manufacturer whom she had befriended in the brief time she was a model. He said she sounded 'groggy', but he was certainly not alarmed. Perhaps at that

Peter Lawford is here pictured with June Allyson
MGM

time she was feeling sleepy.

Between making calls she received one, from her Mexican friend Jose Bolanos. He told that he spoke to her from a restaurant where he was having a meal. She had recently been romantically linked with him and he had accompanied her to the Golden Globe Awards on 5 March. The only odd thing he reported was that she did not hang up when they finished talking. She just put the phone down. Bolanos did not find this troubling; he said she had done it before. The phone was not off the hook for long, however, for it was soon after this she telephoned Sydney Guilaroff, the legendary hairdresser. Their conversation was brief, and during their talk he recalls her telling him, 'I'm very depressed.' He remembers she hung up without saying goodbye. He was another who was obviously not alarmed.

And, of course, a comment she made to him relating to depression, even if trivially expressed, is the kind that the mind would retrospectively pluck from a conversation when suicide is later reported.

It was at about 9.30 p.m. Pat Newcomb arrived at Peter Lawford's dinner party and announced that Marilyn was tired and would not be coming. It seems Joe and Dolores Naar had been first to arrive, about an hour before this, and by all accounts they appeared to know that Marilyn would not be coming. By the time Pat arrived, producer George Durgom was there. Durgom remembers Pat arriving and tells how, much later that evening, Peter Lawford expressed concern about Marilyn. As we said in an earlier chapter, it would be incredible if Pat Newcomb were not aware of the telephone calls made regarding Marilyn's welfare that evening. If she was aware, it is even more incredible if she, as one of Marilyn's best friends, was not drawn into the mesh of expressed concern for her well-being that evening. This represents an important and perhaps vital loose end in the recounting of the events of that night.

At about 9.45 p.m. that night Marilyn tried to reach masseur Ralph Roberts, with whom she had tentative dinner plans. If Dr Greenson had not told her he had rung at 6.30 p.m. she would want to find out what had happened to him. If he had told her, she would no doubt want to apologise to her masseur. She did not reach him, however. His answering service told her he had gone out to dinner with friends, and this was the call in which it was said her voice seemed slurred, but, at about 10.00 p.m., in what appears to have been her final call that night to Jeanne Carmen, there was no mention of slurring. That night, again, Marilyn did not put the phone outside the bedroom door.

Here she was, she had said to Dr Greenson earlier that evening, the most beautiful woman in the world and she did not have a date for Saturday night. That Saturday night Marilyn would become what someone else believed was his trump card to play in a bitter struggle to determine who would rule the United States.

18

No Damn Way

It is remarkable, and impressive, the number of people — very different people, most of whom had direct links to Marilyn — who believed, from very early on, that she was murdered, despite the cry of suicide that had been raised by the media at the time.

Perhaps heading the list was John Miner. John Miner, who is now a highly respected lawyer, had no axe to grind. He was present at the Monroe autopsy, one of thousands he attended representing the Los Angeles District Attorney, and this, at the outset, was no different from any other. He watched Dr Noguchi, stage by stage, as he performed the autopsy. He assisted him in examining the body for injection marks, and, together, they drew a blank. Before he left the autopsy room he knew Marilyn had not died from ingesting the drugs that had killed her, neither had she been injected with them. This puzzled him, especially in view of having seen the purple hue of Marilyn's colon. His curiosity turned into worry, so much so that he later wrote to two internationally respected pathologists for new opinions. They both reassured him his own opinion was correct, and to him this meant the drugs had been administered by enema, which, in turn, meant that Marilyn had been murdered.

John Miner has now released the contents of the secret tapes made by Marilyn for her psychiatrist, hoping to achieve a new investigation that will show she was not a suicide. This is the only way the stigma of suicide will be removed. It will not bring her back to life, but it would be a kindness if the truth were universally known about her death.

Thomas Noguchi has always fought shy of saying he believed she was murdered, though he is quoted as having come very close to saying it. Having met him and talked to him, it is my opinion this is his personal belief. He certainly makes no attempt to argue a case for suicide. Noguchi, a junior member of staff at the time, was the victim of the 'tight ship' run by the coroner, Theodore Curphey, in which everyone had to toe the line. Noguchi escaped with his reputation intact, but it was no thanks to those who put him in charge of a case that carried the risk of media explosion and political backlash. It was a 'hot potato' and a

Milo Speriglio,
Los Angeles private eye.
Photo Robert F Slater
Collection

lesser man might have been professionally ruined in the hands of those who were pulling the strings.

Bob Slatzer knew Marilyn for a very long time, and became a close friend. From the very beginning he did not believe the stories that Marilyn had committed suicide. Slatzer was, in fact, Marilyn's second husband. Daringly, since she was dating Joe DiMaggio at the time, he and Marilyn slipped off to Tijauna, on the Mexican border, in October 1952 and had a 'quickie' wedding. Three days later, Twentieth Century Fox boss Darryl Zanuck, faced them both and told them he had a big financial investment in Marilyn and made it clear he was not going to be 'put on a hook' with a marriage. They went back to Tijauna and bribed the official to destroy the marriage certificate which had not been filed.

Bob Slatzer acknowledges that Marilyn had probably thought better of their marriage by the time she returned to Los Angeles, but this did not prevent a lasting friendship. Slatzer knew Marilyn well and he followed her progress — and sometimes the lack of it — with interest. He was stunned when he heard a news broadcast announcing she had taken her own life. It was something he could not accept even before he made an investigation of the circumstances, and his enquiries only served to support his instincts. He engaged a private detective, Milo Speriglio, to use his professional skills in developing the investigation he had made, and for ten years the detective looked into every nook and cranny to find answers. Answers come in all shapes and sizes, however, and one man's answer sometimes presents itself as another man's question. Speriglio made much progress. He unearthed a great deal of detail, fascinating hearsay and many interesting facts. And though hard evidence is difficult to come by, he eventually collected enough material to write two books on the subject. Speriglio's work convinced him Marilyn was murdered, and Bob Slatzer, who has also written on the subject, has not changed his mind. He is convinced Marilyn was killed.

Sergeant Jack Clemmons, the first officer to reach Marilyn's house when the news was officially telephoned to the police, makes no bones of it either. He had the feeling he was at the scene of a crime when he went to the house at Fifth Helena Drive that night. The place was too tidy, and he could not find a drinking receptacle in the bedroom and there was a strange absence of papers and documents of the kind he would have expected to see lying around. Others, too, would seem to have become conscious of the over-tidiness of the place; when pictures were taken later documents were seen strewn around the foot of the bedside table. Then, to Clemmons, the position of the body was odd. It was lying in what he called the 'soldier' position: legs straight, arms by the sides. He thought the people there were creepy, and he 'felt' the presence of others in the house. And he could not forget the sounds of the washing machine and the vacuum cleaner.

He followed the case and was amazed to hear about the drugs passed to the coroner which were said to have been found on the bedside table. When he had been at the house he had made a point of looking into every pill bottle on top of the table and had seen they were all empty. Much would have been explained, of course, if he had known that the house had been alive with activity for hours before he was called, as well as after he left. And he would have been scandalised if he had known that Police Chief Parker had been informed of Marilyn's death some five hours earlier than he, as duty Watch Commander, had been. Clemmons is now dead, but his belief that Marilyn was murdered was unshakeable right until his death.

Among the many journalists who have challenged the suicide verdict, Dorothy Kilgallen

Marilyn with Dorothy Kilgallen,
Also in the picture is Yves Montand.
Photo courtesy Jean Bach

was probably the most prominent. Chicago-based Kilgallen, a radio and television personality as well as a writer, was one of those who first accepted the suicide story, but only until she made a close examination of the then-known facts. Kilgallen was smart and shrewd, and quickly recognised she was looking at a case of murder. She planned to write a book on the subject but, for some reason, never did.

Another journalist, Frank Capell, wrote for a small, little-known newspaper. But Frank Capell was an astute man and within a short time of Marilyn's death he acquired a remarkable grasp of the nitty-gritty surrounding the event, and he and his associates made a great many enquiries about the people who were near to her when she died. He could not accept the suicide verdict and pulled no punches in his book, *The Strange Death of Marilyn Monroe*. Capell complained about 'strong efforts' being made to discredit both him and some of those who carried out enquiries for him. He thought they were 'too well co-ordinated' to be wasted on the editor of a small right-wing publication. But his little book was felt to be important enough to be brought to the attention of J Edgar Hoover, who, in turn, told Robert Kennedy what was in it. The soundness and excellence of Capell's work was spoilt by what appeared to be his compelling motive for writing his book. He was an avid right-winger, and was seeking to discredit Robert Kennedy, whom he saw as a socialist. In those days being a socialist — to those of the Right, such as Capell — was just one step away from being a communist.

Of the various authors who have written on the subject, Norman Mailer is undoubtedly the most important. Mailer, if not completely convinced Marilyn was murdered, leans very heavily in that direction. In his book *Marilyn*, he mentions Bob Slatzer's book *The Life and Curious Death of Marilyn Monroe* and salutes the depth of research featured in it.

A number of the stars who numbered Marilyn among their friends believed, also, that she had been murdered. Frank Sinatra, who kept quiet on the subject during his lifetime, was revealed by biographer Michael Munn[1] as believing she had been murdered. He had remarkably accurate ideas about how it was done, and believed the Mafia were behind her death, even naming the men he thought had killed her. Robert Mitchum, who worked with Marilyn on *River of No Return*, could not accept the suicide verdict. 'I think she was murdered,' he told me. Marilyn had tried to reach Bob Mitchum after the Madison Square Garden birthday party that he persuaded her to go to. Not realising there was anything urgent about it, he did not speak to her again before she died. Pat Newcomb told him later she really did want to speak to him, and afterwards Bob never shook off the feelings of guilt that he had not taken the trouble to contact her. '[It seemed] she wanted so desperately to talk to me,' he told me.

---

[1] Michael Munn, *Sinatra: The Untold Story*, Robson Books, London, 2002

Jeanne Carmen, Marilyn's neighbour when she lived at her Doheny apartment and friend of long standing, told me she couldn't accept the suicide verdict. 'I will never think that,' she said. Marilyn spoke to her on the telephone three times on the day she died, she told me. She so wanted Jeanne to come over to see her, but it was Jeanne's birthday that day and she had her day arranged. Even up till ten o'clock on the night she died Marilyn was asking her to come over. 'I don't think she was suicidal. That's a lie.' She spoke of Marilyn's new deal and reinstatement to *Something's Got to Give* and said, 'She was as happy as I've seen her.' Marilyn had planned to join Jeanne, a professional standard golfer, on the golf course at Monterey the day after she died.

Allan (Whitey) Snyder, Marilyn's make-up man, was as close to the star as any of her best friends. He and his wife, Marjorie Plecher, who was Marilyn's wardrobe mistress, were two of her very favourite people. When Whitey heard Marilyn was dead he was devastated. He found it hard to take in. He drove round to her house and then realised she was no longer there. But he did not forget the last task Marilyn had given him. She was only twenty-seven when, during the making of *Gentlemen Prefer Blondes*, she asked Whitey to make her a promise. ' . . . if something happens to me, promise you'll do my make-up so that I'll look my best . . . ' It was an embarrassing promise to exact, and Whitey responded with a jest, 'Sure. Bring the body back while it's still warm and I'll do it.' But, it seemed, Marilyn was not jesting. Some time later she sent Whitey a gold money clip with the engraving, 'Whitey dear While I'm still warm Marilyn.'

Whitey Snyder would not fail Marilyn now that the time had come. But when he heard a news broadcast saying she had taken her own life, his response was immediate. 'No way. No damn way.'

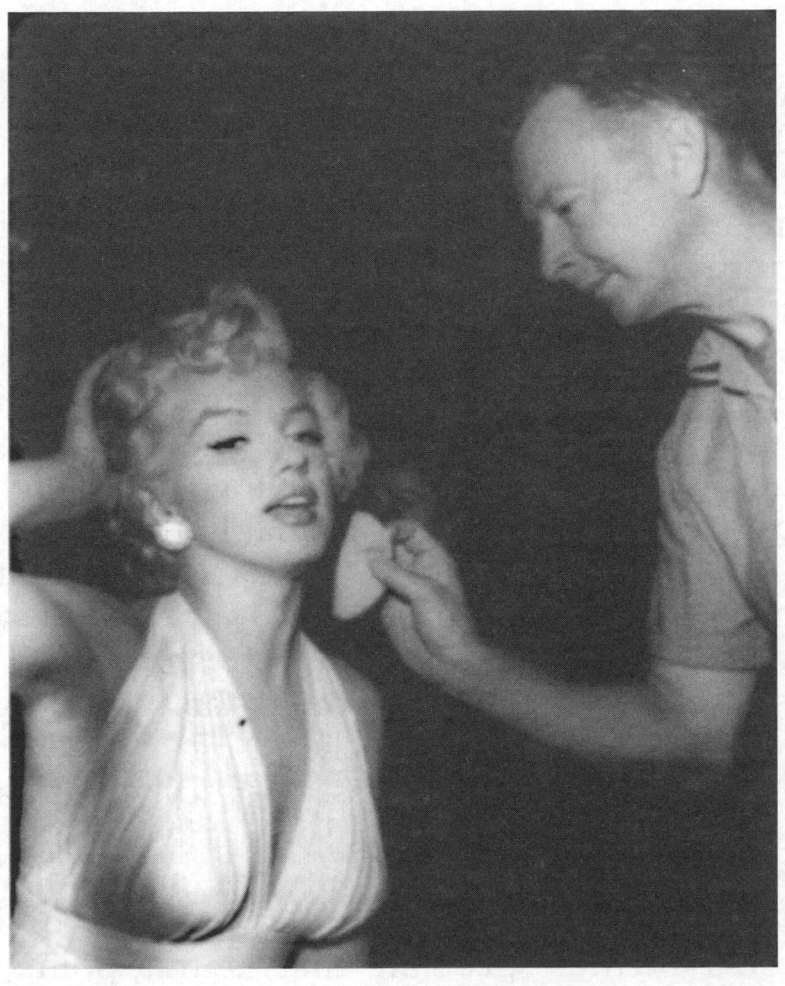

Whitey Snyder makes up Marilyn on the set.
Photo Robert F Slater Collection.

19

No Touch of Silk,
No Hint of Finesse

It would not be wild speculation to suppose that while Marilyn was lying in bed that Saturday night she had a late-night caller. Perhaps he was someone she knew, or perhaps he commanded her attention by who he was and the status he carried. I favour the latter. There is little doubt Mrs Murray let the late caller in, and it is likely he persuaded Marilyn to take him to the guest 'cottage' to talk in private. The guest accommodation was furthest from the living room, kitchen and main bedrooms, and probably the only part of the house not bugged. The visitor had not come to talk, but the evidence suggests he was offered — and accepted — refreshments. This was essential to his plan, for in this way he was able to slip Marilyn a 'Mickey Finn'.

A 'Mickey Finn' contains chloral hydrate, and chloral hydrate is tasteless, so Marilyn would be totally unsuspecting and simply — and probably quickly — go to sleep in the presence of her guest. I further speculate that at this point the 'guest' was joined by others. Since there were people around all during and after the time of Marilyn's death who would open doors for those with lawful and justifiable reasons to access rooms, the fact that the A-1 Lock and Safe Company submitted a bill to Marilyn's estate for repairs made to locks *after* she had died suggests intruders. When Marilyn's secretary Cherie Redmond complained the house had no locks that worked, it is likely she had not included the guest apartment in this. The 'guest' who had been talking to Marilyn in the guest apartment presumably was not able to admit those who joined him without either attracting attention or causing damage.

The intruders knew exactly what they were doing and the effect they were trying to produce. They either brought their own surgical equipment with them, or obtained the equipment that they knew was in the house, with which to administer an enema and by this means inject a huge and fatal dose of Nembutal into her system. Normally the consequences of this method causes the bowel to discharge its contents, which suggests they had come prepared with a plug of some kind, by which means to make sure the barbiturates were retained. No finesse in this murder, a quick and straightforward operation to kill Marilyn, but leaving, on the face of it, all the evidence of her having taken her own life. There is little doubt that when Sergeant Clemmons heard the washing machine being used in the middle of the night it was Mrs Murray making sure that the evidence of faecal discharge was destroyed by washing the sheets.

We know she had been given a 'Mickey Finn'

because of the volume of chloral hydrate in her blood. It was a considerable dose, but by itself not fatal. It was certainly enough to put her out cold, and probably quickly. The killers could then get on with the rest of what they had to do unhampered. Intruders intending straightforward murder might well have finished the job with a higher dose of chloral hydrate, but they had more on their minds than murder. Nembutal being the drug she had been prescribed and would normally have in the house, death from Nembutal poisoning — a huge overdose — would clearly point to suicide.

But if there was no finesse in this murder, there was certainly no lack of cunning and careful planning. This had to be a death that, at first easily identified as suicide, had later to be proven without question to have been murder. It had to give the appearance there had been a clumsy attempt to cover up a murder. Those who carried out this plan did not have the death of Marilyn Monroe as their prime objective. Her death had been designed as a trap in which to ensnare both the Attorney General and the President. When the apparent suicide was found to have been murder, in circumstances where Robert Kennedy had been Marilyn's last known visitor the night she died, he would immediately become a suspect and it would appear to be abundantly clear that he was responsible for the star's demise, and had clumsily tried to make it look like suicide.

Marilyn's relationship with Robert Kennedy over the previous six months was common knowledge among journalists, but, as we have indicated, it was regarded as 'off limits' to the press. They would not sit on a story like this, however, nor would their editors. This was murder, and the murderer was the top lawman in the country, the Attorney General. No touch of silk to bring comfort here, no matter how privileged he was. Even had he been able to prove without doubt that he was innocent, his resignation would be on the President's desk the day the story broke in the papers, and the President's would inevitably follow: the press knew of his involvement also with Marilyn and a case could easily have been made for him being as guilty as his brother. The Kennedy clan would be politically wiped out in one go. But who would want this? And who would be ruthless enough to achieve their aim by such terrible means?

The Kennedys had many enemies, among which was a powerful faction in the CIA. Earlier in this book we told how the Agency — among other 'interested parties' — had been listening in at Marilyn's home by means of bugs and telephone taps. Their interest, they claimed, was national security, though this did not explain why they were carrying out the function of the FBI, who were also listening in. The CIA in general lost no love on the Kennedys, but the faction in question venomously hated them. These were the survivors from the ill-fated Bay of Pigs invasion the previous year, in which Cuban rebels attempted to overturn the Castro regime. The CIA had trained the Cubans, equipped them, fed them, armed them, and they had likely been the inspiration for the invasion, also. They believed the Kennedys — the President and his brother — had abandoned them in their hour of need.

The Bay of Pigs episode was the CIA's baby all the way. They had obtained the support of the Chiefs of Staff for what appeared to concern the formation of guerrilla groups to re-enter Cuba during the presidency of Dwight D Eisenhower, JFK's predecessor, who approved the scheme. John F Kennedy, therefore, found the plans lying on his desk, so to speak, when he took office. It was an ill-conceived plan in which the main weakness was, remarkably, poor intelligence. Kennedy made it clear he would not bring the United States into a war with Cuba. The insurgents would be on their own without back-up. It would be Cuban against Cuban. But this was in the days when the CIA was virtually another, covert, government, operating independently of the government elected by the people. They had failed to tell Eisenhower they had expanded the plans he had approved, and they certainly did not enlighten the new President: far from some bands of guerrillas, they had recruited a small army of Cubans.

The outcome of the invasion was disastrous. The CIA had forecast the Cuban people would welcome the insurgents and rally behind them to overthrow Castro, but this did not happen. They miscalculated the strength of the arms Castro had and the striking power of his air force. They were routed. Blood ran freely on the Cuban shore and among the many killed were CIA operatives. They had desperately sought air cover from the President for their withdrawal from the chaos but, it appeared, the message had gone unanswered. In fact, air cover had been despatched, but, perhaps due to a miscalculation in time difference, the planes had arrived an hour too late.

A story emerged that the President was suffering from his back ailment the day it all happened and that the attempted landing had been monitored by Robert Kennedy. From that time on, therefore, the two Kennedy brothers were blamed by the CIA for the debacle and were intensely hated by the group of agents who survived and, no doubt, the friends of those who had died. Even if the renegade faction in the CIA's ranks was not directly concerned with the monitoring of the relationship between Marilyn and Robert Kennedy from the outset, there is little speculation in believing members of their group were kept informed by their colleagues and then became involved.

Confirmation that the CIA were closely monitoring everything that had been going on between Marilyn and Robert Kennedy later surfaced in a document which indicated that the head of the Agency, James Angleton, no less, was immediately made aware of Marilyn's threat to ' . . . blow the whole damn thing wide open.' This would be no isolated piece of information. It indicated that everything overheard from the CIA bugs and taps in Marilyn's house was being scrutinised, and that the Agency had eyes and ears concentrated on every move being made. It must be accepted, therefore, that the Kennedys' enemies in the CIA were abreast of all developments and knew exactly where, when and how to strike in their bid to discredit the Kennedy Administration by killing Marilyn Monroe.

This was their chance to exact the revenge on the Kennedys they had been seeking for a year. In one dramatic act they could get rid of both brothers from government. But there was only a narrow time slot during which they could operate. The bugs had revealed the relationship was well and truly over, and if they were to carry out their audacious plan it had to be Saturday night or else their advantage would be lost. If the plan was carried out hurriedly, it did not mean the planning was rushed or thrown together at the last minute. They had probably had the scheme worked out for some time, perhaps months, and had just been waiting for the appropriate time to put it in motion. It appears they struck shortly after ten o'clock and were probably out of the house well within 30 minutes.

Such a timescale would fit the movements of those involved in what came later. First to be called to the scene was publicist Arthur Jacobs, who was probably at Marilyn's house at 11.00 p.m. and found that she could not be roused. After speaking to Mrs Murray, who no doubt gave him an account of the man she had admitted to the house, they are likely to have spent some time trying to revive her, though with

Marilyn's bedroom photograped immediately
after her death.
Photo copyright Robert F Slatzer

little idea of what it was she was suffering from. When they found they could do nothing they then called an ambulance. Marilyn, it seems, died on her way to hospital and was returned to her home, where she was placed on her bed to assume the role she was to be given as a suicide. Arthur Jacobs, having put two and two together from the details supplied by Mrs Murray, would next call Police Chief William Parker in person.

Parker was an astute man who would quickly grasp what he was being told and the implications of it. This was the chance of a lifetime dropping into his lap. A grateful Robert Kennedy, rescued from a bomb blast which would have blown him, the President and the rest of the Kennedys out of the water, could not fail to reward him with the post he wanted above all others, the Directorship of the Federal Bureau of Investigation. It is likely he would go directly to Marilyn's house to confer with those already there. Apart from Arthur Jacobs and Eunice Murray, Peter Lawford was there, no doubt acting as the go-between for the group and the Attorney General, as he had in the past acted as go-between for Marilyn and the Kennedy brothers with such disastrous consequences.

It would appear that neither of the doctors was available when Mrs Murray first rang. The timing of their respective arrivals suggest Ralph Greenson first heard the news immediately he returned home from his evening out with his wife, while Hyman Engelberg did not get home for some time after this and arrived at Fifth Helena Drive more than two hours after Greenson. It was inevitable they were drawn into the conspiracy. The logic, no doubt, would be that nothing could now be done for Marilyn while the Kennedys, who were innocent of her murder, were totally exposed and they — this small group — had the means of protecting the First Family. Eunice Murray, who cleared up the mess and — and with remarkable audacity — washed the evidence while the police were in the house, would have to be included in their number, as would Milton Rudin, Marilyn's lawyer, who was called to the scene fairly soon. Chief Parker's cooperation in protecting the Kennedys would, no doubt, give the others contributing to the cover up a great deal of comfort. His participation may well have made them feel they had a degree of protection in what they did.

There were meetings and consultations all day Sunday, culminating in a final gathering on Sunday night, where all those involved in the deception met to come to terms with what they were doing. Held this time in Arthur Jacobs' offices, Rupert Allan, a Jacobs man, spoke of it as a 'strategy meeting'. Another of Jacobs' staff present was Michael Selsman, and someone representing the Kennedys was also present. Peter Lawford was like the proverbial cat on hot bricks after Marilyn died and it is probable he was there, too. It was said the meeting was noisy from time to time as they consolidated plans to keep what had really happened under wraps. In their skilful planning, the murderers had provided them with a cover story they could, with the co-operation of key people, make stick. The superficial suicide story would be developed for consumption across the world: Arthur Jacobs, the consummate publicist, was the man to sell it.

On the face of it, it would be easy to believe the Kennedy brothers plotted to have Marilyn killed to extricate themselves once and for all from their entanglements with her, but the evidence surrounding Marilyn's death does not allow this to stand up. To begin with it would require that all the people we have just named were prepared to be complicit in the crime, and others, besides. Every single one would have been guilty of murder after the fact: the Chief of

Police, Arthur Jacobs, doctors Ralph Greenson and Hyman Engelberg, Eunice Murray, Peter Lawford, Milton Rudin, and Pat Newcomb, if she was involved. And then came others including the coroner, who did his version of a fudge in respect of the autopsy, and police officers, including some of high rank, who were bound to find out what had been going on.

The Kennedys had had plenty of time and opportunity to kill Marilyn if they had wanted to. But think of the enormous risk they would have been taking if they had decided to go that way. One false move, one person speaking out of turn, and it would have been all over for all of them. It is inconceivable that the Kennedy family would risk everything on one throw of the dice, as it were. They were people who took risks, but they were not gamblers of that order. If any one party among those who were recording what happened in Marilyn's house during that night had been Kennedy-friendly, they might have been able to enlighten us about many things, but they were not. Not that those involved in her murder would have been likely to record Marilyn being killed. I am assuming it was carried out in the guest apartment partly because it was geographically the remotest part of the house, but mainly because they knew it was the only part of Marilyn's house not bugged. They would not be recorded, and did not, therefore, run the risk of being hoist by their own petard. The position in which the body was found in her bedroom suggests she was killed elsewhere and taken there, and the dirty bed linen going

Bernard Spindel. His New York home
was raided for the Marilyn tapes.
Photo copyright AP World Wide.

through the washing machine suggests a mess
had been made, wherever she was killed. The
guest apartment would provide the likely murder
room.

The tapes recorded by those who monitored
what was happening in Marilyn's house were
only as reliable as those who explained them, as

we have already said. The recordings were made at a speed of 15/16ths of an inch per second, which is incredibly slow. The set up was designed to cater for continuous recording over an extended period, and, even allowing for top-of-the-line early 1960s equipment being used, the sound quality was going to be poor. The very nature of a bugging operation imposes limits that restrict what can be obtained by those who listen. It should also be remembered that bugs have to be concealed and are not necessarily placed in the best locations to collect sounds.

There was no doubt that Bernard Spindel carried out quite a professional bugging operation at Marilyn's house, and that copies of the tapes survived the raid on his house carried out by the police. We have recounted that several people have heard soundbites from them and have reported on what they contained. We have already mentioned the sounds of Marilyn and Robert Kennedy arguing on the day she died and Marilyn ordering Kennedy out of her house. We have also mentioned the sounds recorded at a later meeting that day, when Kennedy stormed through the place searching for 'it', and we have speculated this was a file of documents Marilyn promised to return to Jack Kennedy before her relationship with Robert broke down. It would seem likely Jack Kennedy had made a pact with Marilyn in which she promised to keep his secrets, though this would not prevent him from wanting to retrieve the various tangibles still in Marilyn's possession. It is likely, again, that she promised to give them to him, but it appears to be quite clear that in the light of Robert's clumsy handling of the situation she had changed her mind. They were probably recovered in the plundering of Marilyn's possessions when she died.

A box of 15-inch quarter-inch tape spools were used for Spindel's bugging operation and, remarkably, the pertinent recordings occupied only two 7-inch reels after the long periods of silence were edited out. This invites speculation as to what else may have been edited out or, for that matter, edited in. It also reminds us that tape sequences can be put in different order, to produce different meanings. But if the tapes really did contain evidence that Robert Kennedy was present when Marilyn died, the most remarkable thing is they were never used to blackmail the Attorney General. And Jimmy Hoffa would not be likely to miss a trick like that. Robert Kennedy continued to fight Hoffa until, after the assassination of his brother, President Kennedy, in November 1963, he was relieved of his post. It is also interesting to note that when Robert Kennedy was in line for election to the Presidency his enemies sought the services of Ralph de Toledano — as we said earlier — to buy the tapes, hoping to use them to discredit the then-Senator Kennedy. If there was not enough there for Hoffa to use it would appear the tapes did not contain clear, indisputable blackmail material, and de Toledano's sponsors were clutching at straws.

Hoffa would not be likely to send in a hit squad to murder Marilyn. It was far more profitable for him to control the Kennedys rather than oust them. Control was a far more realistic goal, hence the elaborate surveillance operation he paid Spindel to install and run. The scale of the operation was considerable and must have cost Hoffa a great deal of money, since Spindel's services were unlikely to come cheap. They had started their bugging operation in the apartment Marilyn had rented at the Beverley Hills Hotel before she moved to her house, and included cover of the Lawford mansion on the beach road at Santa Monica. To maintain his position at the head of the powerful Teamsters' Union and fight off the constant attacks made by the Justice Department, Hoffa's need was for a means of spiking Kennedy's guns and turning the heat back on the Attorney General.

J Edgar Hoover was kept informed of what was happening in Marilyn's house and he was another with blackmail intent. We do not know what was overheard by the FBI agents who were listening in, but Hoover's dossier on Robert Kennedy must have grown at that time. The Kennedys, who despised Hoover and were quite conscious that this was reciprocated, remarkably did not appear aware that the Director had his eyes and ears everywhere. But Hoover would not, in any case, have been likely to send in a team to kill her. He, too, wanted to have a measure of control over the Kennedys, and that was exactly what he was achieving.

As we have said, the team of two or three men who were admitted to Marilyn's house were most likely from the ranks of the CIA, whose

Robert Kennedy talks to J Edgar Hoover.
No love lost here.
Photo Courtesy John F Kennedy Library

smouldering, deep hatred of the President and the Attorney General would find satisfaction in a plan which would exact revenge for their abandonment and the deaths of their comrades and rid the country for ever of the influence of the Kennedys.

Fred Otash must have known the Lawford and Monroe houses as though they were his own. By his own admission, his operatives planted bugs in both houses and he was in a position to know that others were listening in, too. He saw surveillance grow like topsy. Otash claimed 'certain elements' within the Republican Party engaged him to bug Lawford's house in the first place, their interest no doubt being in the activities of the actor's visitors, the Kennedys. When Spindel — for Hoffa — came into the picture, Otash was sent on further bugging and tapping operations involving not only the Lawford house but the home of Marilyn Monroe. Then there was the FBI and the CIA. As Otash saw it, 'You had the CIA who wanted to neutralise them [the Kennedys] because they didn't want them to take over control of the Agency.' No doubt that accounted for the interest shown by the Agency per se. It did not account for the deeper interest shown by the Bay of Pigs survivors.

20

LAWFORD AND 'MR O'

Peter Lawford was one of the Englishmen who made it to the top in Hollywood, though he never achieved superstar status. He was attractive and popular and in demand at a time, during the Second World War, when Hollywood needed English actors. He was successful in both acting and the business side of movie making; he married into the Kennedy family, and also became a member of the Rat Pack, which was made up of Frank Sinatra — the undisputed leader — Dean Martin, Sammy Davis Jr and Joey Bishop.

Patricia, Peter Lawford's wife, was regarded as the prettiest of the Kennedy girls. She married Lawford in 1954, though this did not stop his eye roving. He was accepted into the family by Jack and Robert Kennedy, though father Joe had misgivings: he didn't like Englishmen and didn't like actors. The Lawfords acquired the impressive house which movie mogul Louis B Mayer had had built for himself, superbly located at the beach at Santa Monica, and Peter enjoyed everything the sun, the sea and the sand could offer when his busy life allowed him to relax.

Pat Lawford and Marilyn Monroe hit it off and became good friends. Marilyn was an exception to Pat's dislike of Peter's friends. She was a frequent visitor to the beach house, the invitations becoming more pointed when Jack Kennedy was expected, though she took exception on the occasions when she found the other 'guests' included local prostitutes. Lawford and Marilyn were said to have had a fleeting romantic interlude at one time, but it amounted to nothing. Lawford was said to do the chasing but Marilyn did not respond.

As far as Marilyn was concerned, Peter Lawford was a procurer of women for the sexual pleasure of John F Kennedy and, later, Robert Kennedy. Jack Kennedy had been dazzled when he first saw Marilyn at a reception given by agent Charles Feldman, and had asked Lawford to introduce them. Marilyn was in awe of Jack Kennedy. He was handsome, strong and hugely intelligent, all the attributes she sought in the man of her dreams, and the affair that followed some time later became one of those best kept secrets which everyone in Hollywood knew about. For her part, it seemed not to matter that she was recently married to Joe DiMaggio when the relationship began. Baseball legend Joe had married the sweet, wholesome girl he saw in Marilyn, and expected her to become a loyal and faithful wife. The marriage was over in nine months, but DiMaggio continued his love affair with Marilyn from afar, while Marilyn clung to the security she felt in him still being there for her.

Peter Lawford had access to President Kennedy and to the Attorney General. During the time Marilyn could not reach Robert Kennedy, Lawford could, and Robert Kennedy therefore knew what was happening in Los Angeles — and with Marilyn — at all times. It appeared to be Ethel finding out about her husband's affair with Marilyn that changed the course of events on Friday 4 August, the day before Marilyn died. The Attorney General, it seemed, was prepared to meet Marilyn — in fact knew it was imperative he met Marilyn to retrieve a photograph and documents required by his brother — but did not want it to be at her house, as apparently arranged. It was as if he had been alerted that Fifth Helena Drive was being watched by someone who would get the word back to Ethel. If this is so, the stormy Friday night meeting at the restaurant must have triggered something approaching desperation in Kennedy, for he threw caution to the wind the next day, when he went to Marilyn's house not once but twice.

Peter Lawford was like Mrs Murray in some respects. He was desperately anxious to establish that Marilyn had taken her own life and tailored his story to support this. He spoke to Marilyn once, perhaps twice, the day she died, but exactly when is a matter of conjecture. It seems likely the claim he rang at 5.00 p.m. is correct. At least, this does not conflict with other incoming or outgoing calls. As for the second call — if, indeed, there was a second call it is anybody's guess what time it took place. Presumably, in the 5.00 p.m. call Lawford tried to persuade Marilyn to come over for dinner that night. That, no

*Hollywood's Fred Otash, private eye to the stars.
Photo Corbis-Bettmann UPI*

doubt, would have suited Robert Kennedy, who still had to settle with her the collection of the photograph and documents that were vital to Jack Kennedy. But, after the ill-tempered meeting of earlier in the afternoon, it would seem she was neither in the mood for a social engagement nor to oblige Robert Kennedy.

Deborah Gould, who was married to Lawford in 1976 for only a few weeks, professes to know a lot about what went on when Marilyn died because, she says, Peter confided in her. Lawford's attempt at giving the timing of the second call was 7.30 p.m., which could not have been correct since we know Marilyn was happily talking to Joe DiMaggio Jr at that time. Gould corrected this to being at about 10.00 p.m., but this time conflicted with a call Jeanne Carmen said she received from Marilyn. There were several versions of the content of the telephone call or calls made by Peter Lawford to Marilyn. In the call at first claimed to have been made at 7.30 p.m., she was said to have been explaining why she had not turned up for dinner, though this was strange if she had declined the invitation in the earlier call. Lawford said her speech was slurred and her voice became distant. She then became less and less audible until he could not catch what she was saying. Then the line went dead. He hung up and tried redialling but could not get through, he said.

Lawford then said he contacted his agent, Milton Ebbins to ask his advice. Most people would have jumped into a car without delay to find out what was happening to a friend if a crisis was suspected, but Lawford contacted his agent. Ebbins, he said, told him it would be a mistake for the President's brother-in-law to get involved so he should not go to her house. He (Ebbins) would get in touch with Marilyn's lawyer, Milton Rudin, and let him know there was a problem. Unbelievable! He did so, however. He traced Rudin at 8.45 p.m., a guest at a party, and Rudin called Marilyn's home at 9.00 p.m. asking if she was all right. Mrs Murray evidently went and looked in at Marilyn's bedroom and told Milton Rudin there was no problem.

It is likely, however, that Peter Lawford was at Marilyn's house later that night, when she died. Presumably he was one of those sent for when she was found to be dying, and before she was sent to the hospital at Santa Monica, where they thought she might be revived. According to ambulance boss Walter Schaefer, there was a 'famous actor' with her in the ambulance when it raced to hospital, which leaves little doubt it was Peter Lawford. Once Marilyn died, it was probably Lawford who suggested that her body be returned to her house. It would have been difficult for him to 'control' the situation and keep the Kennedys out of the equation if the hospital became involved.

We know much more about Lawford and his movements than he ever admitted because, years afterwards, the private detective he engaged, Fred Otash — 'Mr O' — opened up and told what he knew. Gaps became easier to fill and speculation became less speculative in view of what he said. But there was no speculation needed for the fact that Lawford telephoned President Kennedy just after six o'clock on the morning of Sunday 5 August (9.00 a.m. in Washington). He was put straight through to Jack Kennedy and the conversation lasted 20 minutes. On the grounds of 'national security' the record of this call remained hidden until 1991, when British writer Anthony Summers found that the telephone system had automatically logged it. The call was traced to a 'Pacific Coast Highway' residence at Santa Monica. It was claimed Lawford had telephoned the White House earlier than this from a phone at Marilyn's house, but hard and fast corroboration of this would only be obtainable from the records of Marilyn's phone calls, and these were confiscated by Chief Parker. In respect of the earlier call, the White House log, unfortunately, did not cover the time in question.

Otash had been a Los Angeles vice cop and had left the LAPD to become a private detective. He worked for many well-known Hollywood stars including Frank Sinatra, Judy Garland, Anita Ekberg and Errol Flynn, in addition to mob figures, including Jimmy Hoffa. Lawford had engaged Otash to tap his own telephones during the years he was married to Pat Lawford, and gave the impression he was keeping tabs on her. Later, it seems, Otash returned to do further work at the beach house, this time so that Bernard Spindel could listen in for Jimmy Hoffa. Since Fred Otash was also involved, in the surveillance work carried out by Bernard Spindel at Marilyn's house, and had listened to the tapes made there, he knew quite a lot about what was going on.

Otash told how Peter Lawford had telephoned him 'shortly after midnight' on Sunday 5 August, to tell him something traumatic had happened. He agreed to a meeting at his office in Laurel Avenue, and Lawford turned up at about 2.00 a.m. Otash said he looked 'half crocked and half nervous'. 'Lawford said he had just left Monroe and she was dead and that Bobby had been there earlier. He said they got Bobby out of the city and back to Northern California and would I go on out there and arrange to do anything to remove anything incriminating out of the house. He (Lawford) said: 'I took what I could and I destroyed it — period.' But he told Otash he wanted him to go out and finish the job. Otash protested he was too well known to put in an appearance at Marilyn's house, but he agreed to send one of his men, a man experienced in installing listening devices, together with an off-duty LA cop whom he used, to do the job. As it turned out there were people swarming all over the place by the time they arrived there, which greatly inhibited their activities. Nonetheless, they identified items that Lawford had missed and they were removed.

Otash said that Lawford told him Marilyn and Robert Kennedy had had a fight — over whether he would marry her — before the Attorney General had left her house. Kennedy went back to Lawford's house, Lawford said, and complained, 'She's ranting and raving. I'm concerned about her and what might come out of this.' Otash said Lawford told him he phoned her and she said she was passed around like a piece of meat. She had had it. She didn't want Bobby to use her any more. She called the White House and there was no response from the President. She was told he was in Hyannis Port and she didn't connect with him. Lawford, Otash said, had tried to reason with her to quieten down and come to the beach house and relax. She said, 'No, I'm tired. There is nothing more for me to respond to. Just do me a favour. Tell the President I tried to get him. Tell him goodbye for me. I think my purpose has been served.' Lawford tried to call her back but the phone was off the hook. Bobby got panicky,

Lawford told Otash. Bobby asked 'What's going on?' Lawford said, 'Nothing. That's the way she is.' Otash spoke from Cannes, where he had gone to live. He died some years ago.

The Otash version of this call sounds to be much more reliable than the one Peter Lawford gave in which Marilyn sounded to be dying of despondency, particularly because before he began to circulate this story, Lawford himself was quoted as saying he spoke to Marilyn and ' . . . there didn't seem to be anything wrong with [her]. She sounded fine.'

Peter Lawford's Saturday night guests included Joe and Dolores Naar, who said they had evidenced nothing to do with Marilyn's problems while they were at dinner. They left the beach house shortly before eleven o'clock but had a curious experience when they got home. Peter Lawford telephoned to say that Marilyn had taken too many pills and he sounded anxious about her. Joe Naar offered to go and find out what was happening. He dressed in readiness but Lawford called again before he set off. He said it was unnecessary to go, that it had been a false alarm. Dolores Naar recalls Lawford telling them that Marilyn's doctor had given her a sedative and she was resting.

Producer George Durgom was another of Lawford's guests that night. He recalls Pat Newcomb arriving and telling them Marilyn was not coming because she was not feeling well. Fred Otash knew George Durgom, who quoted Lawford as telling him Robert Kennedy had said he was worried about Marilyn being loose-tongued. 'She won't talk to me,' he had told Lawford. 'Get her to the beach.' Lawford's chief anxiety was keeping the Kennedys out of trouble. He appeared to have manipulated the Narrs by using them to register his anxiety about Marilyn. But he determinedly kept them away from her house.

I cannot say that what Deborah Gould had to tell ever inspired much confidence in me. When I telephoned her to make an appointment to interview her, after travelling from Los Angeles to Miami, she made it clear there would be no interview without payment. Before Peter Lawford died in 1984, he denied much of what she said about Marilyn's death. There was one quite remarkable thing Gould claimed, however. She said that when she asked Lawford how Marilyn had died, he answered, 'She took her last big enema.' This was a very long time before an enema had been mooted as a means of her being killed.

21

The Secret Tapes
of Marilyn Monroe

When Deputy District Attorney John Miner was asked to interview Dr Ralph Greenson by the coroner three days after Marilyn died he was going to talk to a man he knew and respected. He had attended lectures and seminars given by the psychiatrist at the University of Southern California. Greenson, a man of outstanding ability, had written what had become a standard volume to those in his field, *Explorations in Psychoanalysis*, in addition to other papers and textbooks.

Greenson had informed the police that Marilyn had committed suicide on the night she died, but now wanted to rectify that. By all appearances he was caught up in the conspiracy to protect the Kennedys at the time of her death, but, a man of integrity, when he'd had time to consider what he was involving himself in he wanted to set the record straight. He made it clear he believed she had not taken her own life, and agreed to play to Miner two sound tapes Marilyn had made to support the position he was now taking. There would be certain conditions attached to playing the tapes. Though

Miner could report his conclusions as a result of listening to the tapes, he was not to divulge their contents to anyone, ever, not even the DA or the coroner. Miner agreed and listened to the tapes that he recreated as a transcript.

He kept his promise until, more than 20 years after Greenson's death and after seeing the doctor maligned as a murderer while Marilyn's memory continued to be taintcd with the stigma of suicide, he was finally released from his promise by Hildi, Greenson's widow. Miner spoke out on Greenson's behalf when the psychiatrist was attacked by authors such as Donald Spoto, Marvin Bergman and others. He quoted sparingly from the transcript he had of the tapes and released only a small segment of the contents until now, when he agreed to let them be featured in this book in their entirety.

There are the strongest reasons for accepting that the tapes were recorded by Marilyn very shortly before she died, and they survived only because she passed them to Dr Greenson, probably on the very day she died. Here then is the voice of Marilyn. This is the only surviving contribution made by the star herself, in which she tells of her disposition at the time she died. Among other things she talks about what was happening to her, about Jack and Robert Kennedy, about her marriages and why they failed, about her friends — Clark Gable, Frank Sinatra, Joan Crawford, Laurence Olivier and others — about her sexual deficiencies, the book she was reading, experiments in lesbianism and, most important of all, her plans for the future.

238

It should be noted that, in spite of Dr Greenson's protective attitude towards the contents of the tapes, they did not, strictly speaking, constitute medical records. They were made outside the treatments Greenson arranged for her. She had difficulty in his free-association analysis sessions, because she was unable to let herself go in his presence. The tapes were made by Marilyn on her own, in private, when she could completely let herself go. They were an experiment, a new idea she had, which would allow her to get into free-association analysis as the tapes could be listened to later by Greenson and analysed during her presence at their next session. She tells him of her idea on the tape itself.

These then, are, as she puts it herself, ' . . . the most private, the most secret thoughts of Marilyn Monroe'. Unless otherwise indicated, the text shown in italics in the following chapters represents Marilyn's voice from the tapes.

22

The Secret Tapes: Sex, Literature and Daddy's Little Girl

Marilyn begins her tape:

> *Dear Doctor,*
> *You have given me everything. Because of you I can now feel what I never felt before. She comes by herself and with somebody else. So now I am a whole woman (pun intended — like Shakespeare). So now I have control — control of myself — control of my life.*

Those writers who have speculated that Ralph Greenson, regardless of professional ethics, had had a sexual relationship with Marilyn receive a sharp rebuff in what follows as she continues to talk to her tape. This will be underlined by what she says later about Greenson adopting her.

> *What can I give you? Not money — I know that from me that means nothing to you. Not my body — I know your professional ethics and faithfulness to your wonderful*

wife make that impossible. What I am going to give you is my idea that will revolutionise psychoanalysis.

Isn't it true that the key to analysis is free association? Marilyn Monroe associates. You, my doctor, by understanding and interpretation of what goes on in my mind get to my unconscious which makes it possible for you to treat my neuroses and for me to overcome them. But when you tell me to relax and tell you what I am thinking, I blank out and have nothing to say; that's what you and Dr Freud call resistance. So we talk about other things and I answer your questions as best I can. You are the only person in the world I have never told a lie to and never will.

Oh yes, dreams. I know they are important. But you want me to free associate about the dream elements. I have the same blanking out. More resistance for you and Dr Freud to complain about.

I read his Introductory Lectures. What a genius. He makes it so understandable. And he is so right. Didn't he say himself that Shakespeare and Dostoevsky had a better understanding of psychology than all the scientists put together? Damn it, they do.

You told me to read Molly Bloom's mental meanderings (I can use words, can't I) to

Marilyn with her tape recorder.
She used it for many things including making
the secret tapes featured in this book.
Photo Robert F Slater Collection

get a feeling of free association. It was when
I did that I got my great idea.

As I read it something bothered me. Here is
Joyce writing what a woman thinks to
herself. Can he, does he really know her
innermost thoughts? But after I read the
whole book, I could better understand that

Joyce is an artist who could penetrate the souls of people, male or female. It really doesn't matter that Joyce doesn't have breasts or other female attributes, or never felt a menstrual cramp. Wait a minute. As you must have guessed I am free associating and you are going to hear a lot of bad language. Because of my respect for you, I've never been able to say the words I'm really thinking when we are in session. But now I am going to say whatever I think, no matter what it is.

I can do that because of my idea which, if you'll be patient, I'll tell you about.

That's funny. I ask you to be patient, but I am your patient. Yet to be patient and to be a patient makes a kind of Shakespearean sense, doesn't it?

Back to Joyce. To me Leopold Bloom is the central character. He is the despised Irish Jew, married to an Irish Catholic woman. It is through them Joyce develops much of what he wants to say. Do you agree that the scene where Bloom is looking at the little girl on the swing is the most erotic in the book? What is a Jew? In my business I have known more Jews than I can count. There are those who, I suppose, look Jewish but so do Arabs; there are others who are more blond and blue-eyed than Hitler ever was. And some in between that you can't tell if

243

they are Jewish or not. How do you think Hitler knew who were Jews to be killed? Couldn't be by looks alone. I have met too many German Jews who sure could be Hitler's Aryans by their looks.

I couldn't tell if you were Jewish by looking at you. Same with women.

Keep getting side tracked. Well, that's what free association is.

OK, my idea! To start with there is the doctor and the patient. I don't like the word analysand. It makes it seem like treating a sick mind is different from treating a sick body. However, you and Dr Freud say that the mind is part of the body. That makes the person getting treated the patient. I'll bet Gertrude Stein would say a patient is a patient, is a patient. See, free association can be fun.

Anyway, you are in his office and the doctor says I want you to say whatever you are thinking no matter what it is. And you can't think of a damn thing. How many times after a session I would go home and cry because I thought it was my fault.

While reading Molly's blathering, the IDEA came to me. Get a tape recorder. Put a tape in. Turn it on. Say whatever you are thinking like I am doing now. It's really easy. *I'm lying on my bed wearing only a brassiere. If I want to go to the refrig or the bathroom, push the stop button and begin again when I want to.*

And I just free associate. No problem. You get the idea, don't you? Patient can't do it in Doctor's office. Patient is at home with tape recorder. Patient free associates sans difficulty. Patient sends tape to Doctor. After he listens to it, Patient comes in for a session. He asks her questions about it, interprets it. Patient gets treated. Oh yes, she can put her dreams on tape too — right when she has them. You know how I would forget what I dreamed or even if I dreamt at all.

Dr Freud said dreams are the via regia to the unconscious and so I'll tell you my dreams on tape.

OK, Dr Greenson. You are the greatest psychiatrist in the world. You tell me. Has Marilyn Monroe invented an important way to make psychoanalysis work better? After you listen to my tapes and use them to treat me, you could publish a paper in a scientific journal. Wouldn't that be sensational? I don't want any credit. I don't want to be identified in your paper. It's my present to you. I'll never tell anybody about it. You will be the first to let your profession know how to lick resistance. Maybe you could patent the idea. And license it to your colleagues. Ask Mickey. [Marilyn here refers to Milton (Mickey) Rudin, her lawyer.]

Marilyn now lets go in the privacy of her bedroom, and talks to Dr Greenson as she has been unable to in his office.

You are the only person who will ever know the most private, the most secret thoughts of Marilyn Monroe. I have absolute confidence and trust you. What I told you is true when I first became your patient. I had never had an orgasm. I well remember you said an orgasm happens in the mind, not the genitals.

Marilyn then goes on to a consideration of explicit language saying she prefers coarser language to the more polite equivalents.

I don't think the problem is the words themselves, it is the way people use them.

It doesn't bother me, but this damn free association could drive somebody crazy. Oh, oh, crazy makes me think about my mother.

Marilyn lived in fear of madness. Her maternal grandfather, Otis Monroe, died with a brain disorder and her maternal great grandfather, Tilford Hogan, had hanged himself at the age of 82. Her maternal grandmother, Della, died at the age of 51 in an asylum just a year after Marilyn was born, while her mother was committed to Rock Haven Sanitarium. With our more advanced knowledge of mental disorders we now know that Otis Monroe died from a diseased brain and not, by any means, insanity. He contracted syphilis, which was rife in Mexico, where he lived, transmitted by deplorable living conditions rather than sexual relations. Tilford Hogan may have taken his own life 'while the balance of his mind was disturbed' as the lawyers express it, but there is no evidence he suffered from mental disorders. Gladys Baker was a skilled film cutter who had, apparently, induced anxieties through her religious convictions. She was committed to an asylum, though today it is exceedingly unlikely she would have been. By all accounts she was certainly disturbed but by no means insane. More than likely Marilyn worried for absolutely nothing, but there is no doubt she worried a great deal and lived in fear that she was doomed to follow her family into insanity.

I am not going to free associate about her [her mother] right now. Let me finish my thoughts about orgasms. You said a person in a coma or a paraplegic doesn't have an orgasm because the genital stimulation doesn't reach the brain, but that an orgasm can happen in the brain without any stimulation of the genitals.

She develops this idea, speaking of her dreams and discussing the problems Dr Greenson had raised relating to her inability to have orgasms.

You said there was an obstacle in my mind that prevented me from having an orgasm; that it was something that happened early in my life about which I felt so guilty that I did not deserve to have the greatest pleasure there is; that it had to do with something sexual that was very wrong, but my getting pleasure from it caused my guilt.

Dr Greenson, however, appeared to have conquered her fears.

Bless you Doctor. What you say is gospel to me. What wasted years. How can I describe to you, a man, what an orgasm feels like to a woman. I'll try. Think of a light fixture with a rheostat control. As you slowly turn it on, the bulb begins to get bright, then brighter and brighter and finally in a blinding flash is full lit. As you turn it off it gradually becomes dimmer and at last goes out.

I have a dream for you. I dreamt that I was sitting on Clark Gable's lap with his arms around me. He said: 'They want me to do a Gone With the Wind sequel. Maybe I will if you will be my Scarlett.' I woke up crying. They called him King, and what respect and deference he had from the actors and crew, even Huston. (Marilyn was here referring to the making of her most recent film, The Misfits.) Some day I hope I'll be treated like

Marilyn with *Clark Gable* on the set of The Misfits.
Photo Twentieth Century Fox

that. He was Mr Gable to everyone on the
set, but he made me call him Clark.

He had such concern for the animals. Even
though there were Humane Society inspec-
tors all over the place, he kept ordering that
nobody hurt the horses. Ironically, it was a

horse that hurt him. I was told after he was dragged and the horse calmed down, he stroked his muzzle and gave him a piece of sugar. He was so nice to me and I didn't deserve it. I was having problems with Arthur and being sick and I held up the shooting a lot. Clark protected me from Huston who kept giving me a bad time.

The Misfits was the last film Clark Gable made before he died. The weekend after the film was completed he complained of severe chest pains and died of a heart attack. His wife, Kay, was said to blame his death on the tension he had worked under on the film, where he had to wait interminably to begin shooting, and without saying so she was reported as blaming Marilyn for his tension. There is no doubt that Marilyn was a perpetual latecomer, and also no doubt this can cause a lot of tension. Reporters asked Marilyn if she felt guilty about this, but as we discover a little later in what she said on her tape, far from guilt she felt rather the opposite. She felt she had given him something. Whatever was the case, Kay sent Marilyn an invitation to the christening of Clark's son, John Clark, who was born after his father died.

★ ★ ★

Marilyn had seen a photograph of the man who she was told was her father. He wore a slouch hat and had a pencil-like moustache rather like Clark Gable, and it is often thought she looked

250

upon him as a sort of substitute father. *The Misfits* proved to be Marilyn's last film, too. The film she worked on when she died, *Something's Got to Give* was never finished. She continued to talk about Gable in her tape:

In the kissing scenes, I kissed him with real affection. I didn't want to go to bed with him, but I wanted him to know how much I liked and appreciated him. He told me he had been a hunter for a long time, but he had decided not to kill animals. He said if he had children, he would teach them to hunt with a camera instead of a gun.

When I came back from a day off the set, he patted my ass and told me if I didn't behave myself, he would give me a good spanking. I looked him in the eye and said: 'Don't tempt me.' He burst out laughing so hard it was tearing. Because of his performance I've seen Gone With the Wind over and over again. He was perfect. It makes me so mad I could scream that those Academy idiots didn't award him the Oscar. He should have won hands down.

All that was a long time ago. I must have been about thirteen. I have never seen a man who was as romantic as he was in that picture. It was different when I got to know him. Then I wanted him to be my father. I wouldn't care if he spanked me as long as he made up for it by hugging me and telling me

I was Daddy's little girl and he loved me. Of course that's fantasy.

This sparked off another train of thought relating to her need for a family.

Ever since you let me be in your home and meet your family, I've thought about how it would be if I were your daughter instead of your patient. I know you couldn't do it while I'm your patient, but after you cure me, maybe you could adopt me. Then I'd have the father I've always wanted and your wife, whom I adore, could be my mother, and your children, brothers and sisters. No, Doctor, I won't push it. But it's beautiful to think about it. I guess you can tell I'm crying. I'll stop now for a little bit.

Marilyn had always longed to belong to a stable and loving family. Here she expresses her desire in no uncertain terms. Then she resumes . . .

When Clark Gable died, I cried for two days straight. I couldn't eat or sleep. It was some comfort I'd made him laugh like that. Is there a God? He must be cruel for not letting Clark live to teach his son to hunt with a camera.

She then embarked upon a tirade about her past lovers and how they had meant so little to her. She made an exception of Johnny Hyde, however. Johnny Hyde had been her agent until he died.

252

Johnny Hyde was special. He wasn't a hell of a lot to look at. A little shrimp. Little shrimp, is that redundant or tautological? I always get them mixed up. Anyway he only came up to my chin. Johnny was a cocky character. There was no better agent in the business. The studio bosses and casting directors respected him. His word was gold. You didn't need any damned lawyers when he made a deal.

How that man took care of me. He divorced his wife and bought a house for us to live in, bought my clothes, paid my hairdresser and cosmetic bills and medical expenses. He was my agent and got me better parts and more money that I had before. Funny, though. He always took his agent fee. Said it kept me professional and then he'd turn around and spend a fortune on me.

There was a lot of talk that he did all this to get me to marry him. And I probably would have if he'd wanted me to. But the truth is he thought marriage would hurt my career. He said if I did what he told me, he'd make me a big star. I was everything to him: wife, mother, sister, daughter, mistress. Nobody will or could love me as much as Johnny H. I loved the little guy, but I was never in love with him. I'd do anything he wanted and I've only skimmed the surface in what I've said. But I just couldn't have

*the kind of love for him that he had for me.
We both knew he had a bad heart. His
doctor told him if he wanted to stay alive,
he should stop seeing me and retire from his
work. He didn't and died suddenly before
he could keep his promise to put me in his
will. C'est la vie.*

When Johnnie Hyde died Marilyn had to quit
the house she lived in with him without delay.
His family had no time for Marilyn.

*The talk went around that his relationship
with me killed Johnny. They are wasting
their time trying to make me feel guilty. I
gave Johnny the greatest happiness he ever
had. He wouldn't have traded a day of it for
a year of life.*

Marilyn completely changes the subject, and
next relates how she went out one day to
conduct an experiment. She got the idea from
hearing about some Caliph or Sultan who went
out incognito among his people to find out what
they thought about him. She disguised herself
with a brunette wig and horn rimmed spectacles
and wore no make-up, then got into nine taxis
just to ask the drivers a question. Giving each
driver a ten-dollar bill she asked them: Name the
woman you would most like to be dating tonight.
Six said Marilyn Monroe.

23

THE SECRET TAPES:
THE OLIVIER IMPACT

There's someone on radio trying to restart a
fire under the so-called [Joan] Crawford
— Monroe feud. OK, she said some mean
things about me a while back. What do I
care? I don't know why she did. Crawford
and I started out friendly. As always,
Shakespeare said it best: 'He that takes from
me my good name robs me of that which
not enriches him and makes me poor
indeed.' No, Doctor, I did not look it up.
I've memorised a lot of Shakespeare. That
reminds me of Prince and the Showgirl.

Olivier came into my dressing room to
give me hell for screwing up. I soothed him
by telling him I thought his Hamlet was one
of the greatest films ever made. You know
he won an Oscar for it. But the Prince was a
real clown. He was superficial — no, that's
not the word — supercilious, arrogant, a
snob, conceited. Maybe a little bit anti-
Semitic in the sense of some of my best
friends are Jews. But damn him, a great,
great actor.

255

Sir Laurence Olivier and Marilyn did not hit it off too well when *The Prince and the Showgirl* was being shot. Marilyn's production company was funding the making of the film, and that spoke well of the confidence she had in Olivier. As co-producer and director of the picture also, this was to be his first attempt at comedy, and Olivier did not appear too comfortable with the character he was playing. Marilyn, however, felt her natural flair for comedy fitted her part well. Olivier was critical of Lee Strasberg, her coach. He ventured he had missed her natural talent which he repressed rather than promoted. Paula, Lee's wife, flitted about the set as ever. *The Prince and the Showgirl* attracted every kind of conflict possible in the making of a picture.

Marilyn had just been married to Arthur Miller before starting the picture, and Miller accompanied her to England where the film was made. He was supposed to be getting on with his writing, but somehow managed to interfere with the production and alienate Marilyn into the bargain by siding with Olivier when she felt she needed his support. They had only been married for a few weeks when Marilyn came across some notes Miller had been making that mentioned her. She was thunderstruck to read that he wrote of his disappointment with her. She told those near her that he wrote ' . . . *his first wife had let him down, but I had done something worse. Olivier was beginning to think I was a troublesome bitch, and Arthur said he no longer*

256

had a decent answer to that one.'

Marilyn, forever late, got later and later each day and this, even though he had been warned to expect it, nonetheless exasperated Olivier, who responded with rather cutting 'amusing' remarks. Clashes between those exerting their influence on what was happening on the set created tensions. At one point there was a showdown in which Olivier ordered Paula Strasberg and Hedda Rosten — wife of Norman Rosten, the poet who was acting as Marilyn's secretary, to quit, but faced with the ultimatum from Marilyn, they stay or I go, they stayed. But in spite of all, the movie was reasonably successful and Marilyn survived with a warm glow for Shakespeare that had rubbed off from Olivier, and the highest regard for her leading man's acting.

At a party he [Olivier] told a couple of Jewish jokes. Arthur says his Yiddish accent was perfect. I told him Lee Strasberg said I had Shakespeare in me. What did he think? Olivier said, 'Marilyn, if you worked with Lee harder than you ever worked and get the basics, come to me and I'll help you do it. Here's what you're in for . . . ' And Olivier recited Shakespeare for two hours. Everything from Hamlet to Shylock. It was magic. I've never heard anything so magnificent. He ended with: 'She should have died hereafter. There would have for such a word. Tomorrow and tomorrow and tomorrow creeps in this petty pace from day to day to the last syllable of recorded time. And all our yesterdays have lighted fools the way to dusty death. Out, out, brief candle. Life's but a walking shadow, a poor player that struts and frets his hour upon the stage and then is heard no more. It is a tale told by an idiot, full of sound and fury, signifying nothing.' Olivier said: 'That says it all,' smiled and left. I sat and cried with joy for being so privileged.

The Prince and the Showgirl was released by Warner Brothers in 1957. Marilyn made this tape in 1962, just before she died, and the impact Sir Laurence Olivier had made on her had survived five years as strong as ever. It changed her ambitions. She now saw herself as a great Shakespearean actress in the making. She was very positive about this in what she said to Dr Greenson.

If I have to do any more pictures for those b — s at Fox, I am going to be the highest paid actress in Hollywood, double what they pay Taylor, and a piece of the gross. I'll choose the script, director and cast. The pictures will be box office hits. I'll put part of the millions I make in no-risk invest-ments. The rest I'll use to finance my plan. I'll take a year of day and night study of Shakespeare with Lee Strasberg. I'll pay him to work only with me. He said I could do Shakespeare. I'll make him prove it. That will give me the basics Olivier wanted. Then

I'll go to Olivier for the help he promised. And I'll pay whatever he wants. Then I'll produce and act in the Marilyn Monroe Shakespeare Film Festival which will put his major plays on film.

I'll need you to keep me together for a year or more. I'll pay you to be your only patient. Oh, and I made you another present. I have thrown all my pills in the toilet. You see how serious I am about this?

I've read all of Shakespeare and practised a lot of lines. I won't have to worry about the scripts. I'll have the greatest scriptwriter who ever lived working for me and I don't have to pay him. Oh, Monroe will have her hand in. I am going to do Juliet first. What with what make-up, costume and camera can do, my acting will create a Juliet who is fourteen, an innocent virgin, but whose budding womanhood is fantastically sexy.

I've some wonderful ideas for Lady Macbeth and Queen Gertrude. I feel certain I'll win an Oscar for one or more of my Shakespearean women. Yes, Doctor, this is what I am going to do. I owe it to you, Doctor, that I can.

Marilyn craved learning, she had an insatiable appetite for it, and longed for serious artistic achievement. Among the many books she had in her possession was a copy of Michael Gorchakov's *How Stanislavsky Directs*. In his book,

Goddess, The Secret Lives of Marilyn Monroe, Anthony Summers comments that this title ' . . . reflected the goal that Marilyn held in deadly earnest — her determination to become a serious actress.' And even John Huston who directed *The Misfits*, and did not get along with her very well, recognised something special in her. He said, 'She could turn into a very good actress.' And that was praise indeed from the master director.

None of the 29 movies Marilyn Monroe made ever gave her the chance to show herself as a serious actress. It is true she had greater opportunity to demonstrate her ability in some films more than others, but she was not thought of as a serious actress by producers, and the scripts she was given reflected this. Although the 'dumb blonde' image had begun to be eroded in pictures such as *The Misfits*, this was predominantly the way she was perceived by writers, producers and the public at large.

The problem involved more than merely having to enlighten those she worked for. Probably schooled to do so by her publicists, Marilyn tended too often to sink into the part of the dumb blonde she played so frequently on the screen when she made public appearances. She appeared effervescent, breathy voiced and just a bit feather brained, which did nothing to promote her cause to be recognised as a serious actress. Her friends were not patronised in that way, and, therefore, had no problem with accepting her ambitions for a change in direction, but stepping outside of the studio image was going to involve a total rethink. It would be a brave and quite dangerous move to make, and possibly one in which having closed a door behind her she might find it difficult — if not impossible — to reopen if things went wrong.

But by the time she made these tapes, Marilyn was happy enough with the progress she had made in landing the script for *Something's Got to Give,* in which she played the part of the smart and far-from-scatty Ellen. Ellen had survived years on a desert island before being rescued and was about to re-establish herself with husband and family, regardless of discovering her husband had decided to choose a new wife in her absence and finding the wedding bells had just finished ringing the very day she got back to civilisation. This movie would be a step in the right direction, a distinct move away from *Gentlemen Prefer Blondes* and the tarty Cherie in *Bus Stop*.

After recovering from the saga of being fired from the set and having settled the terms for her return to making *Something's Got to Give,* Marilyn had decided to make some sweeping changes in her life. She had dismissed Paula Strasberg, wife of Lee, for interference on the set, and had also trimmed Dr Greenson's wings by forbidding him to negotiate for her at the studio. Now she wanted to get rid of Mrs Murray.

But let's get to something serious. Doctor, I want you to help me get rid of Murray. While she was giving me an enema last night I was thinking to myself, lady, even though you're very good at this, you've got to go. But how? I can't flat out fire her. Next thing would be a book, Secrets of Marilyn Monroe by her Housekeeper. She'd make a fortune spilling what she knows and she knows too damn much. How about this. You tell her you have a seriously sick or suicidal patient or locate one somehow: that the patient is in urgent need of Murray's services. I graciously, with tears in my eyes, agree to part with her. I'll give her a substantial severance bonus, but she'll have to sign a contract not to write or give interviews about me. Ask Mickey [Milton Rudin, her attorney] if a contract like that can be made to stick. Doctor, the fact is we just plain don't like each other. I can't put up with her insolence and disregard for anything I ask her to do. If you have a better idea please let me know what it is.

This was quite clever of Marilyn. Dr Greenson and Mrs Murray were old friends. Dr Greenson had bought Mrs Murray's house from her and he had 'found' her for Marilyn. It would appear she had only recently discovered that Mrs Murray was acting more in the way of a spy for Dr Greenson than a housekeeper, and, in fact, it seemed likely Greenson had planted her there more because of her nursing background than any talent she had as a housekeeper. But Marilyn was anxious not to offend Dr Greenson, and her ploy to involve him in getting rid of Murray — or

262

for him to suggest another idea for getting her to go — was a clever way to put the ball in his court. What she didn't tell Greenson was that when Mrs Murray had arranged to take a holiday, Marilyn had paid her a month's salary and told her she need not return until September. This gave her a month to resolve the problem with Greenson, but the hint was she was going to fire her whether the doctor liked it or not.

Though there is no telling what Marilyn had at the back of her mind, the content of the tapes would not support in any way that Marilyn was planning to get rid of Dr Greenson, as some writers have suggested. She still appears to lean heavily on him, and her long term plans clearly include him and his services also, while the suggestion made in the tapes that she would like him to adopt her so that she became part of his family would indicate considerable affection.

Mrs Eunice Murray. It was time for her to go.
Photo Robert F Slatzer Collection

24

THE SECRET TAPES: HUSBANDS, FRIENDS AND OTHERS

Joan Crawford and Marilyn were close friends.

We went to her house from a cocktail party. She asked if I minded waiting while she gave her daughter an enema the doctor had ordered because of the flu. But the little girl screamed that she didn't want an enema and wouldn't let her mother give it to her. I could see that Crawford was getting so angry she was going to hit the child.

Marilyn intervened and offered to do it for her, since it was clear Joan's technique was lacking if the child found it so upsetting.

I gave it to the sweet angel so gently she giggled. Joan gave me a sour look and said, 'I don't believe in spoiling children.' I felt she had a cruel streak towards the child.

For those who have wondered about Marilyn's sexuality, another question was settled in her tapes. She described an intimate´ moment in some detail and how she and Joan Crawford had sex. Crawford, she said, wanted this relationship to continue, but Marilyn decidedly didn't.

I told her straight out I didn't much enjoy doing it with a woman. After I turned her down she became spiteful. An English poet best described it: 'Heaven hath no rage like love to hatred turned; and hell hath no fury like a woman scorned.' Most people wrongly credit that to Shakespeare. William Congreve is the author. That's me, Marilyn Monroe, the classical scholar.

Marilyn makes a number of remarks of this kind, as though she is anxious to demonstrate her knowledge and establish that she has a familiarity with literature and books of learning.

Then there was more talk about enemas. She remembered what Greenson had had to say about their psychological effects and referred to what she had learnt about Freud. This linked to what she had said (see Chapter 22) about difficulty with orgasms and the problems in her childhood.

You know I have a very poor memory of my early childhood. After the enema thing with Crawford's daughter I remember a little bit about the enemas I had as a child. They were what you and Dr Freud called repressed memories. I'll work on it and give you another tape.

But Doctor, I don't understand this big taboo about enemas. Most of the actresses I know use them, even some who won't admit it. Mae West told me she is given an enema every day. Mae says her enemas will keep her young until she is 100. I hope she makes it. A nice lady, even though she turned down making a picture with me. That just shows how smart she is. Before she told me I knew about her enemas from Jim Bacon. He said Gloria Swanson takes two to three enemas a day. Well look at them. They look pretty good for post-menopausal gals.

Peter Lawford showed me some piston syringes he got in France. He says the Queen and noblewomen of the court of Louis XIV were given frequent enemas by special servants called apothecaries. The purpose was to give them peaches and cream complexions by preventing pimples caused by constipation. I asked my gastroenterologist. He says it's true that constipation can cause pimples. Something about intestinal toxins getting into the blood. So there you are. Those ladies were doing the intelligent thing.

Yes, I enjoy enemas, so what! They sure beat the cramps and diarrhoea you get from laxatives. We have had fun with those piston syringes at beachhouse parties. Peter swears . . . one . . . belonged to the Countess du Barry.

Marilyn speaks of a problem she has. Someone has rattled her and she is uncertain how to respond.

I asked Frank Sinatra what I could do. He said, 'Marilyn baby, ignore it. If you take on one of those bastards you make him bigger and yourself smaller.' I suppose if anyone knows Frank should. He is a man at the top of his profession and is a fine actor as well. You know he got an Oscar for From Here to Eternity. He has helped more people anonymously than anybody else. And the miserable press smears him with lies about his being involved with the Mafia and gangsters. And Frank just takes it. What a wonderful friend he is to me. I love Frank and he loves me. It is not the marrying kind of love. It is better because marriage can't destroy it. How well I know. Marriage destroyed my relationships with two wonderful men.

Marilyn was here generous to Sinatra in more ways than one. They had been romantically linked some time before this, the episode ending with Sinatra becoming engaged to dancer Juliet Prowse without so much as having the courtesy to tell Marilyn their affair was over. But long afterwards they had become friends again and Marilyn, as can be seen in the contents of the tapes, staunchly defends his character.

What she says may well have been for the benefit of Doctor Greenson, however. It belies

Marilyn with her little dog Maf.
Photo Robert F Slatzer Collection

she knew all too well that Sinatra rubbed
shoulders with underworld figures. After she and
Arthur Miller divorced, Miller kept the basset
hound they had, of which she had become fond,
and a friend — some say Pat Newcomb, others
Frank Sinatra — made her a present of a small
white poodle. She named it 'Maf' after Sinatra's
friends. In spite of Marilyn's protestations, his
friendship and dealings with mafiosi in general
and Sam Giancana and Johnny Rosselli in

269

particular became well known. Giancana, for instance, was known to stay at Sinatra's Palm Springs house, and was said to have become a partner in the singer's hotel and casino, the Cal-Neva, at Lake Tahoe. Two years after Marilyn died, when the business relationship became known to the FBI, Sinatra withdrew from the Cal-Neva and lost his gambling licence. Almost 20 years later he protested that from 1960, though he knew Giancana slightly, he did not know he was connected to organised crime. Sam Giancana, in fact, was in his — and Marilyn's — company only a few days before she died.

On the face of it, it seems that Marilyn had, at this point, accepted Frank Sinatra as a true friend, and would not have a harsh word said about him. It is possible there may have been another reason for Marilyn's enthusiasm, however, which had more to do with staving off Greenson's criticism of the friends she kept. When her friend Norman Roston commented on their friendship, he said that on Marilyn's part, what he saw was 'not eagerness, but panic'.

Joe DiMaggio loves Marilyn Monroe and always will. I love him and always will. But Joe couldn't stay married to Marilyn Monroe, the famous movie star. Joe has an image in his stubborn Italian head of a traditional Italian wife. She would have to be faithful, do what he tells her, devote all of herself to him. Doctor, you know that's not me. There is no way I could stop being Marilyn Monroe and become someone else to save our marriage. It didn't take too long before we both realised that and ended our marriage. But we didn't end our love for each other. Any time I need him, Joe is there. I couldn't have a better friend.

Marilyn then goes on to make it clear she had firm plans to see Joe DiMaggio again, and her plans were far from platonic. What she says was quite consistent with her having agreed to the remarriage he had been seeking. His devotion was certainly impressive and extremely touching. While there was no specific reference to the wedding rumoured to have been set for the Wednesday after she died, there was enough here to justify belief that they had reached some kind of compromise in their warring attitudes and that reconciliation was on the cards.

It's different with Arthur [Miller]. Marrying him was my mistake, not his. He couldn't give me the attention, warmth and affection I need. It's not in his nature. Arthur never credited me with much intelligence. He couldn't share his intellectual life with me. As bed partners we were so-so. He was not that much interested; me faking with exceptional performances to get him more interested. You know I think his little Jewish father had more genuine affection for me than Arthur did.

I loved the little man and his quaint Jewishness. But the Jewish religion never got to me and I think Arthur didn't care about it. Maybe he is a fine creative writer. I suppose so. Arthur didn't know film and how to write for it. Misfits was not a great film because it wasn't a great script. Gable, Monroe, Clift, Wallach, Huston. What more could you ask. I'll tell you. There has to be a story as good as the talent who play it. You know why those religious theme pictures like Ben Hur *and* The Ten Commandments *are so successful? Because the Bible is a good script.*

The *Misfits* opened to mixed reviews and much criticism of the story. In a cruel review *Time* magazine called it ' . . . a dozen pictures rolled into one. Most of them . . . terrible'. They wrote of it being ' . . . [a] fatuously embarrassing psychoanalysis of Marilyn Monroe, Arthur Miller and what went wrong with their famous marriage.' During filming things got so bad that Marilyn would not ride to the lot in the same car as Miller, and the not-unexpected announcement that the marriage was over came soon after the film was completed. Marilyn had expected great things of that marriage. She thought she had found a solid foundation on which she could build her life, but it proved not to be so. It gave the appearance of being yet another mismatch.

25

THE SECRET TAPES:
JACK AND BOBBY

Marilyn leaves no doubt she holds President Kennedy close to her heart. What she has to say would support all that has been said about their relationship, and serves to pour scorn on the idea being peddled by some that she was somehow black-mailing JFK:

Marilyn Monroe is a soldier. Her Commander-in-Chief is the greatest and most powerful man in the world. The first duty of a soldier is to obey her Commander-in-Chief. He says 'do this', you do this. He says 'do that', you do that.

This man is going to change our country. No child will go hungry. No person will sleep in the street and get his meals from garbage cans. People who can't afford it will get good medical care. Industrial products will be the best in the world. No, I'm not talking Utopia — that's an illusion, but he will transform America today like FDR did in the thirties. You don't think you're hearing me, do you? You're right. And he'll

273

do for the world what he'll do for America — transform it for the better. I tell you, Doctor, when he has finished his achievements he will take his place with Washington, Jefferson, Lincoln and FDR as one of our greatest Presidents.

President John F Kennedy and brother Robert. Photo Courtesy The John F Kennedy Library

I'm glad he has Bobby. It's like the navy. The President is the captain and Bobby is his executive officer. Bobby would do absolutely anything for his brother. And so would I. I'll never embarrass him. As long as I have memory I have John Fitzgerald Kennedy.

There is a clear indication here of the affection Marilyn still feels for President Kennedy. But by the time she was making this recording Robert Kennedy was a problem. After chasing Marilyn he had suddenly dropped out of sight, refusing even to speak to her. She was offended — mad at him — that he didn't even say goodbye, but upon reflection she was happy to let him go, and it appeared she was anxious that she was not seen to be dumping him the way he had unceremoniously dumped her.

Marilyn then embarks on a sequence of free association in which she compares the bodies of Jack Kennedy and his brother, Robert, following her mention of Robert as Executive Officer. The difference, she says, is Robert is covered by dense hair.

But Bobby, Doctor, what should I do about Bobby? As you see there is no room in my life for him. I guess I don't have the courage to face up to it and hurt him. I want someone else to tell him it's over. I tried to get the President to do it, but I couldn't reach him. Now I'm glad I couldn't. He is too important to ask. You know when I sang Happy Birthday for him I sweated profusely; I was afraid it would show. Maybe I should stop being a coward and tell him myself. But because I know how much he'll be hurt I don't have the strength to hurt him. His Catholic morality has to find a way to justify cheating on his wife, so love becomes his excuse. And if you love enough, you can't help it and you can't be blamed. All right, Doctor, that's Marilyn Monroe's analysis of Bobby's love for me. And now I understand it for what it is, I'm not going to have any problem handling it myself. What is amazing is I solved my problem just through the free associating I did for you.

Well, there's something for you to sleep on, Doctor.

Goodnight.

26

THE SECRET TAPES: HIDDEN IMPLICATIONS

Marilyn's words about Bobby Kennedy have to be placed carefully in context and sequence. It is clear this was recorded before they met on Friday night, when Robert Kennedy failed to show for dinner at her house, and they later argued at the restaurant. She was unlikely to have said what she says here after the row they had that night, and even less likely after the events of Saturday afternoon and evening. This must have been recorded before Friday evening, then, perhaps shortly before being persuaded to meet Peter Lawford at the La Scala.

The other important indication of sequence is her reference on the tape to trying to contact President Kennedy to get him to call Bobby off. Peter Lawford spoke about this to private eye Fred Otash. Lawford told him of Marilyn trying to contact JFK at the White House and being unable to reach him because he had gone to Hyannis Port. We know from the tapes she changed her mind about speaking to the President and this makes sense of her giving Lawford the message, 'Say goodbye to the President for me,' indicating she knew she was finished with them both. It would appear that Lawford, however, saw the opportunity to link this to other goodbyes he was to say she expressed, which he did in such a way as to turn them into the last words of a despondent Marilyn contemplating suicide.

It should here be noted there is not the slightest hint of despondency to be found anywhere in the tapes, and it is clear they were made *after* she tried to reach the President, and *before* she saw Robert Kennedy on Friday night. The 'say goodbye' phone call to Lawford was made on Saturday, in the sequence of things — what time on Saturday is uncertain, though probably about 5.00 p.m. — and this indicates the calls Marilyn attempted to make to the President were likely to have been made on the Friday, the day before she died, and not earlier than the day before that, Thursday 2 August.

Another indicator of when the last of the recordings was made is that she finishes the tape saying 'Goodnight' to the Doctor. This could not have been late on Friday; she had her row with Robert Kennedy that night and later got drunk. As we have said, she probably recorded the tapes before she was persuaded by Lawford to go out for a meal at the restaurant where Robert Kennedy was waiting for her, though 'Goodnight' might merely have indicated she expected the doctor to be listening to the tapes at the end of his working day.

In these recordings, Marilyn bears Robert Kennedy no ill will. She has recovered from the disappointment she experienced when he dropped her and refused to take her calls, and she has definitely resolved the affair is ended. It appears Kennedy accepted an invitation, probably arranged through Peter Lawford, to dine with Marilyn at Fifth Helena Drive on Friday night. She had arranged for Briggs Delicatessan to deliver nearly 50 dollars worth of food, a tidy sum for two buffet meals in 1962. She probably saw this as her opportunity to pluck up the courage she mentions in her tapes to tell him it was all over. It would appear, however, he didn't show, and this, no doubt, would have upset her. Then followed the invitation to eat with Peter Lawford, and the row with Robert Kennedy in the restaurant, which changed everything and set the scene for what was to come on Saturday.

The tapes reveal a Marilyn who is in command of herself and has made positive changes of direction. There is no hint of aggressive introversion. She is upbeat and full of plans. She has finally decided to finish her relationship with Robert Kennedy. That was a big step. Having already fired Paula Strasberg, another decisive step, she next plans to get rid of Mrs Murray, too. She is quite positive about setting her sights on achieving something really worthwhile in her acting career by aiming at becoming a Shakespearean actress, and the tapes indicate this plan has been well thought through. It is long-term planning she is sharing with Dr Greenson, not as a possibility, but as something about which she has quite made up her mind. The revelation of this hard, fast, forward planning hardly indicates someone who is

279

*Briggs' bill for food supplied to Marilyn's home on
the Friday night before she died.*

teetering on the brink of suicide. Quite the
reverse: she is brimming with confidence and
cannot wait to get on with her life.

Athough it is nowhere mentioned, the context
in which the tapes are made is one where Dr

Greenson must by then have been acutely aware he had overstepped the mark by interfering in Marilyn's professional life. It would not be necessary to raise the issue, but his removal from her work scene would be likely to have reduced tension and increased her confidence yet further.

There is no hint in the tapes of pining for the Kennedys, or feeling sorry for herself. Her plans for the future are positive, robust and realistic, and she has an exciting time ahead. She had many times declared a desire to become a 'serious' actress, and now this is in the forefront of her mind. There are no fears preying on her, excepting for the slight worry about her mother's mental condition, which she reveals and, it is noted, keeps firmly at bay. The yearning to belong to a real family, something of which she was deprived, is apparent in what she says to Dr Greenson early in the tapes. Greenson had, to a measure, already drawn Marilyn into his family circle, and was, after her death, severely criticised for having done so. It was a dangerous and highly unusual manoeuvre on his part, though it is doubtful there was anything untoward intended in it.

The establishing of Clark Gable as a father figure is interesting. He is clearly someone set apart and special for her, not at all the cult figure he had become to many girls. That he had attained such status is expressed in a recording made in the fifties by a young Judy Garland, 'Dear Mr Gable', a song in which a combination of highly respectful adulation, admiration and puppy-love affection is directed towards the star.

Filmgoers of the time had no difficulty in understanding the inspiration for the early teen song, which survives as a Judy Garland classic. To Marilyn, however, he was someone she could admire as a father figure.

In discussing the making of *The Misfits* with Clark Gable, Marilyn totally ignores the tensions and stresses of various kinds that were present under the Nevada desert sun. She was, no doubt, suffering the trauma of her marriage to Arthur Miller having disintegrated into a daily, bitchy, 'give nothing, take nothing' relationship, which would end, shortly after the completion of the picture, in divorce. The movie was not easy for anybody. The cast and the crew sweltered in the heat while waiting for Marilyn to appear, while Marilyn was suffering torments from the fear of appearing in front of the cameras, and was having to be coaxed along by her make-up man and confidante, Whitey Snyder. Marilyn accused Miller, who as writer of the movie was on the set daily, of getting back at her by detracting from Roslyn, the part she played, in rewrites, and the atmosphere between them was frosty at best.

By the time she records the tapes, however, her only mentions of Arthur Miller are philosophical and understanding, and her attitude benign and tolerant. She had confided her marital problems to Greenson at the time *The Misfits* had been made, and, listening to the tapes, the doctor must have been well satisfied with what he had achieved, since there was no evidence of malice or churlishness.

In the tapes Marilyn reveals there was no romantic entanglement or any improper relationship between her and her doctor, so spiking the guns of those who have suggested otherwise. She clearly indicates the high regard in which she holds him and the whole tenor of what she says underlines a healthy esteem for a man of integrity.

It should also be noted that she tells Dr Greenson she has thrown all her pills down the toilet. This represents another huge step forward, and is an indication that she is moving with confidence to meet her future and is prepared to be brave about it. It should be doubly underlined that Dr Hyman Engelberg led the police to believe Marilyn had a prescription filled for 50 Nembutal capsules, which he suggested she had in her possession the day she died. In fact this was later found to be incorrect: the prescription he gave her had been for 25 capsules. Dr Engelberg also said she had had it renewed 'a few days before her death'. If this is so, and there is doubt about it, it appears they were among the capsules she had flushed down the toilet on the day before she died.

As for the coroner sagely talking about some 40-plus Nembutal capsules having caused Marilyn's death, a representative of Abbott Laboratories, who made the Nembutal capsules, said that to account for the large volume of the drug found in Marilyn's liver and bloodstream she would have had to have ingested the contents of up to about 90 capsules. All this would tend to support, therefore, that the Nembutal that killed

Marilyn was brought to the house by her murderers, probably in liquid form, rather than in any way involving capsules.

It is small wonder Dr Greenson played the secret tapes for John Miner to listen to. If one can possibly, for a moment, 'hear' what has been written above coming from Marilyn's lips, the very idea is enough to indicate Miner heard an excited — perhaps breathy — voice that expressed enthusiasm about everything of which it spoke. John Miner had no other option than to write to his superiors and tell them in no uncertain terms that Marilyn Monroe did not take her own life.

27

Two-Act Tragedy

The dramas of Marilyn's courtships and marriages were easily recounted against the backdrops of the movies she made in the corresponding periods of her personal life and career. The movies acted like bookmarks, and a number of those who worked with Marilyn became involved in whatever part the saga had reached by that particular time.

When she made *Gentlemen Prefer Blondes*, Marilyn worked with Jane Russell. They had met in the days when Marilyn was Norma Jean and she was married to Jim Dougherty. Marilyn and Jane were not strangers to each other, since they had attended the same high school. During the making of *Gentlemen* they became good friends and Marilyn had a lot to discuss with Jane in view of her latest boyfriend, Joe DiMaggio. Jane had married Bob Waterfield, who had been a well-known football player before he quit, and Marilyn was anxious to know how football and movies had mixed.

She had started dating DiMaggio in 1952. Joe had been married to an actress before; she was Dorothy Olsen, and Joe Jr, with whom Marilyn got on so well, was their son. The 1939 marriage lasted until 1945, when they divorced upon his discharge from the Army Air Force, in which he had enlisted in 1943. The cause of their break up had been, it seemed, the incompatibility of their careers, and it was somewhat astonishing, therefore, that Joe was prepared to savour the same recipe in his involvement with Marilyn.

The courtship progressed throughout 1952, moving into the limelight and attracting much publicity during that year, when she moved on to making *How to Marry a Millionaire*. In *Millionaire* she worked with a distinguished cast that included Betty Grable and Lauren Bacall. Betty Grable allied herself to Marilyn at once and Bacall made up a loyal and trusty trio. When Joan Crawford unleashed a catty attack on Marilyn in the press it was Betty Grable who sprang to her defence. Marilyn impressed Betty Grable with the concern she expressed in frequent telephone calls when she heard her daughter had been injured in a horse riding accident.

Lauren Bacall, who got on well with Marilyn also, recalled the discussions she had with her while the picture was in production. Marilyn asked about her marriage and her children. She also remembered Marilyn telling her she would rather, at that time, be with Joe in some spaghetti joint in San Francisco. Bacall liked her, and was later to say she found ' . . . no meanness in her, no bitchery'. Joe, all the while, made it clear how much he despised Hollywood ballyhoo, celebrity parties and a scantily clad Marilyn.

After *How to Marry a Millionaire*, Marilyn was hurtled, almost literally, into the *River of No*

Return project. The Canadian Rockies were not really her scene, and she did not think much of a story that cast the scenery — incredibly beautiful as it was — in the starring role. From the actors' point of view the script left a lot to be desired. They would have to work hard to make their mark in this movie. She played opposite Robert Mitchum in this action-packed western, which was a huge plus, and enjoyed playing with the young Tommy Rettig, who took the part of Mitchum's son. The production ran over budget, drawing the quip, '*Picture of No Return*' from Mitchum, with Marilyn adding to the cost by her antics in the river featured in the film. She claimed to break a leg — though this was not so — obtaining much attention from a concerned production team and bringing an attentive Joe DiMaggio swiftly to the location when he heard about it.

It was not until January of 1954 that Marilyn finally married Joe DiMaggio, who had distinct ideas about the changes he wanted to introduce to the person Marilyn was; frequently if not usually a fatal ambition to bring to a marriage. Twentieth Century Fox had a new picture lined up for Marilyn after *River*. This was *Pink Tights*, a remake of *Coney Island*, which had been made as recently as 1943 with Betty Grable in the lead part. Though in *Pink Tights* she would have been cast opposite Frank Sinatra, after reading the script, Marilyn promptly said she would not do it. She adamantly refused to go along with Fox in doing another picture that she recognised as a cul-de-sac, as far as acting opportunities

Marilyn with Joe DiMaggio. Their unyielding careers were not compatible.
Photo AP World Wide

were concerned. And that was that. Her next move would be to leave with her new husband on her honeymoon.

Her marriage to Joe DiMaggio was tempestuous and, according to reports that began to surface, degrading. She refused to quit Hollywood and settle into the role Joe had cast for her as the little wife who ran after him, ironed his shirts and darned his socks. He was staunchly set in opposition to the glitz that went with Tinseltown, and wanted Marilyn to give up making pictures. Joe was dedicated to his ball-player background and, though now retired from the game, was firmly committed to retaining his identity in the world of sport. It was against this background that Marilyn was making *There's No Business Like Show Business*, in which she played a part which was little more that an addendum to the plot, a plot which was hard to find. The picture was little more than a showcase for Irving Berlin songs, though cinema audiences would accept the slight story in return for being given Berlin's magic music performed by Marilyn with Ethel Merman, Dan Dailey, Donald O'Connor, heart-throb Johnny Ray, and Mitzi Gaynor. From time to time Marilyn won awards of one kind or another, but Joe would not accompany her to the ceremonies where she received them.

Show Business did nothing to help Marilyn's marriage to Joe. He was on the set to watch her performing for the shooting of the *Heat Wave* number, an embarrassing sequence which cocked a snook at the censor and revealed hidden 'depths' to the meaning of the lyrics. To Irving Berlin, they were so hidden he had never realised they were there in the first place. Joe stormed off the set, not prepared to get involved in applauding what was going on.

Marilyn was determined to progress in movie making, widening her horizons and finding more-demanding acting parts. Joe wanted none of it; he was assertive and believed the man should rule the household. Marilyn sought to continue her own interests and be free to entertain her friends as she chose, establishing a degree of independence. The two clashed head on. It became no secret he hit her. The bruises showed but were then covered up by make-up.

Her next picture was *The Seven Year Itch*, which was released in 1955, and it was during the making of this film that the fiery mismatch with Joe burnt out. The premiere of *The Seven Year Itch* proved to be an exception when Joe agreed to escort Marilyn, and he arranged a party at which to celebrate afterwards. During the party, however, they had a row, and Marilyn left. The marriage had lasted only nine months. It appeared neither was prepared to budge in accommodating the wishes of the other, and the common ground between them evaporated. Joe, it was said, was incredibly jealous and became suspicious she was seeing other men. If all reports are true, he had every right to be. Marilyn did not accept that marriage should preclude her becoming involved with other men, and it was during the time she was married to Joe DiMaggio she first met Jack Kennedy. Her friend, journalist Sidney Skolsky, was shocked to hear her declare, quite early in their marriage, that she had set her sights on marrying Arthur Miller. Marilyn told how Joe had threatened to divorce her while they were on honeymoon, so angered was he over other men in her life and the ballyhoo over her performances for the troops in Korea. She reportedly said, ' . . . *deep down I didn't want to marry him.*'

Between the time of their divorce and the end of Marilyn's life, Joe, regardless of his past rigidity, jealousy and refusal to compromise, gave the impression he wanted to change. He appeared to soften, became gentler, and anxious to be more accommodating in what was left of the relationship he still had with Marilyn. He wanted very badly to try again with her, and interestingly, this reflected a desire he had had for reconciliation with Dorothy Olsen, his first wife, after his first divorce. He tried then and it came to nothing, but it is strongly believed by some that, if Marilyn had survived, he would have succeeded this time, and they would have remarried, prepared this time to give and take and accommodate each other's wishes. What Marilyn has to say in her tapes, while not confirming this absolutely, gives a definite indication she was heading that way.

After Joe, one affair followed another. In 1955 she became close to Henry Rosenfeld, a wealthy New York-based dress manufacturer whom she had known for some time. His proposal of marriage came to nothing, but he had become a friend, confidante, consultant and financial adviser, and this continued for the rest of her life. She spoke to Henry Rosenfeld on the telephone the very day she died. Then it was Marlon Brando. Brando had also been a student at Lee Strasberg's Actor's Studio in New York, and Marilyn had long admired him. He, too, became a life-long friend. It was also during that year that she began to be linked to Arthur Miller.

Miller had been married for some 15 years when he got to know Marilyn Monroe. He had two children and a wife who had supported him devotedly, providing for his needs, checking his manuscripts and, when he was hard up, working to bring in the money they needed to live on. The marriage had, however, become stale, and he was seeking to end it. He had met Marilyn several years before and had been greatly taken with her. Now they began a courtship that would lead to marriage. The novel part of the courtship was the two of them cycling quite anonymously in parts of Brooklyn, where Arthur Miller belonged. For all his literary and theatrical connections, Miller was an outdoor man. He hunted and he fished and he spent time in the countryside.

It was during the time of their courtship Marilyn made *Bus Stop*, the screen version of a work by leading playwright William Inge. The story of *Bus Stop* took Marilyn away from light-hearted comedy and musicals, but the film, as successful as it was, still did not point in the direction she wanted to go. She did not want to replace the dumb blonde image with that of *Bus Stop*'s sluttish Cherie.

Marilyn with Arthur Miller, in London when she made The Prince and the Showgirl. Their marriage might have survived but for her miscarriage.
Photo AP World Wide

Marilyn in Bus Stop
Photo Twentieth Century Fox.

Marilyn was 11 years younger than Miller, but it meant nothing to her. She had been 12 years younger than Joe DiMaggio. A secret registry office marriage was followed by a traditional Jewish wedding, for which Marilyn had opted. Those of the Jewish faith had been all around her; many of her best friends were Jewish. She took an instant liking to Arthur's father, Isadore, and they began a friendship that would outlast her marriage to his son. The next film on Marilyn's agenda was *The Prince and the Showgirl*, playing opposite the illustrious Laurence Olivier, and this would be made in England.

Miller accompanied his wife there, but it proved not to be the best of moves in their new marriage. He was supposed to be spending his time writing while Marilyn made the movie. He spent a great deal of time in the studio, as it happened, and the outcome was not helpful to their relationship. In spite of Marilyn's tremendous admiration for Olivier's work, their relationship on set was somewhat abrasive, and not improved at all by her perpetual lateness. When Olivier, who was directing the film as well as performing in it, parried with some cutting remark, she expected Arthur to speak up and defend her. This he did not do. He had a good relationship with Olivier and left them to it. This was a disastrous way to begin a marriage.

It seemed that at this stage Marilyn contributed a lot less to the marriage than she might have done. When his daughter took ill, Miller left his wife and flew home to the United States to see her. Marilyn was offended that he went and let everyone know it. She claimed she was ill and brought filming to a halt for all the time he was away. As a consequence, Miller cut his trip to just one week. The set became a battlefield on which a war was fought between Olivier and Marilyn's entourage. Marilyn preserved the status quo by laying down the law, the whole process lurched forward and, remarkably, a workmanlike movie emerged which, generally, people liked. Before leaving England Marilyn was criticised for not being responsive to the kindness and courtesies extended to her when the film was being wrapped up. Next, it was back home and a long break from making movies.

Marilyn expected a great deal from her marriage to Arthur Miller. Most of all she sought security and the opportunity to acquire culture and learning. They were very happy and deeply in love. The frosty atmosphere of England was behind them. They took an apartment on East 57th Street in addition to the farm in Connecticut that was Arthur's home. When, in 1957, Marilyn became pregnant, life seemed complete, but their joy would be short lived. After two months, Marilyn suffered a miscarriage and their hopes and dreams were dashed. She met and mingled with Arthur's intellectual friends and took an interest in his particular brand of left-wing politics and liberal ideas. When he was pilloried for them during the McCarthy witch-hunts she defended him magnificently and supported him with money to fight his corner when he had need.

The following year Marilyn went back to Hollywood to make a new film, *Some Like It Hot*. Billy Wilder directed this movie, which was filmed in black and white to accommodate the demands of a hilarious story in which Marilyn's co-stars, Jack Lemmon and Tony Curtis, were to spend much of the movie dressed as women. If Marilyn had problems to share while she was making this film, her co-stars would likely not have been the people to share them with. Jack Lemmon and Tony Curtis were at their wits' end coping with the delays that followed delays that followed delays that had become Marilyn's stock in trade. During the making of *Some Like it Hot*

Some Like It Hot
Photo Twentieth Century Fox.

Marilyn developed an inability to handle the words in her script. In one incredible instance — which no doubt qualified at once to enter cinematic history — she required 65 takes to complete a three-word line satisfactorily. But *Some Like it Hot* was hugely successful at the box office, and Fox were anxious to follow it quickly with another hit. This, they decided, was *Let's Make Love*.

Let's Make Love featured a story Marilyn disliked from the outset. She felt it took her back to the kind of movie she had grown out of a decade before, and though the script was by the able Norman Krasna, she demanded wholesale rewriting. Gregory Peck, who had been signed to play opposite her, didn't like what was happening and quit, and the hunt for a co-star ultimately resulted in the part being offered to the French actor Yves Montand. Despite distinguished support players in Tony Randall and England's Wilfred Hyde White, and the directing skills of George Cukor, whose services Marilyn had demanded for the film, it was something of a disaster. During the making of *Let's Make Love* Marilyn's marital problems became such as she required the ear and support of a psychiatrist, rather than sympathetic friends.

Her marriage, it seems, took another nose-dive when Marilyn became involved with Yves Montand. Arthur eventually became aware of Marilyn's infidelity and likely realised Montand was probably not the only man with whom she had been unfaithful. The marriage was spinning out of control. When Ralph Greenson became Marilyn's psychiatrist she brought her problems to him, and Greenson decided to talk to her husband. Recounting his interview with him, Greenson spoke of Miller's concern for Marilyn and his anxiety to help her. He had become like a father to her and had done more than most fathers would in his attempts to support her, but he was reaching the end of his rope.

Marilyn's next project would be the movie Arthur Miller had written for her, *The Misfits*, which he adapted from a short story he had written. Shot in the Nevada desert, a distinguished cast, which included Clark Gable, Eli Wallach and Montgomery Clift, struggled with an unwieldly script which served to underline that, though Miller had undertaken script revisions for *The Prince and the Showgirl* and *Let's Make Love*, scriptwriting was not his forte. In the Nevada wilderness the progress obtained by director John Huston was hard earned. All the while Marilyn's marriage to Arthur Miller was quickly running out of time. Huston said of Miller, 'He had done everything in the world to make that marriage survive. She embarrassed him . . . It was sheer malice, vindictiveness.' Whether this was so or not, the marriage ended in divorce soon after *The Misfits* was completed. As her secret tapes reveal, she at least came to terms with the failure she experienced and accepted her share of the blame for the problems that arose in the marriage.

28

BIG JOE D

Joe DiMaggio had loved Marilyn deeply, but he could not accept her infidelity. An extremely jealous man, it was claimed he at one time had Marilyn's apartment bugged to keep tabs on what she was doing. At a party given by Marilyn's agent, Charles Feldman, Joe saw the attention paid to Marilyn by the up and coming Jack Kennedy, and so did Jackie, Jack's wife. Joe tried to persuade Marilyn to leave several times and the two had a spat. Joe, not unreasonably he no doubt thought, expected Marilyn to settle down with him in an unpretentious marriage, where the honest, Italian values he embraced would become their rule, in a 'happy ever after' relationship. Marilyn, however, neither shared his values nor his dream. Joe DiMaggio was said to have expected Marilyn to become a housewife, to fetch the beer and watch the television movies with him.

She was not interested in that kind of life and made it very clear. They quarrelled. 'Joe is a sweet guy, but we don't have much in common,' she said, and as time went on bitterness showed. She spoke of Joe's 'coldness and indifference'. She could not see herself as the exclusive property of one man, and it took but nine

300

months for the magic that might have been to be wrapped up in an eight-minute divorce. Inez Melson, Marilyn's business manager, told at the divorce hearing how, 'Mr DiMaggio was very indifferent and not concerned with Mrs DiMaggio's happiness. I have seen him push her away and tell her not to bother him.' They had, in fact, separated in late September 1954, about a month before the divorce.

DiMaggio, nonetheless, still loved Marilyn and his jealousy persisted even after they split up. Some weeks before their divorce — in October — Joe engaged a private detective, Barney Ruditsky, to find out if Marilyn was seeing someone else. It was not until 5 November, several days after the divorce, that Philip Irwin, who worked for Ruditsky, reported Marilyn as entering an apartment block where her friend Shiela Stewart lived. They suspected she had some sort of assignation planned, and they were right, for Shiela Stewart's other guest was Marilyn's current lover, Hal Schaefer, her singing coach. Word was quickly passed to Ruditsky and then to DiMaggio. DiMaggio enlisted the help of his friend Frank Sinatra, and they made haste to the apartment block at Kilkea Drive. DiMaggio was not seeking to do violence to whoever it was with Marilyn: he hoped his intrusion would be instrumental to a reconciliation. With Ruditsky, Irwin and another of Ruditsky's men leading the way and Joe DiMaggio not far behind, they rushed inside the building, identified a door, and broke it down.

It turned out they came face to face with

Stewart's neighbour, Florence Kotz who, at 11.15 p.m., when the raid took place, had been in bed. They had identified the wrong door. Marilyn quietly slipped away during all the commotion, while the detectives and Joe DiMaggio were all recognisable by the egg on their faces. This famously became known as the 'Wrong Door Raid', and the outcome took years to resolve. The injured Florence Kotz was finally recompensed in a settlement of $7,500, a far cry from the $200,000 she claimed, but enough to put the matter to rest.

Sinatra sat in a car about a block away while the raid was being carried out, but a witness identified him as one of the intruders. The story was sold — probably by an investigator — to *Confidential* magazine, and their September issue made great capital of it. The matter did not die when the publicity faded. Two years later the magazine came under scrutiny by the Kraft Committee, who were conducting an investigation into exposé magazines. The Wrong Door Raid was again in the news, and this time the enquiry was being publicly conducted. This was shaping up to cause a lot of damage to the singer's reputation, and he sent for private detective Fred Otash to get him out of the mess. Otash, who wrote in his book, *Investigation Hollywood*[1], ' . . . the resurrection was more sensational than the burial,' was at first unwilling to take the case, since he also carried out

[1] Fred Otash, *Investigation Hollywood*, Regnery, Chicago 1976

investigative work for *Confidential*, and feared a conflict of interest. Eventually he was persuaded to take it on, and by using a combination of doubt on the original witness's ability to recognise anyone in the particular location on a moonless night, more doubt on the integrity of the man believed to have supplied the story to the magazine, and a witness that firmly placed Sinatra in his car, he got the singer off the hook.

Shortly after this, Joe DiMaggio and Frank Sinatra had a serious falling out. DiMaggio thought Sinatra was exposing Marilyn to influences she could well do without. Such was the state of things when Marilyn died. DiMaggio, who arranged the funeral, would not allow Sinatra to attend.

After the divorce, Joe spent a few weeks as a house guest with Dr Leon Krohn, a gynaecologist who had become friendly with both Marilyn and Joe. While he was there Joe received an early morning call from Marilyn each day to see how he was doing. He went to see her at her apartment the evening following the 'Wrong Door Raid', and spent several hours there. Talk of reconciliation began. Marilyn was preoccupied that night, however, with a landmark celebration in her career.

It was a big night for Marilyn. Any time she stepped into a room, heads turned and her presence could not go unheeded. This occasion would certainly be no exception. Radiant in her gown of red chiffon, she was fêted at the famous Romanoff's restaurant at a party to celebrate the completion of her latest film, *The Seven Year*

Itch, that also featured Tom Ewell. Arriving late, she found waiting for her producers Darryl Zanuck, Sam Goldwyn and Jack Warner, and director Billy Wilder. The guest list was no less illustrious, for it included James Stewart, Humphrey Bogart, Gary Cooper, Doris Day, Susan Hayward, Claudette Colbert, Lauren Bacall, William Holden, Clifton Webb and Loretta Young, and the man she would dare to make a father figure, Clark Gable. Her success in this reception finally marked her acceptance by her peers in the Hollywood motion-picture world. A delighted Marilyn said to her old friend Sydney Skolsky, 'I didn't think they'd all show up. Honest.'

After dancing 'til three in the morning, Marilyn went later that day into the Cedars of Lebanon Hospital for 'correction to a gynaecological problem [she] had suffered from for years', as it was described by her doctor. Joe drove her to the hospital, and the following night, which she spent there, he was to be found dozing in a lounge when not pacing the corridors.

Joe put in an appearance not long before Marilyn died. It was the weekend before the fatal Saturday, when Frank Sinatra invited Marilyn with Peter and Pat Lawford to his hotel for a couple of days. The Cal-Neva Lodge was so named because it straddled the border between California and Nevada. Nevada laws permitted gambling whilst Californian law did not, so the tables were located in that part of the building which was in the State of Nevada. Sinatra owned it in partnership, at one time, with Mafia boss Sam Giancana, and Giancana was there this weekend with, it is believed, another top Mafia figure, his side kick Johnny Rosselli. Dean Martin, Marilyn's leading man on her current movie *Something's Got to Give*, and scheduled to play opposite Marilyn in another film, *I Love Louisa*, was there. But Joe DiMaggio was not a guest. He and Sinatra were still at loggerheads and Joe was not invited. He would not have accepted an invitation to such a weekend, anyway: he hated Hollywood parties. But it appeared he was worried about Marilyn's well-being that weekend, and his anxiety brought him to the Cal-Neva. He probably also knew that Marilyn and Sinatra were friendly again.

When he reached Lake Tahoe on the Friday night the Cal-Neva was full and he booked into the Silver Crest Motor Hotel nearby. Still jealous of other men, DiMaggio was enraged that Sinatra invited Marilyn to weekend parties of this sort. They were little more than opportunities for drugs, sex and booze. It eventually emerged that Robert Kennedy planned visiting Los Angeles that weekend and, anxious not to see Marilyn, had asked his sister, Pat Lawford, to arrange for Marilyn to be elsewhere, hence the invitation to the Cal-Neva. Marilyn found out later what had been going on behind the scenes and, outraged, she felt let down by her friends who had been party to the deception. It turned out to be a disastrous weekend for her. She occupied Bungalow 52, which Sinatra reserved for his special guests, but the star was not much in evidence those few days.

Lots of rumours circulated afterwards that Marilyn had overdosed and was given coffee and had had to be paraded about her room to revive her. The other tales which circulated of Marilyn looking ghastly on one of the few times she was seen would lend support that something of that kind had happened. Was Harry Hall, an old friend of Joe DiMaggio, gifted with insight, in possession of hard information, or just plain guessing when he said, 'She went up there and they gave her pills'? It was the weekend following this that Marilyn died, and Peter Lawford did not miss a trick. He quickly took advantage of the stories going around to make out that Marilyn had failed in an attempt at suicide at Cal-Neva, but succeeded a few days later at home.

A touching story surrounds another sighting of Marilyn at the Cal-Neva party. It was early on the Sunday morning that she was seen, dressed in her white robe, trailing a foot in the water of the swimming pool. She was seen by one of the staff of the Lodge, who said she gazed up to a driveway on a ridge above the hotel. He followed her gaze, and in the early morning mist he saw Joe looking down on her. This may have been the defining moment for DiMaggio. He went back to the east coast and resigned from his $100,000-a-year job as vice president of VH Monette Incorporated, a supplier of military post exchanges. He told Valmore Monette he still loved Marilyn and believed she may now be prepared to leave Hollywood behind and re-marry him. The date he resigned was 1 August, five days before Marilyn died, and rumour had it they planned to marry during the week after her death. The day set for the wedding was said to be the Wednesday. But it was her funeral Joe DiMaggio went to that day.

Found among Marilyn's belongings was a letter which had been started but not finished. It, too, might be thought to lend support to the theory she and Joe had come to terms and had found a basis for a new marriage. It ran . . .

Dear Joe,
If I can only succeed in making you happy, I will have succeeded in the biggest and most difficult thing there is — that is, to make one person completely happy.
Your happiness means my happiness, and

That was all.

29

THE SHADOW

It is impossible to make any appraisal of what went on during the period before Marilyn Monroe's death without considering the influence upon her of Dr Ralph Greenson, her psychoanalyst, who became so close to her he might have been mistaken for her shadow. Greenson was an extraordinary man by any standards and, some would have it, an exceptionally helpful influence on Marilyn. Others, however, saw a different man who was hurtful and even destructive.

Ralph Greenson was of Russian stock, born in the United States in Brooklyn in 1910. He was given the name Romeo Samuel Greenschpoon, and was one of four children. He qualified with a medical degree in 1935 after studying at Columbia University and Berne University, Switzerland. It was in that country he met and, in 1935, married, Hildegard Troesch. They settled in Los Angeles, Greenschpoon acquiring the name Ralph. The change from Greenschpoon to Greenson followed later. Shortly before war broke out in Europe, he studied Freudian psychology in Vienna, and became close to Sigmund Freud. During the Second World War he served in the US Military, and returned to Los Angeles after his discharge, where he began to practise in the developing discipline of psychoanalysis. He was appointed Clinical Professor of Psychiatry at the University of California.

In affluent Los Angeles during the forties and fifties it became fashionable to have one's own 'shrink'. In a field where problems might be real or might be imagined, the need was often equal, though the treatment might vary from highly beneficial therapy to dangerous tinkering. Not surprisingly, the views held of those who practised this new and contentious science were likely to vary according to the dispositions and points of view of those expressing them. To some Ralph Greenson was 'the backbone of psychoanalysis in the western United States'. To others he was a shallow pedlar of pop psychology.

During her years in New York, Marilyn had an analyst, Marianne Kris. It was when she returned to Los Angeles and was distressed while making the film *Let's Make Love* that Kris recommended Ralph Greenson to her. Greenson was quite willing to give immediate assistance to Marilyn, and though at first he was not prepared to accept her as an ongoing patient, Marilyn succeeded in persuading him. He considered her symptoms and decided against deep psychoanalysis. He had found her in a state of disorientation when he first attended her, slurring her words and appearing to be under sedation. Marilyn needed supportive therapy, he determined, and patiently listened to her complaints about those around her. One of her problems, she told him, was she didn't like her role in the film she was working on, though she had been keen enough when she accepted the part. He heard how she was plagued by chronic insomnia, and how she had collected a variety of drugs by visiting various doctors, which he found appalling, blaming the doctors involved.

He recommended Dr Hyman Engelberg to her, and insisted she stick to one doctor only. Greenson soon detected that Marilyn's marriage to Arthur Miller was beginning to disintegrate. She claimed Miller was cold and unresponsive and unkind to his father and children, of whom she was very fond. It appeared that the basic causes of their problems were sexual, and Marilyn thought she had become frigid. Miller was anxious about Marilyn but at his wit's end as to how he could help. Greenson's recommendation of unconditional love, no doubt, proved a tall order in the circumstances. To Greenson, Marilyn appeared as the orphan child, the fragile waif which, in terms of her inner self, well represented her delicately balanced state. Marilyn leaned on Greenson during the making of her next picture also, and it was while *The Misfits* was in production her marriage to Miller collapsed. To Marilyn the best thing about *The Misfits* was her leading man, Clark Gable. She was scathing about the script, which her husband wrote.

The relationship between Greenson and Marilyn began early in 1960, and he appeared to make a good deal of progress in the early months. It would not be long before he began to wean her off drugs. In the months which followed he achieved getting Marilyn to reduce her medication until, as she indicated in the tapes she made shortly before she died, she was strong enough to flush away all she had in her possession. But her 'shadow' gradually over-shadowed her. He may have accomplished a great deal in making Marilyn less reliant on drugs, but he engendered another dangerous dependency upon himself.

Ralph Greenson has been much criticised by those who have written about Marilyn for the manner in which he conducted her therapy. He saw her an increasing number of times, as often as daily and on some occasions several times a day. He treated her at her home and received her into his, a practice which was regarded as distinctly unethical. As her tapes reveal, she saw Greenson as a father figure and wanted to integrate herself into his family. She became anxious to please him, and it was suggested she even invented responses to therapy, though it is not certain whether this was to please him or merely to satisfy him.

Greenson was a popular lecturer both to his fellows in the profession and interested lay people. His devoted wife Hildi saw him as a charismatic speaker, though his attempts at humour alienated some who found this trivi-alised his subject matter. He was once described as a 'hard living man with passionate enthusiasm and even flamboyance, [to whom] psychoanaly-sis was ... a way of life'. A regular caller at Bungalow 21, Beverley Hills Hotel, where

Ralph Greenson.
A brilliant psychiatrist but not for Marilyn.
Photo Matthew Smith Collection.

Marilyn lived when he began treating her, Greenson was not only a frequent visitor to Marilyn's new house at Fifth Helena Drive, but he installed Mrs Murray as housekeeper, to report on what the star was doing when he was not there.

Greenson asserted more and more control over Marilyn, and she began to be more and more dependent on him. It was not long before he began to make inroads into her professional life. With his brother-in-law, Milton Rudin, Marilyn's newly appointed lawyer, he began to act as her manager, promising to Fox he could 'deliver' Marilyn to the set of Something's Got to Give when she was due, making guarantees about her performance and undertaking other negotiations on her behalf. This was an astoundingly unethical position for him to adopt, and he was meddling in something he did not understand. At the time of his negotiations with Fox, Greenson realised quite well how he must look to the studio executives. In notes that were made at one key meeting, someone present wrote, 'He did not want us to deem his relationship as a Svengali one, but in the next breath the psychiatrist admitted that . . . 'he, in fact, could persuade her to do anything he wanted.' I said that it appeared,' continued the writer of the notes, 'that he would have to be the one to determine . . . what scenes she would or wouldn't do, what rushes were favourable or unfavourable, and all the other creative decisions that had to be made . . . Dr Greenson seemed ready to assume responsibility in all creative areas.' Indeed, Dr Greenson actually offered to go into the editing room, if it was necessary.

When Marilyn was fired for attending President Kennedy's birthday celebrations at Madison Square Garden, she recognised Greenson was quite ineffective at what he was attempting. Conversely, he could hardly avoid noticing how highly skilled Marilyn was as a negotiator when she later put together a greatly enhanced deal to resume making the picture.

Marilyn had arranged to take time off for the birthday celebrations quite some time beforehand. The trouble arose because she had lost so much time due to ailments and, at the time she flew to New York, she was supposedly sick. And basic to all the superficial problems, the studio, facing bankruptcy, could not decide whether it would be financially better for it to finish the picture or to make this an excuse to abandon it. Having decided to continue, the dispute was soon settled, though not without insistence that Dr Greenson be dropped from his new role as 'negotiator' as part of the deal. Pat Newcomb was also to be dismissed from the set.

The other person who had to be dropped at this juncture was Paula Strasberg, Marilyn's acting coach, who imposed herself on all the proceedings on set. There were times when, at the end of a 'take', Marilyn would look for approval, not to the director, but to Paula. To add to the mayhem, at one point Newcomb, Strasberg and Greenson were not on speaking terms with one another. Between Ralph Greenson and Paula Strasberg in particular, the patience of the production team must have been in shreds. When both were dismissed from endlessly interfering in Marilyn's professional life it must have breathed new life into the production crew, let alone Marilyn herself. In the clean sweep Fox were also to replace George Cukor with Jean Negulesco, whom Marilyn liked. Marilyn's decision to carry the clean sweep further and reorganise her personal life did not go as far as severing relations with Ralph

Greenson. This may well have been the consequence of the dependency he had created.

Several weeks before Marilyn died, she was taken by Greenson to see Dr Michael Gurdin, a well-known and highly discreet plastic surgeon, at his Beverley Hills clinic. The date of the visit is reported variously as 7 June or 14 June. Marilyn, wrapped up in a scarf, was disguised with dark suit, black wig and dark glasses. When she unwrapped, Gurdin found her to have a bruise on her cheek and a black and blue nose. Her eyelids, also, were black and blue, and Greenson explained she had had an accident using the shower, and had fallen on the tiles.

Gurdin did not take x-rays as he was asked not to, but after careful examination was able to give the assurance that nothing was broken. He noted that Marilyn appeared to be under the influence of drugs, and that she said virtually nothing, leaving all the talking to her analyst. Marilyn and Greenson left as furtively as they had entered. Curiously, there were no tiles around Marilyn's bath and she seldom used the shower. A fall might well have accounted for Marilyn's injuries, though they were also consistent with her receiving a beating. But who would do such a thing? The mystery of this event remained so, and no further explanation ever came to light.

There would seem to be no doubt that Ralph Greenson was swept along in the conspiracy to cover up the truth when Marilyn died. It was he who told the police she had committed suicide, and indicated empty medicine bottles as evidence of how she had killed herself. He acted as spokesman during questioning, and readily conformed to what appeared to be an agreed story of the events of that night and early morning. But within days he had thought better of his participation and recanted his opinion that she had killed herself. But by waiting that few days, when his change of mind was lost in the media tumult of the suicide story, those who conspired to cover up the truth and inflict the ignominy of suicide on Marilyn were well on their way to success. Nevertheless, it must have taken courage for him to pull out of the conspiracy. He was clearly declaring his opposition to it, but by then nobody was listening.

Greenson was undoubtedly a talented and able man, whose brilliance as a psychoanalyst earned him international respect. There is no doubt his dealings with Marilyn Monroe were always honest and well intentioned. Greatly criticised for his unprofessional approach in his treatment of Marilyn, particularly allowing himself to become emotionally involved with her, this was not something he stumbled into. He considered well and deep how he should treat this fragile patient and decided on the path he took as the best way he knew to help her. Undoubtedly ill advised in certain of his decisions — particularly in respect of her professional life — it was a catastrophic mistake to make Marilyn so dependent on him. He also jeopardised his integrity in getting himself involved in the conspiracy to conceal the truth after her death. Though there have been murmurs that he fell in love with his patient and had ulterior motives for some of his actions, there is absolutely no evidence of this. There is nothing to contradict that he was honest and upright in all that he did in his relationship with Marilyn. He suffered, personally and professionally, after Marilyn died, and he did not deserve that.

30

MONTAGE

It is not uncommon for writers to draw the conclusion that Marilyn was two different people. She was Norma Jean — or Norma Jeane as she came to style herself — for a large part of the time. For the rest of the time she became this different person, Marilyn Monroe, specially created for the movie world and her countless admirers. Except she was not by any means just two people; that would be to ignore the variations she could make on her selves. Marilyn certainly was not the great movie icon each and all of her days. It took a great effort and much time for the 'girl next door' to become the sophisticated screen idol.

In 1953 Marilyn was scheduled to make *River of No Return* with Robert Mitchum. She felt low before she left Los Angeles to make her way to a deep-country area in Canada where the movie was to be shot, as reporter Jim Bacon could well testify. He interviewed her, and wrote, 'Her hair was in tangles. She had cold cream all over her face and her eyebrows were smeared . . . on the outside she was Dracula's daughter. I couldn't get out of there fast enough.' Marilyn was hiding behind a mask of which Norma Jean would have been horrified. Allan 'Whitey' Snyder, her

Robert Mitchum recalled the saga of Marilyn's accident in River of No Return.
Photo Matthew Smith Collection.

make-up man, certainly was, too. 'Get that rubbish off your face,' he said. 'You scare people.' But the grease had been symptomatic of her depression and Marilyn tended to become who she felt she was at the time.

River of No Return was not without problems

for Marilyn. She had director trouble in the shape of the overbearing Otto Preminger, although there was good company to make up for it having Robert Mitchum working with her and Shelley Winters visiting from the set of another movie being made not far away. They were two very old friends. Mitchum had known her since he worked at Lockheed with her first husband, Jim Dougherty, when she really was Norma Jean, and in less affluent days before she reached the heights of stardom she had shared digs with Shelley Winters. Having friends there didn't prevent her from getting into trouble, however. Bob Mitchum told me he had just come out of the river and told her, 'Those rocks are slippery in there. Be careful or you'll break a leg.' He continued, 'She paid no heed, ran into the water and, sure enough, broke a leg.' While newspaper headlines ran MISS MONROE INJURES LEG IN CANADA, Shelley Winters later told how she was unconvinced of the severity of her injury. The team of doctors who flew in from Los Angeles, after having the leg x-rayed, declared it was not broken. 'Perhaps a sprain,' they suggested, and Shelley chuckled to herself. Marilyn enjoyed the fuss made of her and capitalised on her 'martyrdom', and Shelley drew the conclusion Marilyn had found a way to bring director Preminger to heel.

Actress Terry Moore, who knew Marilyn well, told of how she could change her whole appearance simply by taking off her make-up and applying a little Vaseline. In this Marilyn was reverting to Norma Jean. She was still very beautiful, but in a sweet way. She went unrecognised in the streets. It brought anonymity and freedom when she was out walking and wanted privacy, but it also had disadvantages. Once, when her car did not arrive at her home in Beverley Hills to take her to the studio, she walked most of the way from her home because people did not recognise her with her Vaselined face, and, therefore did not offer a ride. Her preoccupation with Vaseline stemmed from a belief that it would keep her skin young.

Terry Moore also spoke of the reverse procedure; the incredible transformation into Marilyn Monroe when her make-up was applied. No one was more conscious of this than Whitey Snyder. Applying the oils and powders specially blended for her by Max Factor and specially modified and developed by Whitey himself, he watched her emerge as this vibrant, shining star. But this was not easily achieved; it took time, usually as long as two hours, though nowhere near the record nine hours one occasion demanded. But when it was finished she was the unique, radiant, impeccable Marilyn Monroe to her fingertips.

Whitey's devotion to Marilyn was well known. He knew her weaknesses, her strengths and her needs at any time. He had frequently been known to make her up before she got out of bed on those mornings she could not be roused and was so shattered. Probably no movie took more out of her than *The Misfits*, and Whitey, who had long before this time added mentor and personal assistant — with special responsibility for getting her on the set each day and in front of the cameras — to his job specification, knew where to begin and how.

There were many ways to view what became thought of as Marilyn's overdose sagas. On one hand it appeared she was highly knowledgeable about which drugs she could mix and how far she could go. On the other, some of her problems could be explained by her being taken by surprise by dangerous cocktails of prescription and recreational drugs. Her friendship with Charlie Chaplin Jr and Edward G Robinson Jr, both of whom were hardened drug addicts, appears to have accounted for her introduction to the kind of drugs her doctor would not be prescribing, and added a new and dangerous dimension to her concoctions. Both Chaplin and Robinson were suicidal, and while they both tried to help Marilyn, perhaps surprisingly, it was Marilyn who was the strong influence, and it was she who gave support to the other two and held them together. The sad culture of drug abuse that would be emulated across the world, however, had its deepest roots in Hollywood. At the height of Marilyn's career, drug abuse in Tinseltown was said to be rife.

Dress designer Billy Travilla was a man who had worked frequently with Marilyn and had vivid memories of her. Quoted by Anthony Summers[1], he said, 'I've dressed many women in

---

[1] Anthony Summers, *Goddess, The Secret Lives of Marilyn Monroe*, Victor Gollancz, London 1985

*Billy Travilla designs for Marilyn as 'Lorelei'. He
was deeply hurt when Marilyn cut him dead.
Photo Robert F Slatzer Collection.*

my life, but never one like this lady. She was for
me a dual personality. She was not well
educated, but an extremely bright woman, and
she had the whims of a child . . . She'd come in
the office, as people would, to complain about
something; but Marilyn would always have a

little tear, a real tear, in one eye, and her lips would tremble. Those lips! And a man can't fight it. You don't want that baby to cry.' Billy Travilla had an unhappy experience on one occasion he bumped into Marilyn, when the problem was not drugs but drink. It took place on the night before Marilyn died, when the dress designer saw her in a restaurant — on Sunset Boulevard, he recalls — with Pat Newcomb and Peter Lawford. This must have been after Robert Kennedy, who had been with Marilyn at La Scala, had left. Travilla greeted her but she cut him dead. Through eyes which spoke of too much to drink, she looked at him blankly and he persevered and spoke to her again. It made no difference; she embarrassed him by demanding, 'Who are you?' Billy Travilla, extremely hurt, just walked away.

The change from Norma Jean to Marilyn, which usually happened daily, might have been painful from certain points of view, but it was not to be regarded as unpleasant, by any means. Neither was the reverse procedure, unless there was some dread influence that might introduce a 'Jekyll and Hyde' element. Such was the case when she was recuperating after her gall bladder operation. Suffering a great deal of pain, she worried the operation would leave a scar, and became very depressed. It was at times like this when she particularly suffered from not having family looking in, helping her out and talking about things. For a while she was said to have become an unpleasant character, foul mouthed and unkempt. The very idea of it is so uncharacteristic as to be mind-boggling.

To be realistic, not all that was said and written about Marilyn was complimentary. James Spada[1], in his biography of Peter Lawford, *The Man Who Kept the Secrets*, draws attention to stories reported in which, ' . . . she could be charming, giving, and thoughtful one minute, vicious and hurtful the next.' She had no compunction about demanding an extra be fired from a film merely because she had platinum blonde hair like her own — Marilyn would brook no competition. Stories, however, abound of her kindness and compassion, from those telling of her deep feelings for crippled children — and her generosity in this direction — to numerous examples of her love of animals. No doubt all this revealed what we already really knew: Marilyn was human like us all.

Marilyn's friend Jeanne Carmen also knew that, where Marilyn was concerned, what showed did not always represent what was inside. 'When she went inside her house she became Norma Jean. She was just a nice person, but oh, so insecure. From the doorway back inside, a lot of the happiness folded. So when she was Norma Jean, she was insecure, but when she was Marilyn Monroe the world was hers,' she said, 'but getting her to step over the threshold was something else. She was scared. She would go back to check her make-up. 'Do I look OK?' she would ask. You know, she was just beautiful.'

---

[1] James Spada, *The Man Who Kept the Secrets*, Bantam, New York, 1991

But by the time Marilyn made *Gentlemen Prefer Blondes* — released in 1953 — with Jane Russell, her insecurity problems were at their height. Marilyn was simply terrified of the cameras. Jane conspired with Whitey Snyder to 'drop in' to her dressing room in the mornings, where she wasted considerable time, to accompany her to the set.

Jeanne Carmen told me she thought part of her general insecurity problem related to her lack of education. 'She was afraid of being criticised for not knowing things,' she said, 'and another thing was that a girl needs a dad to tell her she's wonderful, and Marilyn didn't have that.' Jeanne told how Marilyn, when she became Norma Jean, was a fun person, just an ordinary, nice person, and this was meant as a high compliment. But when she made the change to Marilyn Monroe she glowed. 'When she waved at people through her car window, she was a queen,' said Jeanne.

Anthony Summers recounts in *Goddess, The Secret Lives of Marilyn Monroe* the impression Marilyn made in her early days on German actress Hildegard Knef, when they met in a studio dressing room. 'This sleepy-looking girl, with the transparent plastic shower cap over her white-blonde hair and a thick layer of cream on her pale face, sits down beside me. She digs around in a . . . bag and takes out a sandwich, a pillbox, a book . . . 'Hi, my name's Marilyn Monroe, what's yours?' Knef saw 'a child with short legs and a fat bottom . . . ' But then, 'An hour and a half later only the eyes are still recognisable. She seems to have grown with the make-up, the legs seem longer, the body more willowy, the face glows as if lit by candles . . . '

In her 1951 movie *Clash by Night*, Marilyn achieved co-star billing with Barbara Stanwyck, Robert Ryan and Paul Douglas. Something of an afterthought for the part she played, she managed to upstage the other members of the cast, some of whom were distinctly piqued. After seeing the film the *New York Times* critic declared she could not act, but one of her co-stars knew otherwise. Barbara Stanwyck said, 'This girl is going to go a long, long way and become a big star.'

England's *Manchester Guardian* reporter, W J Weatherby, was favoured by Marilyn to the extent he was granted a whole series of interviews and became, as time went on, her friend and confidante. In her he identified ' . . . chameleon moods that could make her body convey anything she wished . . . How foolish those people were who underrated her as a dumb blonde! What I didn't yet know and couldn't guess was how much was natural — or as natural as a human being can be — and how much was a calculated performance.' Weatherby was an astute man and an able writer. He really got to know a great deal about Marilyn, and in doing so was insightful enough to realise how much he didn't know about her, and would never know about her. But there was a chemistry between them that sparked and rubbed off. He quoted from Virginia Woolf, ' . . . that we all may have a thousand selves. Whichever way she died, there were always murderers in her life, trying to kill off 999 of her selves and leave her as a dumb blonde. They do the same today with her memory.'

31

In Search of a Family

We have already introduced some of the feature players in Marilyn's life in earlier chapters: husbands Joe DiMaggio and Arthur Miller, Dr Ralph Greenson, Eunice Murray, Peter Lawford and his wife, Pat Kennedy Lawford, Frank Sinatra and, of course, President John F Kennedy and his brother, Attorney General Robert Kennedy. There were others mentioned briefly who, nonetheless, played an important part in Marilyn's life and, in particular, those last days of her life. In many cases they became like family to her, and a family was her greatest need.

Agnes M Flanagan was one of the people Marilyn liked to have around. A long-time friend, the Fox hairdresser had taken on the washing and styling of Marilyn's hair and was never far from her when she was on the set. Agnes had done her hair for the important meeting she had with Fox executives on 12 July when it was decided they would resume the making of *Something's Got to Give* and reinstate Marilyn with a huge salary hike. It was merely her usual feat to perform this expected magic for the star. Marilyn was attached to Agnes and to her stylist's two children. She sent a gift of a garden swing for them after she heard Agnes admiring one just like it. Agnes told how she had to take care when looking at clothes for the children when Marilyn was there. They were likely to turn up the next day. Marilyn used the services of other hairdressers, too. The distinguished Sidney Guilaroff, whose other clients included Greta Garbo, designed and styled for her, and in particular for those special occasions, such as the 25 July one-to-one meeting with studio boss Peter Levathes, which would decide the next direction for her future. She also enjoyed the services of colourist Pearl Porterfield, who had originated Jean Harlow's 'hot platinum', and Mae West's superb white, and who would introduce the breathtaking shade of pale which would be known as 'pillow slip white' for Marilyn. And it had been Robert Kennedy who had introduced hairdresser Mickey Song, whose famous clients included Raquel Welch. But Agnes Flanagan was much more than a hairstylist to Marilyn; she was a friend.

Another of Marilyn's special friends, make-up man Allan (Whitey) Snyder, had said the exact same thing as Agnes Flanagan. He told that he had to be careful not to say how much he liked, say, a shirt or else it would be delivered to him. Whitey was Marilyn's make-up man from the beginning of her film career until it ended. But he had been much, much more than just a make-up man to her. When she was filming *Niagara*, and suffering all the fears that tormented her before she faced the camera, Whitey was asked by the director to comfort her and help sort her out. He did, and from then on

*Allan 'Whitey' Snyder looked after
Marilyn's best interests.
Photo Robert F. Slatzer Collection.*

it became just as much a part of his job as
making her up. Whitey married another good
friend of Marilyn's, Marjorie Plecher, who was a
wardrobe mistress.

Whitey knew Marilyn very well and was
anxious for her. He noted the effect of the people
around her and was not always complimentary
in what he said about them. He got on well with
Joe DiMaggio though, and had encouraged
Marilyn to marry him, but he did not like Dr
Greenson, and made no bones about it. He did
not think he was good for her, and he was very
critical that he took so much money from
Marilyn. Greenson did not like Whitey, it should

also be said, but then Greenson did not like Ralph Roberts, Paula Strasberg or Pat Newcomb, either, and tried to persuade Marilyn to get rid of them. But of all those around her, Whitey Snyder was in the least danger of being dropped. In fact on the Thursday before Marilyn died, when she had secured her massively attractive deal with Fox, it was Whitey and Marge she invited round to celebrate with her. When they arrived it was champagne and nibbles and the news that Jean Negulesco would replace George Cukor and his entourage and, no doubt to her great delight, Negulesco — unbelievably — had negotiated a return to the original Nunnally Johnson script. The revised arrangements, in the long run, turned out to suit George Cukor very well, also. His commitment to Fox completed, he went on to Warner Brothers, where he finally got to make *My Fair Lady*, and won an Oscar for his direction into the bargain.

Whitey worked a great deal for Marilyn, not just on the set of her movies, but in preparing her for important social engagements. Interestingly, one of these was on 26 June, when he made her up for a party she was attending at the Lawford's in honour of Robert Kennedy. But things moved fast and changed dramatically in the weeks that followed that party, the last few weeks of her life.

Marilyn's first drama coach was Natasha Lytess, who was probably German by birth, and who, with her husband had fled Germany at the rise of Nazism, before the Second World War. Columbia gave her the task of coaching, among

332

others, a young Marilyn, and this developed into a six-year-long association in which the two grew together in a crisis-torn relationship from which both, apparently, benefited. Natasha was a tall, thin, woman with cropped brown hair. She was a daunting, aristocratic figure who, in spite of her abrasive manner attracted respect from Marilyn, and bestowed on her the cultural and intellectual stimulation she sought. Natasha admitted, much later, that she needed Marilyn more than Marilyn needed her. Not unsurprisingly, Natasha became a mother figure to Marilyn, as did so many others, and the star was happy to become Natasha's 'daughter', as well as protégée. It was quite a shock when Marilyn decided to end the relationship, and the break was sudden and clean cut. Marilyn had found 'the method' and Lee and Paula Strasberg.

For perhaps too long, Marilyn leaned on her drama coaches, Lee Strasberg and his wife, Paula. They were exponents of the 'method' school of acting, and while there were many who criticised them and their handling of Marilyn, there is no doubt she prospered as an actress while they taught her, and she appeared to be on the threshold of blossoming into a fine serious actress when she died. Strasberg had coached James Dean, Marlon Brando, Steve McQueen, Paul Newman and Eli Wallach among others. His credentials were impeccable.

It was the Strasbergs' domination of Marilyn that made her friends hostile toward them. Paula became a huge problem, by interfering on the set while production was in progress. She was in charge, and what the black-garbed coach said went, though in the end the situation got out of hand and her activities became too much for the studio to bear. By this time it seems that Marilyn had developed serious doubts herself over the so-called benefits of having Paula *in situ*. When the studio insisted she go, Marilyn went tamely along with their wishes. And she did not stop with having Paula barred from the set, either. She dismissed her from her life altogether.

With Lee it was different. Though he was capable of coldness and tyranny — and criticised for it, too — Marilyn still felt a need for him. The 'method' guru told her she needed psychotherapy really to find in herself what she needed for the Stanislavsky Method, to give it its full name. Otherwise known as the 'total immersion system', it required actors to explore their scenes and themselves intensely and draw on their own experiences. Self analysis was obligatory, psychoanalysis desirable.

At one time Lee became a father figure to Marilyn and she had become a part of his family. This same situation would occur again later with Dr Greenson, when Marilyn attempted to attach herself to him as a father figure, his wife, Hildi as 'mother' and their two children as her siblings. Lee Strasberg influenced her greatly, she had confidence in him, and she wanted to make progress. She talked about being rushed from one picture to another without a chance to learn. She felt the studio simply wanted her to give the same performance each time and she wanted to develop, to give more. She was aware that Paula was the driving force in the Strasberg family. She ran Lee, and this went on after their marriage, as such, had ended.

Financially, the Strasbergs did well out of Marilyn. Apart from fees for services rendered, Paula, when she was stoking up resentment by interfering on the sets of Marilyn's pictures, also received fees from the studio she was antagonising. When Marilyn died, Lee Strasberg became her principal beneficiary. She bequeathed to him money and her personal effects, which she asked him to give to her 'friends, colleagues and those to whom I am devoted'. And, of course, the film rights which went on earning money. Strasberg married again after Paula died, and his second wife, Anna Mizrahi and subsequently her family, inherited the rights to what became a multi-million dollar 'Marilyn' business. Interestingly, the appointment the star had with her lawyer Mickey Rudin, for the day after she died, might have changed everything. She wanted to revise her will, and it was thought by some of those close to her that she had in mind a revision of the Strasberg legacies. Since the rift with Paula happened just shortly before she died, it does not seem too speculative.

Press secretary Pat Newcomb, the daughter of a judge, studied psychology at university and ranked as one of Marilyn's best friends and closest confidantes. Though pay-rolled by top press agency, the Arthur P Jacobs Company, she was specifically attached to Marilyn. This was a friendship that had taken time to grow. When Arthur Jacobs first sent her to Marilyn — when she was working on *Bus Stop* — she had not lasted long. They did not get on together and Jacobs wisely separated them. The hostility on Marilyn's part appeared to stem from her believing Pat was becoming sweet on a man in which she, herself, was interested. It was not true, but the atmosphere had been created. It was a further four years until a renewed acquaintanceship developed into a firm and lasting friendship.

The night she died, Robert Kennedy had tried to get Marilyn to go over for dinner to Peter and Pat Lawford's house. She refused, but Pat Newcomb went. One of the other guests, George Durgom, spoke of her arrival and telling them, 'Marilyn's not coming. She's not feeling well.' That was at 9.30 p.m.

Pat Newcomb's role in the events of the last few hours of Marilyn's life and what happened afterwards has never been understood. She will not discuss it. One thing is certain, however: she was a strong supporter of Robert Kennedy and even campaigned for him. After Robert Kennedy was murdered, Pat Newcomb remained firm friends with his wife, Ethel. She stonewalled those investigating Marilyn's death and even to this day there is no statement of any consequence from her on record. What she has said is peripheral. Of course it is not impossible that Deputy District Attorney Manley Bowler's investigator, John Dickie, finally got her to talk to him, but if so — and I greatly doubt it — her statement, with the greater part of a voluminous report, has vanished. And Ms Newcomb does not assist researchers.

Pat Newcomb's movements after she was dismissed by Arthur Jacobs was, to many people, somewhat mystifying. It came as a surprise that she took off immediately to spend time as the guest of the Kennedy family at Hyannis Port, and then left soon after that for an extended six month vacation in Europe. Conspiracy theorists were not slow to note that she was then, of course, far away from those who would have persevered in questioning her, and remained far away when she returned to the United States, taking up government work in Washington. Her first appointment was that of information specialist for the Information Agency. She was to promote international co-operation and American prestige abroad through motion pictures. It was said that at one point during the time she worked in Washington, the office she occupied was not far from that of Robert Kennedy.

From the references made in books about Marilyn, it would be easy to reach the conclusion that her relationship with publicist Arthur Jacobs was purely one of publicity and the cold business of promotion. This was far from the truth. Arthur Jacobs and his wife, Natalie, were good friends to Marilyn on a personal level. They were in her confidence and knew about her affairs with Jack Kennedy and Robert Kennedy. They had been known to sit with Marilyn for hours — right through the night — just talking to her and persuading her to go easy on drink and pills. Marilyn would say to Natalie, 'I love Arthur. He'll take care of me. He'll always be here when

I need him.' It was not Arthur's fault he had not rescued her at her time of need. He dropped everything to race to her side as soon as he heard she was in trouble, but he could not undo the terrible things which had been done to her before his arrival. Arthur Jacobs became a producer, his best-known film being *Planet of the Apes*. He was another who succeeded in avoiding being questioned by the police about the role he played on the night of Marilyn's death.

Arthur Jacobs 'was the architect of the cover up', Rupert Allan, one of his staff, later told. Rupert Allan knew Marilyn well; they had had a solid friendship for many years. Although born in St Louis, he was educated at Oxford University and became the quintessential Englishman. He had been an editor for *Look*, and had met Marilyn while writing for that magazine. When he joined Arthur Jacobs' staff, he was appointed as Marilyn's personal press aide, a post he held until he began to spend a great deal of time in Monaco in connection with another of Jacobs' clients, Grace Kelly, when she became Princess Grace. Princess Grace asked him to become Monaco's Consul General, and he accepted. It was at that time Pat Newcomb stepped in as Marilyn's press aide.

Arthur James had also known Marilyn for a long time and she had tried to reach him by phone not long before she died. Arthur James, with Charlie Chaplin Jr and Edward G Robinson Jr, had made up a threesome Marilyn had met in the days of her early career, and her friendship with Arthur was the one that survived to become close. He went into the real-estate business and by the mid-fifties had become very successful. Arthur was the one she could ring at any hour of the night, and he would dash off to help her out regardless of the time or inconvenience.

Arthur told a story of how he was approached by someone who was probably speaking for Hoffa or some other mafioso, with the request he used his influence to get Marilyn to visit him for a few days while they bugged her new house. James knew about Marilyn's relationship with Robert Kennedy and guessed he would be the target of the bugging. That was in March, 1962. He refused, saying later he did not tell Marilyn because he thought she had enough to worry about. He knew his refusal would not stop them getting in with their taps and bugs, and he was, of course, right. There were workman coming and going to her house while she had it altered and that would be opportunity enough. Ironically, as time went by, Marilyn felt so insecure she began calling Arthur from phone booths, as she did Robert Slatzer, to protect her privacy.

Marilyn spent a weekend at Arthur James' Laguna Beach house only a few weeks before she died. Charlie Chaplin Jr and Edward G Robinson Jr were also there. It was Arthur's understanding that Marilyn had, long before, been introduced to drugs by Edward G Robinson Jr. It was well known Robinson had drug problems, but whether his was the influence that led to her addiction and had such an effect on her young life is not at all sure.

Another friend said she believed Marilyn was into drugs from as young as 17 or 18. Arthur James is the only person who Marilyn told about her pregnancy personally. He had misgivings and wondered if she had been fantasising. If she lost a baby, James believes she must have miscarried, though others thought she had had an abortion.

When Marilyn tried to telephone Arthur James on the Wednesday before she died he was not at home. Given a message, he later called her back but hung up when another woman's voice answered. She had also tried to reach Robert Mitchum shortly before her death and did not get through to him, either. He told me Pat Newcomb told him after Marilyn's death she really did want to speak to him, and afterwards he always felt guilty that he had not tried to return the call.

Poet Norman Rosten and his wife Hedda were good friends of Marilyn's. Rosten had studied at Michigan University with Arthur Miller and it was he who introduced Miller to Marilyn. Based in Brooklyn, he saw Marilyn on many occasions, including at New York champagne parties, and recalled how he had watched her in a reverie while staring out of a window at one of these affairs. 'Come back,' he had said, to which Marilyn, whose insomnia was making her feel very low, replied, 'Who'd know the difference if I went down there?' Rosten looked at her. 'I would,' he responded.

If we all have weaknesses, Hedda's was reputedly drink, and that was not the best thing for Marilyn, who went out with her on occasions. Nevertheless the Rostens were solid-gold assets to Marilyn. Norman inspired her to try her hand at poetry, which she found she enjoyed. She was herself with them, and they became part of her.

Norman and Hedda were the kind of people Marilyn was glad to have around when she desperately needed true friends, intimates she trusted with her deepest secrets. With the Rostens Marilyn tended to be herself rather than the creation of the publicity machine. The poet brought comfort and warm friendship to her, and this was a three-way deal because Rosten's wife Hedda was a full partner in the relationship. With this man and his wife she was the private Marilyn. But that did not relieve her of her problems and weaknesses, nor did it in any way release the Rostens from the responsibility that came with knowing and loving Marilyn. Rosten remembered the occasion when he and his wife had been called to the star's apartment at three o'clock in the morning to find that she had overdosed and had come perilously close to losing her life. And that was not the first time. He also recalled visiting Marilyn when she was ill and had later declared, 'She was ill, not only of the body and mind, but of the soul, the innermost engine of desire. That light was missing from her eyes.' But Marilyn bounced back, time after time, a true survivor.

She sometimes stayed at the Rosten's beach house and, during the time she was married to Arthur Miller — when they spent those times Miller loved out in the country — left the keys to her Manhattan apartment with an invitation for Norman to use the place. Marilyn spoke to Norman Rosten on the telephone shortly before she died. Hedda became Marilyn's New York secretary, looking after her mail and other matters which arose in the East. She went with her to England for the making of *The Prince and the Showgirl*, and in London became Marilyn's personal secretary.

As with Ralph Greenson, Marilyn had first claim on the time of Ralph Roberts, her masseur. The tall, handsome Roberts — 'Rafe' she called him, the English pronunciation — who had been an actor and had appeared on Broadway, met Marilyn in the mid-fifties at the home of Lee Strasberg. When he decided to give up acting in favour of developing his skills as a masseur, Marilyn snapped up his services, and used them till the day she died. He became a firm friend and confidante, the kind of rock-like person Marilyn needed to have around her.

This well-read gentle giant was much more than a masseur to the star. He acted as chauffeur when required, driving her to Greenson's for therapy, though he took a dim view of the psychiatrist. He was to comment — along with Whitey Snyder, Pat Newcomb and publicist Rupert Allan — that the more Marilyn got into psychotherapy the more miserable she became. As with Whitey Snyder, Greenson did not like Ralph Roberts either. At one point he delivered the ultimatum that she had to give up Roberts and Strasberg else he would stop his analysis work. For a while Marilyn appeared to comply, though Roberts came to give Marilyn her massages late in the evening when Mrs Murray had gone and could not report his presence to Greenson. This episode provides an illuminating insight into the power Greenson held over Marilyn. Ralph Roberts was one of those who believed Marilyn was on a countdown to getting rid of Greenson, though her secret tapes do not support this. It is fair to say, however, that if she was coming round to that way of thinking she would not be likely to jump the gun by showing her hand before she was quite ready.

When Marilyn bought her new house at Fifth Helena Drive, Roberts helped her to move in. One thing he was particular to do for her was to black out her bedroom. He knew she could not bear any light at all in her bedroom, and because it would take time to choose material for her drapes, more time to have them made up and — as the decoration work was carried out to her satisfaction — even more time to have them fitted, he installed temporary black curtaining brought from her apartment. This is an important point, as it throws much doubt on the story Mrs Murray told of pushing curtains back with a poker from outside the window to reveal the body of Marilyn. The black material was not conventionally hung, and it would have been difficult to part it or open it from outside.

Ralph Roberts was in close touch with Marilyn until the day she died. During the Saturday morning they spoke and talked about an evening meal together — a barbecue — the arrangements for which Greenson promptly

Marilyn with her long-time friend, Robert Slatzer,
who wrote the introduction to this book.
Photo Robert F Slatzer Collection.

scotched when Roberts telephoned to confirm.
Roberts rang at the time Greenson was at
Marilyn's house and, without reference to her,
the psychiatrist simply told him she was not
there. Roberts was no doubt mystified, and so,
apparently, was Marilyn, who tried to contact
her masseur during the evening, only to find he
had made revised arrangements with other
friends.

Robert F Slatzer knew Marilyn from the
forties. He ranked as one of her oldest friends.
From the days when he was a reporter in Ohio,
he spoke to Marilyn on the telephone and made
trips to see her, until he made one too many and

344

was fired from his job. He found work writing in Hollywood and became involved in production work. Marilyn confided in him and though they did not live 'in each other's pockets', he kept in touch with her and she with him until she died. I recount elsewhere the saga of their 'quickie' marriage over the border into Mexico, and the equally quickie unpicking of it by the Fox studio. Featured in other pages also are references to the knowledge he revealed about the red diary Marilyn had shown him. She told Bob Slatzer why she was keeping this diary and a little of what was in it. It disappeared at the time of her death.

Bob Slatzer is entirely convinced Marilyn was murdered. As we noted elsewhere, towards the end of her life she began to telephone him from phone booths, a probable indication that she suspected her phones were tapped and the world was closing in on her. She told him about her relationships with the Kennedy brothers and how she believed Bobby would divorce his wife, Ethel, and marry her, but she received no encouragement from her old friend regarding this particular marital ambition.

Bob knew full well about her previous supposed 'attempts' to take her own life, but he also knew that at those times she always had people around her who would be there to 'save' her. He understood the 'cry for help' syndrome used by the psychiatrists to explain these actions, but he also knew this did not relate to the events of that fatal Saturday night. Robert Slatzer knew she would not have killed herself, neither intentionally nor by accident. Bob was one of those people she could always count on. He was always around for her, and it should be noted he was one of the few friends she had who was not employed by her.

There were others who were important to Marilyn but who did not feature to any extent in the events of the days leading up to her death. There was May Reis, who had worked for Arthur Miller and was engaged by Marilyn to do secretarial work. May was the kind of devoted person who had supported and cared for her ailing mother, grandmother, and brother, too. An able and astute lady, she became no less devoted to Marilyn, working for her in New York. When Marilyn moved to Los Angeles May moved out there also. In her fifties, she worked for Marilyn until it simply became too much for her. Inez Melson became Marilyn's business manager and Marilyn also gave her the responsibility for acting as guardian to her mother, Gladys, liaising with the authorities at Rockhaven Sanitarium, where her mother was a resident, and seeing to the regular payments for her upkeep.

There were others around her apart from secretaries of one kind or another. Her long-time stand-in, Evelyn Moriarty; Lena Pepitone, her New York maid; and Hazel Washington, her studio maid, all played their respective roles. Hollywood journalist — turned film producer — Sidney Skolsky was counted a good, personal friend, and it would be a daunting task to list the numerous actors, actresses and production staff she befriended.

Among Marilyn's friends, there is a curious repetitive pattern that is both interesting and worthy of note. She made a pact with Norman Rosten that if ever either of them felt themselves drifting towards suicide the other would be contacted so that whichever was affected could be talked out of it. Marilyn agreed the same pact with her drama coach, Lee Strasberg and with publicist Rupert Allan, too. With Allan she agreed a code word for any message related to ideas of suicide. It was 'Truckee River'. Having said all this, her so-called suicide 'attempts' were dubious. As we have already noted, she was a person with real and deep needs. Psychiatrists are well aware of those supposed attempted suicides which involve people who have no intention of letting go on life, but who are frantically trying to find a way to express a desperate need.

Of all Marilyn's friends, it is remarkable how few were not on her payroll. Those around her whom she came to rely upon and trust became more than hired help. They were drawn into a personal relationship with her. She bestowed a gift of friendship upon them that was seldom withdrawn. Marilyn had many acquaintances, but outside her relatively small circle of daily contacts, she had not many real friends and saw little of her relatives. In many respects she was a lonely person.

32

THE PATIENT

One of the worst experiences of Marilyn's life — if not the very worst — overtook her when she was admitted to the New York Hospital-Cornell Medical Center early in 1961. Her New York psychiatrist, Dr Marianne Kris, pressed Marilyn to go there to receive the treatment she needed to countermand her depression and increasing dependence on sleeping pills, and Marilyn agreed. To her horror, however, she was not admitted to the private room she had expected. Dr Kris had booked her into that part of the hospital known as the Payne-Whitney Psychiatric Clinic.

Given a room on a floor designated for 'moderately disturbed' patients, she realised she had been admitted to an insane asylum, her worst nightmare. She also, eventually, discovered that once there she could not leave of her own volition. Dr Kris had to authorise a discharge. Her clothes were removed. She was locked in her cell-like room, the bathroom of which had no door, and was later, by all accounts, moved to a padded cell on a floor designated for seriously disturbed patients. This, no doubt, was because she responded to her situation in a completely normal way. She wept, screamed to be released and banged her fists on the reinforced door. At one point, in an account she later gave, it appeared she was put into a straightjacket. She was in a state of absolute shock, not helped at all by members of staff who were totally impervious to patients' protestations. In a letter she later wrote, 'I felt I was in . . . prison for a crime I hadn't committed.'

It was a nurse's aide who finally brought her paper on which she could write a letter of sorts and, when it was written, made sure that it reached Lee and Paula Strasberg. The letter ran,

Dear Lee and Paula,
Dr Kris has had me put into the New York Hospital psychiatric division under the care of two idiot doctors. They both should not be my doctors. I'm locked up with all these poor nutty people. I'm sure to end up a nut if I stay in this nightmare. Please help me. This is the last place I should be. Maybe if you called Dr Kris and assured her of my sensitivity . . . Lee, I try to remember what you said once in class 'that art goes far beyond science . . . ' and the science memories around here I'd like to forget — like screaming women . . . Please help me, and if Dr Kris assures you I am all right you can assure her I am not. I do not belong here.
I love you both
Marilyn

In a postscript she apologises for spelling errors she made in her note and explains the reasons for her apparently crude writing by telling them there is nothing to write on where she is. ' . . . They lied to me about calling my doctor and Joe, and they had my bathroom door locked so I broke the glass [to use the bathroom] and outside of that I haven't done anything that is uncooperative.'

But the Strasbergs were no help in her hour of need. Whatever they might have tried to do they achieved nothing. Marilyn continued trying — under phone call rationing restrictions — to reach various people who could have helped her, but they were not at home; her calls went unanswered. It was Joe DiMaggio, all those miles away in Florida where he was coaching, with whom she finally made contact, and who caught a plane immediately to rescue her. When he reached New York he demanded Marilyn be released into his custody and was told Marianne Kris would have to approve. Joe rang Kris and told her that if she did not agree he would 'take the hospital apart brick by brick.'

Marilyn was discharged. Badly affected and wanting to avoid publicity, she sneaked out of a basement door with Ralph Roberts and at first went to her apartment. Marianne Kris accompanied them, but this appeared not to be from Marilyn's choice; Kris was there purely to formalise the discharge, it seems. The psychiatrist was reported as saying, 'I did a terrible thing, a terrible, terrible thing.' Marilyn saw her long enough to give her a generous piece of her mind and never saw her again. Henceforth she would become a patient of Ralph Greenson in Los Angeles, whom Kris had some time previously recommended for temporary consultation.

Since it was felt she needed sympathetic help and attention after her Payne-Whitney experience, the star agreed to be booked into a room at the Neurological Institute of the Columbia University-Presbyterian Hospital Medical Center, provided Joe would stay at the hospital and be with her each day.

All things considered, Marilyn's psychiatrists seemed to commit some unthinkable blunders. Marianne Kris must have known about Marilyn's fear of insanity and her belief, no matter how ill founded, that it ran in her family. For her to trick her patient — for it was clear Marilyn had no idea as to what she had agreed — into entering what amounted to an insane asylum would appear to be unbelievably crass. And on the face of it, the psychiatrist she turned to after Kris, Dr Ralph Greenson did not come out very well, either. When Marilyn was in clear need of people around her that she could trust and rely upon, Greenson, who did not like some of the star's friends, notably Ralph Roberts, delivered the ultimatum that she either get rid of him or else he would curtail her therapy. High-handed, to say the least, it hacked at the roots of what would have been expected of a caring psychiatrist. This continued until the day Marilyn died, when Greenson, while present at her house, answered the telephone to Roberts, who was seeking to confirm Marilyn was expecting him for dinner, and baldly told him she was, 'Not here', before hanging up. This deprived her of companionship on the last night of her life and gave rise to her comment, 'Here I am, the most beautiful woman in the world, and I have no date for Saturday night.'

When Joe so dramatically came to Marilyn's aid, it was not unnatural that rumours should begin to fly about a reunion between them, but she was emotionally drained and quite unready for decisions of this kind. Besides, she would become a hospital patient twice more in the months immediately ahead. The first time, in Los Angeles, was so that she could have corrective gynaecological surgery that had become necessary due to earlier unsatisfactory surgery relating, it appeared, to a miscarriage or an abortion.

She was in New York a few weeks after her gynaecological surgery when she was rushed into the Manhattan Polyclinic Hospital suffering from gall bladder problems. It turned out she had impacted gallstones as well as an inflamed gall bladder. Once again, Joe DiMaggio was with her. It was on 29 June she was successfully operated on, though it would be another ten days before she left hospital. 1961 was not a good year for Marilyn. There was talk of her letting herself go for weeks on end in the period after her gall bladder operation. She seemed empty and elsewhere, particularly during the time she was still changing wound dressings, which neither inspired pleasure nor feelings of well-being. Those around her spoke of her becoming coarse and vulgar, far from the gentle-voiced creature who had been Marilyn.

During the time spent filming *The Misfits* in the desert, Marilyn was reported to have been saved from death only by having her stomach pumped out. The cause of the mishap and its seriousness is unclear, but there were those who saw it as another 'cry for help' suicide attempt, perhaps the consequence of the extreme tensions she was working under, both on and off the set. Her constant lateness antagonised the sweltering cast and crew, and her marriage to Arthur Miller was disintegrating at a rapid rate. A news agency telephoned in the early morning to ask if there was any truth in the report Marilyn had committed suicide. A studio press officer tartly responded, 'Why, that's impossible. She has to be on the set at 7.30! Besides, Paula Strasberg would never stand for it.' Black humour — intended or accidental — apart, there has to be some sort of commentary in this response to the state of things. Marilyn was flown back to Los Angeles where she spent ten days in Westbrook Hospital — in the care of Doctors Greenson and Engelberg — before being returned to the desert location to resume filming.

Marilyn suffered all her adult life from abnormally severe menstrual periods. The cause of it was termed chronic endometriosis, and her medical records were strewn with details of operations she had on both the east coast and the west coast because of this problem. Her surgeons, Dr Mortimer Rodgers in New York and Leon Krohn in Los Angeles were never quite able to achieve the 'correction of a female disorder', as Krohn called it, when she was admitted to hospitals in either of those cities. Further to all this, in New York she had been admitted to the Doctors Hospital in Manhattan after collapsing into unconsciousness as a consequence of a miscarriage. The child was Arthur Miller's. Marilyn was devastated.

There was much talk about abortions to which Marilyn was said to have admitted. In the autopsy carried out on Marilyn's body, the proceedings had not reached the point where abortions could have been identified before they were suspended due to essential specimens having been disposed of. Dr Noguchi could therefore neither confirm nor deny there was evidence of abortions to be found. Certain of her friends claimed she had told them about having had abortions, however, and there was fresh speculation at the time she was making her last film, *Something's Got to Give*. It was reported that she had a pregnancy terminated on 21 July, two weeks before she died, and following this time she was said to be looking poorly. Several of those near to her spoke of her having had an abortion. Agnes Flanagan said Marilyn told her about it and publicists Rupert Allan and Michael Selsman both said they knew. This coincided with the time she had been conducting a relationship with Attorney General Robert Kennedy. Perhaps significantly, this was the point at which she was dropped like a stone by Kennedy.

It was astounding that little or no attention was paid to the fact that the Fox studio's doctor, Lee Siegal, said he detected clear symptoms of hypoglycaemia in Marilyn. This condition relates, generally, to a deficiency of glucose in the bloodstream, and is grossly affected by diet — or the lack of it. Sufferers are, these days, given strict food charts to stick to which involve radical modifications to a normal diet. Small meals to be taken each two hours of the day is typical of a modern treatment, for instance. No sugar, bread or potatoes, and no alcohol. The consequences of ignoring this condition can be quite severe, including being listless and tired, finding it hard to cope with everyday life, and, in extreme cases, lapsing into a coma-like condition from which it is difficult to be roused. On the face of it the problems from which Marilyn suffered were entirely consistent with this condition, which would be severely aggravated by her lack of controlled diet and alcohol excess. Her intake of barbiturates was not likely to alleviate the condition, either.

There was some evidence that Marilyn was also, to some extent, dyslexic. She was inclined to transpose words in her script and sometimes developed a block to speaking them in the correct order. This combined with Meniere's Disease, which, at times, caused her to mis-hear what was being said to her, could make for difficulties on the set and make her appear vague. It did not help at all that there were those who were prepared to put the worst construction on difficulties that arose on the set. Bandied in gossip columns, the word 'confusion' attracted suggestions that Marilyn was now unable to remember her lines, and the Meniere's problem caused her to look vacant on those occasions when she had not properly heard what she had been told.

Marilyn was thought to be a hypochondriac, but when the conditions she regularly had to cope with are added up I would disagree. She suffered tortures from her menstrual periods and other gynaecological problems, periodically had mild attacks of Meniere's Disease and had some degree of dyslexia, which was liable to interfere with her ability to read scripts. In addition to this she was tormented by fear before daring to appear before the cameras, from whatever cause. The depressing effects of drug excesses and the wretchedness of hangovers added to her burden, though in the light of the discovery she suffered from hypoglycaemia, it is now hard to distinguish between the former and the effects of this aggressive blood deficiency condition. Taken together, she had a lot to genuinely complain of and feel insecure about.

Also, in view of the general lack of progress she appeared to make regarding her various health problems, it was incredible that Marilyn, who was not inclined to neglect her various psychological and medical conditions — perhaps this is where the hypochondriac notions came from — spent a fortune for the services of people at the top of their respective professions in her quest for relief from her problems. I would not be the first to point out how ludicrous it was, for instance, for Hyman Engelberg and others to be prescribing the drugs that Ralph Greenson was treating her — with success towards the end of her life — to give up.

But underlying the other medical problems from which Marilyn suffered, it was insomnia that caused her the most grief. This had led to the increased use of drugs and that led to deeper problems still, which haunted her until she died. This situation was well known to those around her and those with whom she worked. When John Huston, director of *The Misfits*, heard of Marilyn's death and that it was being said she had committed suicide, he said, 'Marilyn wasn't killed by Hollywood. It was the doctors who killed her. If she was a pill addict they made her so.'

33

MARILYN AND THE MOB

Even though, in her tapes, Marilyn defended Sinatra from having Mafia connections, there is no doubt that through the singer, Marilyn became acquainted with several mafiosi. This, by itself, did not amount to very much. She became acquainted with people from many walks of life, and it could not be claimed the Mafia figures she met played any kind of decisive role in her life. She dated Giancana's lieutenant, the dark, handsome, Johnny Rosselli, a few times, and occasionally saw George Piscitelle and Sam LoCigno, two of Mickey Cohen's henchmen. The question many people have asked, however, is whether those shady Mafia figures played a role in her death.

Marilyn disliked Sam Giancana. Had she known it — and it was extremely unlikely that she did — her instincts were right. The boss of the Chicago Mafia, Sam Giancana was said to have ordered the torture and murder of some 200 people who crossed him in one way or another. He was credited with controlling most of the bookmakers, loan sharks and extortionists in Chicago, and his other unsavoury activities in that city included prostitution. He had been imprisoned for murder and other

Sam Giancana. Marilyn met him through Frank Sinatra.

felonies, and it was not surprising Frank Sinatra did not advertise his friendship with the gangster. In spite of his protests, however, there was no doubting the singer's affinity with the mobsters. 'Momo', or 'Mooney', as Giancana was called, was at one time Sinatra's business partner in the Lake Tahoe Cal-Neva Lodge and Casino, and may have been involved in other activities with the singer. It was said Sinatra ended his shows by singing 'Chicago' to please the mafioso.

Before her death, Marilyn became of concern to prominent Mafia people, notably Giancana, not because of who she was but rather for what she knew. During her relationship with Robert Kennedy she had found it handy to make notes on what he had told her so that she could converse more intelligently with him when they met again. These notes may well have been kept in her notebooks, of which there seemed to be quite a few around, or, as many thought, in the red diary which went missing at the time of her death. It may have been both, of course; temporary, rough notes scribbled in notebooks later to be refined and copied up in the red diary.

Kennedy apparently talked to her about what was going on in government and told her secrets about which the government were not proud. The main concern with organised crime would be the scandalous alliance that had formed between top mafiosi and the CIA to kill Fidel Castro, the communist ruler of Cuba, which Robert Kennedy had told Marilyn about in 'pillow talk'. This, which eventually became common knowledge after massive shock media headlines, was Top Secret in 1962. The CIA did not want this story spread around and neither, by any means, did the Mafia figures. The Mafia would have benefited enormously from the overthrow of Castro, for in the revolution they had lost all their gambling interests in Havana, while the CIA had the toppling of Castro as one of their prime objectives. They had struck a deal which shocked the world when it was exposed.

The CIA had put into action 'Operation Mongoose', a plan to undermine the communist regime in Cuba by means of propaganda, the instigation of guerrilla warfare on the part of rebels, sabotage, and the stirring up of internal dissent. Murder had not been expected to be part of the plan, and it shook America to learn that, not only was it 'policy', it was sought through a sleazy deal between agents of the government and members of organised crime. And this was not the kind of thing that Robert Kennedy should have been gossiping to Marilyn about. It became known to Jimmy Hoffa and Sam Giancana that he had been talking about it, no doubt, through the bugs placed in her house.

It should be noted, however, that by the same means it also became known to the CIA agents listening that Kennedy was talking about the subject.

When people became aware that Robert Kennedy had told Marilyn secrets relating to a CIA — Mafia relationship, they believed they had found the reason Marilyn was killed and that this pinpointed who her killers had been. Indeed, when I carried out research for this book I came up with two accounts of her murder, both supposedly carried out by mafiosi. The claims made quoted the names of those who had carried out the killing, and gave all necessary details. Unfortunately, they were two *different* accounts, carried out by two different sets of people using two different means of killing her. After his death, a third account emanated from Frank Sinatra, via a biographer. There was no shortage of attempts to credit Mafia figures with Marilyn's death.

For those who read *Double Cross* by Sam and Chuck Giancana, which was published in 1992, I can offer no encouragement that they have heard anything more than the speculation of two of the gangster's relatives cashing in on the notorious name. Sam and Chuck Giancana were 'Mooney's' nephew and half-brother, who wrote of the mobster's involvement in the murder of Marilyn Monroe, John F Kennedy, and Robert Kennedy. I consulted Sam Giancana's daughter, Antoinette, on the subject of the book and she denounced it without hesitation. She said her father would have scorned its contents. She

361

dismisses it as scurrilous. She told me her father was not involved in the death of Marilyn Monroe, and that he had disowned Chuck, who had at one time changed his name to Cain, which her father did not like. Antoinette was so scathing about what they wrote, it would have been difficult to conduct point by point discussion of its contents with her.

It is quoted by those who attribute the killing to the Mafia that they were moved to act quickly by Marilyn's threat to 'blow the lid off the whole damn thing'. This was when she was angry with Robert Kennedy just before she died. She had spoken to Robert Slatzer of holding a press conference the following Monday necessitating, it was thought, an urgent 'solution' to the volatile and unstable Marilyn. It is an interesting enough scenario, but does not stand up to a great deal of scrutiny.

First of all, Marilyn had regular monthly press conferences; another one would not have been regarded as extraordinary. Would she have blown the whistle on Jack Kennedy? As we have seen from the secret tapes, she had great admiration for the President, and it is doubtful she would ever, in any circumstances, have compromised him, even to get even with Robert. It must be clearly understood that Marilyn, regardless of the roles she played in some of her movies, was no dumb blonde, and would not have been likely to get into publicity calculated to backfire on her. She was a very astute businesswoman who knew what she was doing. Would she have been likely to go through with her threat? Had she really decided to go ahead and 'blow the lid off the whole damn thing'? She had no guarantees her story would grab front-page headlines, by any means, and in this respect Marilyn also knew what she was doing. As we said earlier, many of the reporters had all the stories they wanted about Jack Kennedy and his women but would not — or could not — get them into print. To add to the list a story about Robert Kennedy would have been different, but would have been extremely unlikely to alter the prospects of publication.

Hard evidence of the censorship of articles putting the Kennedys in a bad light is to be found in the experience of Ezra Goodman. Ezra Goodman was *Time* magazine's 'man in Hollywood' and he wrote a piece linking Marilyn to the Kennedys after her death. *Time* editors declined to publish it and saw to it that every copy of the article was destroyed. Goodman went on to write a book that was accepted for publication by Macmillan. In spite of paying him a handsome advance on royalties, the book was dumped by the publishers, and no other publisher in New York would touch it. We are left to speculate on the reason.

Any success registered at all would probably have finished up as an 'Outburst by Angry Star' item located in an obscure mid-paper column: buried. Marilyn was, no doubt, aware of this and was not likely to set off a bomb that merely went 'pop'. She would lose far more than she gained, and those reporters who did not believe what she was telling them would have been the ones likely to finish up with the item in the obscure mid-paper column.

Besides, the need for blowing whistles had now gone. She had already achieved the result she was seeking. By Friday night Robert Kennedy was sitting up and paying attention, even if that brought more problems than it solved.

When push came to shove, the very idea of Marilyn really going through with 'blowing the lid off' her relationships in such a vengeful way was out of the question, according to Allan (Whitey) Snyder, Marilyn's make-up man and confidante. 'To think of Marilyn Monroe calling a press conference to air her grievances against anyone is laughably out of character,' he said.

The *modus operandi* for Marilyn's murder lends no credence to it being carried out by the Mafia. It may be true that there were times they poisoned, and when they did they favoured using chloral hydrate. But the dose found in Marilyn's bloodstream, though large, did not constitute a fatal dose, and it would be untypical for the Mafia to miscalculate. When they killed they killed. In any case, this would leave the huge volume of Nembutal in her bloodstream and liver unaccounted for, and the Mafia were not known for Nembutal poisonings. The Mafia killed many people, but theirs was not the subtle poisoning by barbiturates introduced by enema. In the main, mafiosi did not care how many questions were asked about their killings as long as they were somewhere else when it happened. Theirs was more likely a swift bullet or even a hail of bullets. The idea of involving the Attorney General by carrying out a murder dressed up as a suicide does not fit, either. The idea has been located in the wrong place. It does not belong under M for Mafia.

Robert Kennedy was already giving the Mafia a bad time. He was targeting them in many parts of the country and was obtaining a success rate never before achieved in the United States. His success was also inspiring lawmen elsewhere — who would have let cases slide because of the previously small chance of putting well-known mobsters behind bars — to strike out against their local Mafia figures, and they, too, were putting the criminals away. The Attorney General was on a roll, and Giancana and company knew it. Their need was to control the Attorney General, and a convoluted scheme to commit a murder with the idea of the blame landing on Robert Kennedy was not their style. Besides, their logic was likely to be that if any plan to discredit the Attorney General came to light, they would be the first people to be suspected. This was not a risk they were likely to take. It was too 'iffy'. And besides, failure would have been likely to generate greater problems; the backfiring of such intrigue was the stuff of which stepped up campaigns against organised crime was made. The people — the voters — would have applauded even more than they applauded Robert Kennedy's present initiative to see the heat turned further up.

Had the Mafia wanted to get rid of the Attorney General, they could have killed him long since. On balance, they were actually happier with a scheme in which they could exercise control over Robert Kennedy, and every spool of tape recorded at Marilyn's house took them a step further in that direction.

There was an interesting echo of the CIA — Mafia collaboration some years after this. In 1975 Sam Giancana had already answered questions put to him by the Senate Intelligence Committee and they wanted to speak to him again, but this time they wanted to know about plots to kill Fidel Castro. Giancana was found dead, having been shot in the back of the head, then shot again six times in a circle around his mouth. He would answer no more questions. It was much the same with his lieutenant, Johnny Rosselli. Rosselli had been questioned by the Committee also, and was due to return for another session. He was garrotted, stabbed, and his body dismembered and stuffed into an oil drum. This was then dropped in the ocean, but washed up on a Florida beach. Charles Nicolleti, another of Giancana's hitmen, was found in a blazing car, his body riddled with bullets. It would seem that other members of the Mafia hierarchy had decided no one would talk about the infamous CIA — Mafia link. This was pressure being exerted by those inside on those inside. They were concerned with silencing those in possession of all the facts, not loose chatter from a girl, whose word was likely to be challenged.

But this tailpiece is not finished. The man who was one of the original negotiators of the CIA — Mafia liaison was Jimmy Hoffa. Robert Kennedy never succeeded in placing him behind bars, but his successor as Attorney General did. Hoffa never served his full term, however. Although the parole board rejected his appeal three times, he was rescued by President Richard Nixon, no less. Budd Schilberg wrote an introduction to *The Fall and Rise of Jimmy Hoffa* by Walter Sheridan, in which he said, 'George Jackson rotted in jail for nearly a decade for heisting $70. Jimmy Hoffa cops a million, bribes juries, runs with the most dangerous gangsters in America and, thanks to the intervention of his good friend Dick Nixon, does an easy five.'

When Hoffa was released he was completely disorientated. The Teamsters no longer wanted him. On 30 July 1975, just weeks before Sam Giancana was murdered, he disappeared and has never been seen since. It would hardly be rated speculation that he had been included in those who were to die with their CIA — Mafia secrets.

Elsewhere I have shown why I believe the CIA are the most likely candidates for wanting to kill Marilyn in order to discredit and destroy the Attorney General and his brother, the President. An interesting idea which has been mooted, that the CIA may have enlisted the Mafia to kill Marilyn for them as a favour, so to speak, is probably just that: an interesting idea. In view of what has already been said in this chapter, it is hard to see mafiosi risking all for their CIA 'friends'. Besides, do those who think that is true think the CIA, capable of the deepest levels of skullduggery, needed any help in carrying out a murder?

34

MARILYN AND THE FBI

The 1950s saw suspicion of communism in the United States manifest itself in the witch hunts conducted by the House Committee on Un-American Activities, chaired by the fanatical Senator Joe McCarthy. It was not difficult to be listed among those whom McCarthy felt should be investigated, and once placed under a shadow it was difficult to survive the consequences of the relentless investigatory machine. A connection with communism or communist leanings of any kind was enough to ruin reputations and place even the most famous and talented in a wilderness where they became unemployable — 'untouchable'. The slightest taint of communism sparked off a train of procedures that put those with minor or casual connections under a cloud in which they had to fight, and fight hard, to escape the rigours of McCarthyism.

The fact that so many people around Marilyn had left-wing connections of one kind or another became one of those things which right-wing writers, such as Frank Capell, liked to bring to public notice. And if Capell was aware of the background of those near to Marilyn, we can be sure that FBI chief J Edgar Hoover knew about it also. Mrs Murray's husband had been a union activist and made no secret of it. He quite openly held meetings at their house. Dr Ralph Greenson held left-wing views, and Dr Hyman Engelberg, Marilyn's physician, was identified as having direct communist links.

The Strasbergs, Lee and Paula, were both tenuously linked to communist activities, and Paula, in the name of Paula Miller, was identified as a member of the Communist Party. Marilyn's poet friend Norman Rosten, and his wife Hedda, also came under scrutiny. Rosten had many interests that qualified as communist linked — it counted as a link if you subscribed to the *Daily Worker*, for instance — and had once been a member of the Young Communists League. Marilyn struck up a friendship with Fred Vanderbilt Field when she visited Mexico. Field was a well-known communist, in spite of the wealthy Vanderbilt family he belonged to, and had fled America to be able to live in peace. He had married a Mexican girl, Nieves, and the pair enjoyed Marilyn's company. They got on well together. At one time Marilyn was romantically linked to left-wing Mexican Jose Bolanos, though she escaped being caught up in the dissention he created with her friends the Fields, who did not trust him for his declared politics.

Marilyn's husband of four years, Arthur Miller, was accused of being a member of the Communist Party and fell foul of the House Committee on Un-American Activities. Miller was seen not only as a registered Communist Party member, but as one actively engaged in supporting enemies of the United States, since he bravely spoke out at what appeared to be the persecution of a man, Gerhard Eisler, for being a spy. He also raised his voice in defence of 12 people convicted of being communist leaders, in another instance. It was this kind of courage which greatly endeared him to Marilyn, who, probably to please her husband more than anything, took an interest in what left-wing intellectuals had to say. In 1956 Miller was called for questioning by the House Committee for Un-American Activities. He admitted he had signed 'some form' in 1939, though denied knowingly applying for Communist Party membership. But the records show he did, in fact, sign a form applying for membership, his application number being 23345.

He was holding his own in his interrogation until he refused to give his questioners the names of others he met at communist meetings. 'I could not use the name of another person and bring trouble on him,' he said. He was convicted of contempt of Congress, which carried a jail sentence, appealed against his conviction, and was eventually acquitted after spending two years 'under the McCarthy cloud.' He was very fortunate to have the dedicated loyalty of Marilyn, who spoke up in defence of her husband, even though she was told it was unwise. She told English reporter, WJ Weatherby, 'Some of those b — s in Hollywood wanted me to drop Arthur. [They] said it would ruin my career. They're born cowards and they want you to be like them.' And the treatment Miller received at the hands of the House Committee appeared favourably affected by Marilyn's support of him. Afterwards, since his legal expenses were more than he could cope with, Marilyn paid them.

Marilyn's own political views were not what would be described as well defined. She always had sympathy for the underdog, whatever shape, size or form, and this translated into political terms would rank her as a left winger. She was generous with her money and kind to those she came into contact with. Jimmie Haspiel, for instance, a sixteen-year-old boy in New York, pursued her without pencil and paper for an autograph, asked for a kiss, and got more than he could ever have dreamed of; he got his kiss and became a personal friend of Marilyn. When she visited an orphanage to which she intended making a donation of $1,000, she, on impulse, tore up the cheque and wrote another for $10,000, and the sight of a black man being refused entrance to a public place upset her greatly. In his book, *Conversations with Marilyn*, W J Weatherby, who would not publish his book until after Marilyn had died because he promised that to her, wrote of her as being, ' . . . the famous movie star who still had a genuine human interest in a wino in the street, concern for a sparrow among the pigeons. I have known many famous people, but none like that.'

But none of this would explain the close interest taken in her by the FBI. Documents relating to Marilyn that were obtained with difficulty from the grasp of the FBI under the

Freedom of Information Act were liberally censored before release. The classification of the censoring was known as B1. This was invoked to protect the country's interests, coming under the heading of National Security. The FBI's interest was far more likely to have been aroused through Marilyn's friends and contacts who interested them in the steamy climate of McCarthyism. But in a category all on its own, her liaisons with Jack Kennedy and, later, Robert Kennedy would secure the interest of J Edgar Hoover. Of course, both Jack and Robert Kennedy were seen as embracing socialist ideas that to avid right-wingers like Capell placed them close to communism. And there were a great many of those right-wingers who found what they believed to be the Kennedys' 'affinity with communism' disquieting. The FBI Director thought Marilyn's file interesting enough to be copied to the CIA.

The House Committee on Un-American Activities blatantly trampled on the liberties of many loyal Americans, therefore becoming the most prominent perpetrator of un-Americanism itself. Hollywood was among the prime targets for Senator Joe McCarthy, since it was suspected that communism was seeping into the American consciousness through filmscripts and through the popularity of well-known actors. There was, therefore, a ruthlessness in 'weeding out' those who were communist-tainted, regardless of careers being ruined and hardship caused. Highly talented victims of the witch-hunts were eventually to be found carrying out menial tasks

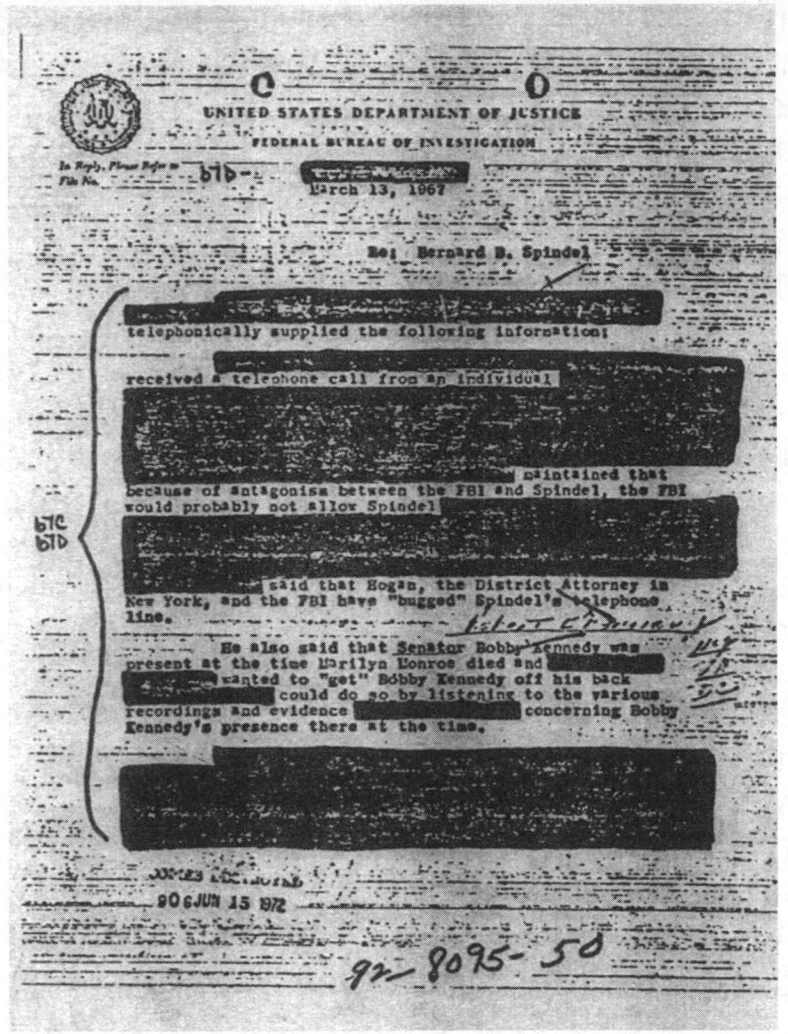

A document 'released' by the FBI.
They were not giving much away.

to sustain life, since no-one dared employ them.

Ludicrous situations arose, such as that of comic legend Charlie Chaplin, who went for a visit to England and found he was barred from re-entering the United States unless he agreed to an interrogation on the subject of his communist leanings. One question he was subsequently asked was why he had used the word 'comrades' when addressing a meeting. And sincere Americans, who saw what was being attempted by the legislation and, in basis, approved of it, were later to suffer for their compliance with the demands of McCarthyism. Almost 30 years after the House Committee on Un-American Activities had ceased its persecution, a television team whose speciality was reviewing the reputations of well-known personalities, many of whom had left this world and were unable to answer back, made the distinguished cartoon movie maker Walt Disney a subject of their series. It appeared the worthy Disney gave them a hard time, and the most damning thing they could find to accuse him of was that he obeyed, like many others, the dictates of McCarthy.

Marilyn's friends being what they were, she was classified alongside them and found 'interesting' to the FBI from the point of view of national security. As absurd as this was, it gave J Edgar Hoover the opportunity to eavesdrop on the star and those she entertained in her home. Similarly, and with the same excuse, the CIA found the chance to bug Marilyn's home because they could argue she was a 'security risk'. But the real interest of both the FBI and the CIA was the Kennedys.

35

KNOCKS AND HARD KNOCKS

A convenient excuse for Robert Kennedy to make trips to Los Angeles to see Marilyn was a proposal to make a film from his book, *The Enemy Within*. This exposé of Kennedy's arch-enemy, Jimmy Hoffa, and organised crime, was hard hitting and made an impact. The *Baltimore Sun* review called it, 'An expose eclipsing the most sensational fiction in every way . . . a story of murder, arson, acid blindings, pitiless beatings, grand larceny, fraud, embezzlement and extortion, all exposed through exhaustive . . . detective work and resulting in instances of heroic personal courage and shocking shame.' Britain's press baron, Lord Beaverbrook, praised the book to the skies. It was, he said, 'a detective story which can be put on the same shelf as the best thriller fiction of the day . . . I feel rather like one who has been sent an account of the Crusade written by Richard the Lionheart himself.'

Twentieth Century Fox had, in 1961, expressed an interest in making a movie of the book, which had been published the previous year. But the news had hardly been released before the producer, Jerry Wald, received the first of many anonymous threats which came by telephone and in the mail. At first he ignored them and pressed on with his plans. But the Mafia had decided it did not want the movie to be made. The studios had been paying 'protection' money to the mob for years, and now they leaned on Fox heavily to abandon this 'offensive' story. *The Enemy Within* represented one round that Kennedy lost to Hoffa, who eventually succeeded, through his lawyer, in halting production.

Such a defeat by the Mafia was not something Kennedy would take lightly. Long before he had become Attorney General, Kennedy had had a well-developed dislike of Jimmy Hoffa, which would be honed into a consuming enmity. Hoffa responded in the same fashion, and descriptions of the occasions when they met face to face, together with background and implications of the meetings, would provide material for a bestseller. Arthur M Schlesinger wrote of each man representing what the other detested most. The two men had a lot to learn about each other, Kennedy admitting he had to guard against losing his temper, and Hoffa being aware of this.

As Robert Kennedy saw it, ' . . . the gangsters of today work in a highly organised fashion and are far more powerful now than at any time in the history of the country. They control political figures and threaten whole communities. They have stretched their tentacles of corruption and fear into industries both large and small. They grow stronger every day.' He was shocked to find out that Hoover's FBI were not aware of the threat posed by organised crime. Hoover did not acknowledge its existence. The Director had communism and communists in his sights. These were his prime concern. This was the age of McCarthyism and the infamous witch-hunts that ruined many lives. Kennedy knew the FBI was not carrying out surveillance on mobsters. 'They do it for suspected spies, but they won't do it for gangsters and racketeers.'

'If we do not . . . attack organised criminals with weapons and techniques as effective as their own, they will destroy us,' said Kennedy. He was speaking at the time of his involvement in the Rackets Committee, but his acquisition of power as Attorney General took him no nearer to achieving his ambition of throwing Hoffa into jail. Hoffa was incredibly elusive, and had people around to give him protection. The mobster boasted he had a way with juries, so much so there was an enquiry into 'jury tampering'. He once said to Kennedy, 'Listen Bobby, you run your business and I'll run mine,' annoying RFK by using his first name. But, somewhat remarkably, there were some who saw clear resemblances between the two men. Writing in the *Saturday Evening Post*, John Bartlow Martin said they were both, 'aggressive, competitive, hard-driving, authoritarian, suspicious, temperate, at times congenial and at others curt.' On one of the congenial occasions, when both were together in a waiting room, they bantered over who could do more press-ups. Hoffa conceded on the grounds that for Kennedy it was not difficult to lift a feather-weight. Neither Kennedy

Jimmy Hoffa.
He and Robert Kennedy were arch enemies.
Photo AP Wide World

nor Hoffa smoked, Kennedy drank little and
Hoffa not at all. Both men were prepared to take
risks, and both were slave drivers; and so the
similarities, in spite of their huge differences,
went on.

In the war of the 'taps', both Kennedy and
Hoffa were adept, aggressive and equipped with
state-of-the-art technology. Hoffa had bugs
placed into the Justice Department and Kennedy
had Hoffa's offices wired out. Hoffa, who had
the advantage of employing ace wire-tapper
Bernard Spindel, had him sweep out Kennedy's
bugs, while Kennedy carried around with him a

briefcase that contained 'debugging' equipment which 'jammed' surveillance transmissions. It was relentless. Hoffa went further and began to keep tabs on Kennedy's brother, the President. But quite remarkably, neither brother appeared to realise Hoffa had bugged Lawford's beach road mansion where they both spent time, and often with Marilyn. Neither was aware either, it seems, that Hoffa had also tapped the phones and planted bugs in Marilyn's apartment, and in her house when she moved to Fifth Helena Drive.

It would not be overstating the Hoffa-Kennedy situation to say that 'getting Hoffa' had become an obsession with Kennedy. It would be untrue to make out a case for another similarity on the part of Hoffa, however, who just wanted the Attorney General off his back. If not an obsession, though, Kennedy was one of his prime concerns. Kennedy took no pleasure in having his likenesses to the Teamster's boss put into print. For him the struggle underlying all this was the war between good and evil. Kennedy never did achieve locking Hoffa away, but his successor under the Lyndon Johnson administration, Nicholas Katzenbach, did. As we recount elsewhere, Hoffa was released by President Richard Nixon after serving only five of his thirteen years' sentence. When he left prison, Hoffa looked to re-establish himself but found he was squeezed out. He disappeared without trace and was never seen again.

At first sight it remains a mystery why Hoffa did not use the product of his taps on Lawford's and Marilyn's homes. There is little doubt he had *some* powerful blackmail material at his fingertips. And if Hoffa held such power, so did his friend and 'colleague' Sam Giancana, the mob's man in Chicago. Or did, perhaps, Hoffa's — or Giancana's — 'intelligence' network find out from the CIA about the 'steps' being taken to get rid of the Kennedys by means of killing Marilyn Monroe? And when that failed, did they learn about new plans quickly put in hand to shoot down President Kennedy in the streets of Dallas the next year? When Jack Kennedy was disposed of Robert Kennedy had no powers. Their work would be done for them; there was nothing for them to stick out their necks for.

When Robert Kennedy journeyed to Hollywood time and again negotiating for the production of the movie, his meetings with Marilyn were sometimes less than discreet. On one occasion, when Jerry Wald attended a meeting with the Attorney General, he found Marilyn by his side. Such indiscretion might suggest that Robert Kennedy had an agenda other than romancing Marilyn when he began paying visits to Los Angeles to see her.

36

THE RED DIARY

In the mystery that has surrounded Marilyn's death, nothing has created more speculation than the red diary she is supposed to have kept. Its existence is important because the diary figures prominently in several scenarios relating to how and why the star was murdered. Some believe it is the very reason she was killed, while others are tantalised by the idea it might still exist, and will turn up somewhere, sometime, and cast some light on what happened to Marilyn.

At least three sources confirm its existence. Robert Slatzer spoke of Marilyn showing it to him and telling him the kind of thing she kept in it; Jeanne Carmen told us she had seen Robert Kennedy open it and, seeing what was in it, throw it across the room shouting, 'Get rid of this'; and Lionel Grandison was partly the cause of raising the 1982 investigation into Marilyn's death by asserting that the diary had been placed in a safe at the mortuary, from where it had been stolen.

Marilyn felt unequal to conversing with Robert Kennedy on some of the subjects he raised. Such things as politics and government were outside her spheres of interest, but she was not ignorant and did not want to appear so. Robert Kennedy would refer to subjects he had raised at previous meetings and it was difficult for her to recall specifics relating to matters with which she was unfamiliar in the first place. For this reason, after their meetings she would make notes about the things they had talked about. In the first place the notes were probably made in common-or-garden notebooks, but they were likely copied into some kind of entry for a diary of sorts that she decided to keep. The pages from her notepads were probably destroyed as she copied the notes up, but her red diary would become a treasured object. It was said that those around her did not recall seeing any such book, but then a diary is a personal thing, and the contents of this particular diary she was unlikely to share with anybody. The nearest she came to doing so was one day, not long before she died, when she was with Robert Slatzer and he got to see it. She told him what it was and why she was keeping it, and gave him hints about what was in it.

If the story Lionel Grandison told was true, he actually read some of the entries. Grandison was employed in the coroner's office, and queried the death certificate made out after the autopsy on Marilyn. He pointed out he had seen three versions, each one slightly different from the others. One gave the cause of death as 'suicide', the second said it was 'possible suicide' and the third, 'probable suicide'. He spoke of the first certificate disappearing, and the second being replaced by the third. His signature was required only as a matter of routine, but he declined to append, attracting the wrath of Coroner Dr Theodore Curphey, whereupon he then signed.

One of his duties was to identify the next of kin to the deceased. Where no next of kin could be found the deceased was cremated, and since no-one had yet come forward to claim Marilyn's body, he set about finding someone who would do so. He asked for one of the coroner's staff to call at Marilyn's house and to locate an address book so that he would be able to carry out his task. Among the items brought back he found a red-covered book that he thought might contain names and addresses, but it was not what he was seeking. It had diary-type entries relating to subjects in which the CIA and the Mafia featured. Grandison commented it was unusual in 1962 to see much reference to either the CIA or the Mafia. He realised he was looking at something containing politically sensitive material and that it should be returned to whoever now owned it. He placed it in a locker-safe for the time being. When he eventually reopened the locker it had vanished. There were few people who had access to the locker-safe, but no-one admitted taking it.

Grandison had an opportunity to press for this to be investigated when the John K Van de Kamp re-investigation was opened in 1982, but as the district attorney did not appear anxious to disturb sleeping dogs, Grandison was discredited and an attempt was made to brand the story of the red diary a fiction. This was a considerable slight to Robert Slatzer, who stood by Grandison in his claim he had seen the red diary, but the investigators said his word was not enough and they had found no one else who could support the existence of the diary.

The investigators had not looked far. When I carried out my research I talked to Marilyn's one-time neighbour and friend, Jeanne Carmen, who told me without hesitation she had seen the red book. 'It was once when I was at Marilyn's and Robert Kennedy was there. I saw them together on four occasions. This time he was reading the book and was not happy with what he saw. He flung it across the room and snapped at Marilyn, 'Get rid of this . . . ' He told her even 'Miss Carmen' should not be allowed to read it. In fact, I hadn't read it. So much for that.' If I found it desirable to be talking to Jeanne Carmen — as someone who had been a friend of Marilyn — it is surely reasonable to expect that those involved in a new investigation would also be asking her questions. To my mind it served to illustrate how inconsequential the new investigation really was.

There was speculation that Robert Kennedy, on the last day of Marilyn's life, was referring to the red diary when he searched her house and angrily demanded, 'Where is it?' I thought this was the case myself at one time, but I am now convinced there were documents which may have formed a file, which was critical for him to recover for his brother, Jack. It seems highly unlikely the red diary would have been overlooked by Peter Lawford and Fred Otash's men when they searched the place while Marilyn lay dead in her bedroom, but they may, of course, like the coroner's men who are claimed to have brought it to Lionel Grandison, have believed it to be an address book.

There is a sequel of sorts to the story of the red diary, however. In 1999 a sale at Christie's, New York, offered, among items of Marilyn Monroe memorabilia, a 'red book' shown as a 'writing case' and described as 'oversized red leather', which was said to have been her personal property. By Smythson of New Bond Street, it was listed in their catalogue as likely to fetch $2,000 to $2,500. It did not contain the 'diary' items that made Marilyn's book so politically explosive, however. Inside it was blotting paper and 18 sheets of cream notepaper embossed *Marilyn Monroe*. There were also 6 matching envelopes with her name embossed on the flap. The existence of this red book has never been questioned though not one of her friends or acquaintances ever mentioned it. Is there any reason, therefore, why they should have been aware she had a red diary? The existence of this unmentioned red book which went to auction clearly undermines the implication raised in the 1982 investigation that there was no red diary because certain of Marilyn's friends had not seen it. Because of the publicity that eventually surrounded the disappearing 'red diary', it is extraordinary no-one ever brought the existence of a red writing case to the attention of investigators.

37

CONSEQUENCES

The group of CIA renegades who, I believe, were responsible for murdering Marilyn Monroe, failed in their aspirations. It had been their intention to involve the Attorney General, Marilyn Monroe's last visitor, in a scandal in which he had appeared to kill the star — or appeared to have had her killed — and attempted a crude cover up making her death look like suicide. Even if — to them — the worst happened and Robert Kennedy was not accused of murder, the scandal of his involvement in a homicide — especially one in which he had been mixed up in a sexual relationship — would have made his position as the country's top lawman untenable, and he would have been compelled to resign.

Such extreme ignominy would have had further consequences, also. His appointment was one of patronage, that patronage emanating from his brother, the President. The fall-out of the scandal would, without question, have resulted in calls for the resignation of John F Kennedy from the Presidency, and, even without leaks about his own involvement with Marilyn Monroe, there was little doubt the President could have been toppled. What likely would have happened was that those newspaper editors who had been sitting on stories about Jack Kennedy's womanising — including his relationship with Marilyn — would now blazon them across their front pages, blasting the President from power. A further consequence would have been a massive fall from grace for the entire Kennedy family, and Edward would like as not have found it impossible to develop a career in politics. Not least of the ripples would have been a severe backwash effect on Kennedy business interests and a decline in their fortunes.

The renegade CIA agents were therefore playing for very high stakes. There would have been massive retribution for the blood that flowed freely at the Bay of Pigs, blood that included American blood. The hatred that had fermented since that day in the previous year, when, as they saw it, Jack and Robert Kennedy had turned their backs on the brave initiative inaugurated by the CIA, would have obtained the desired result. But their plan failed. A seamless blanket of secrecy was thrown over the entire event of Marilyn's demise in a spectacularly successful way, and the killers' own notion of making Marilyn's death look like suicide was promoted to quell further curiosity.

The counter-plan succeeded for a long time, but the renegades determination to destroy the Kennedys survived and took another form. There are strong arguments for believing the renegades combined with another force who had equal zeal to see the Kennedys despatched from the American political scene: the Establishment.

President John F Kennedy. Photo Abbey Rowe.
Courtesy of John F Kennedy Library

Big business had been watching the President
with dismay. His 'breath of fresh air' running
through government had introduced a change of
direction. It meant the prioritising of the Establishment over all else was being eroded. The
people and the needs of the people were being
placed first by the Kennedy administration, which

meant the Establishment's needs took second place. Besides this, the President was vetoing any suggestions made by the Pentagon to enter into hostilities with other countries. The Pentagon represented the greatest military force on earth, and the President would not allow it to flex its muscles.

Apart from the frustrated war machine, the military — industrial complex was stymied. Production in armaments, the steel industry, oil and other enterprises were feeling the effect of the President's quest for peace. The latest initiatives related to the situation in Vietnam, where the President was not committed to all-out war. He never was. History would show he had intentions to defuse the Vietnam situation and withdraw. There were ample reasons here for angry Establishment figures to seek to rid the country of John F Kennedy. Additionally, Kennedy was displaying clear signs of a socialist approach to government. Socialism in the United States in the decade following McCarthyism — even a mild form of it — was perceived as being only one small step away from communism, and during the years of the Cold War, communism was the great enemy.

Whether the CIA renegades made contact with representatives of the Establishment or whether it was the other way around is hard to tell. But a plan was hatched to murder the President when he visited Dallas in 1963. There were clear signs of CIA involvement in the assassination of the President, and ample indication of the involvement of the American

Establishment. If the question of who profited is raised, two clear areas of 'benefit' can be identified. One lay in the direction of the CIA and the renegade agents who had reviled the President and his brother. The other might best be illustrated by events that occurred immediately after John F Kennedy was killed.

President Kennedy had already sent an order for the first 1,000 American personnel to be withdrawn from Vietnam, and indications were he was to pull all American personnel out before they became involved in a full-scale war. President Kennedy was killed on Friday 22 November 1963, and buried the following Monday, 25 November. On the Sunday following his death — the day before he was buried, the new President, Lyndon B Johnson, held a meeting in Washington and Kennedy's Vietnam policy was reversed. It would seem the hawks could not wait. In the bloody war that followed, 50,000 Americans were killed and Vietnam deaths were numbered in millions. That war, however, generated an estimated $200 billion dollars worth of business, which went in the direction of the military — industrial complex; the armaments, steel, oil and aircraft industries among others: the Establishment.

But the CIA renegades' vendetta had not yet ended. Five years after the murder of President Kennedy, in 1968, Robert Kennedy was riding on the crest of an enormous wave of popularity and carried solid support that was clearly calculated to place him in the White House. The California primaries were held, and the votes counted gave Robert Kennedy the victory he was seeking. He was heading for the Democratic nomination and the Presidency. But amid the 1,800 celebrating his success in the primaries at the Ambassador Hotel at Los Angeles lurked those who were determined another Kennedy would not set foot in the White House. Once again gunfire decided who would rule the United States and at 1.44 a.m. on the morning of 6 June, after a three-hour fight on the operating table to try to save his life, Robert Kennedy died from gunshot wounds.

Dr Thomas Noguchi was the autopsist once more, and, again, Police Chief William Parker attempted to draw a blanket of secrecy over what had happened, leaving a hapless Sirhan Bishara Sirhan, a 25-year-old Palestinian refugee, to take the blame for the killing — much the same as Lee Harvey Oswald had when John F Kennedy was murdered. Again there were distinct indications that CIA personnel were involved with this murder.

The tide of popular opinion which had welled up behind Robert Kennedy in the period before the California primaries had by no means dissipated by the following year, when Kennedy supporters considered bringing in the youngest Kennedy brother, Edward, to bridge the gap and satisfy the upsurge of popular feeling. Though he was not ready for the Presidency, they wanted him to run for the Vice-Presidency.

Then a remarkable thing happened. Reports came in that Edward Kennedy, while holidaying at Chappaquiddick, a tiny island off Martha's

Vineyard, itself an island off Massachusetts, had been in the company of a young woman who had been drowned. Mary Jo Kopechne had been one of Robert Kennedy's 'boiler room girls', who had worked hard to support him in his campaigning, and had since joined the Edward Kennedy team. She was one of six girls and a number of men who had been invited to Chappaquiddick by Edward Kennedy to holiday as a 'thank you' for their efforts on his behalf.

Edward Kennedy's reputation as a womaniser went before him, and his association with one of his young supporters was seen in this light. But this time tragedy struck when the Senator's car swung off a wooden bridge that was unrailed, and descended into the deep water of Poucha Pond. Kennedy escaped by some means, but Mary Jo drowned. His career was on the line at this point but somehow he managed to survive. Since then he has twice been a contender for the Presidency, but has never been successful. The chief reason for his failure is the memory of what happened at Chappaquiddick. Thus the third Kennedy was not allowed to occupy the White House. After his second brother had been murdered, Edward Kennedy expected to become a target. He was heard saying, 'I know I'm going to get my ass shot off just like Bobby.' But after two brothers had been gunned down, a third would have clearly shown the hand of the assassins. They were to use a different *modus operandi* here which would be, for their purposes, just as effective. Having closely examined the details of the events related to the tragedy at Chappaquiddick, I can, again, detect the work of the CIA renegades making sure Edward would never become President of the United States.

In my research into the deaths of Jack Kennedy and his brother Robert, and the strange circumstances surrounding the death of Mary Jo Kopechne, I find every reason to link them together. I encountered another very strong reason for linking them together a few years ago, following a telephone call I received from the United States. The caller had heard of me because I had, not long before this time, visited Dallas, Texas, making enquiries of a man who had worked at Red Bird Airfield there. The caller had apparently been satisfied with what he had learned about me, and decided I would be the one to whom he would unburden himself of evidence about which he had kept silent since JFK was killed in 1963. His story was impressive. Though he had moved to Phoenix, Arizona, he, too, had worked at Red Bird Airfield at one time, and had been called back by a company who were selling a Douglas DC3 and needed his specialist knowledge to assist with the 'make ready' for the transfer of ownership.

He went back to Dallas and worked for a few days checking through the aircraft with a pilot who was the purchaser's representative. This was how it worked: one rep from the seller and one from the buyer worked together through the aircraft changing hands so that it was seen to be in good working order and up to specification. My caller was called Hank Gordon, and he began to get to know the buyer's representative well during the few days they worked together. The representative was a Cuban by birth and, though still a young man, had had much experience as a pilot.

A DC3 was a big aircraft for Red Bird Airfield, which saw mostly smaller aircraft such as Pipers or Cessnas. It had been one of a fleet sold off, and the last to go. Hank Gordon saw the military-type who he learned was the buyer, but after the single visit he made to sign the documents, never saw him again. The Cuban pilot was secretive. He would never visit the restaurant for breaks, relying on Hank to bring him sandwiches. They talked and got to know each other. On the Thursday the Cuban pilot startled Hank by telling him he had been recruited by the CIA some time before and had worked for them at the Bay of Pigs. 'Many, many died, far more than was told. I don't know all that was going on but I do know there was an indescribable amount of hurt, anger and embarrassment on the part of those who were involved in the operation . . . I was there involved with many of my friends when they died . . . '

He told Hank how much the CIA people hated the Kennedys and then confided that the President would be killed when he visited Dallas the following day, 22 November. 'They are not only going to kill the President, they are going to kill Robert Kennedy and any other Kennedy that gets into that position.' The Cuban pilot went on to say that their anger stemmed from the failure of JFK to provide air cover. ' . . . Robert

Kennedy talked John Kennedy out of sending in the air cover which he'd agreed to send. He cancelled the air support after the invasion was launched.' The embarrassed Gordon did not know how to handle what sounded like nonsense to him. He said to me, 'What do you do? If I had passed this on to the authorities and it had proved totally untrue they would have thought I was crazy, and they don't let crazy men pilot aircraft, you know.' Hank was a qualified pilot with considerable experience.

The following day John F Kennedy was killed and five years afterwards, as he made his bid for the White House, so was Robert Kennedy. And in 1969, the following year, Edward Kennedy's prospects for reaching the White House were irrevocably dashed by the events which took place on a little island called Chappaquiddick.

There were a great many details supplied to me by Hank Gordon that were verifiable. These were duly checked and found to be correct. He was a reliable witness. Hank Gordon is not his real name: it was a condition for giving me the evidence that I did not publish his name, for he feared for his life and the lives of his wife and family. He agreed to retelling his story to a person I nominated so that it could be validated. I asked a leading researcher in the United States to meet him and talk to him and later received a report that he was entirely reliable.

38

REACTIONS

The news that Marilyn was dead was broken to Marilyn's mother, Gladys, at Rockhaven Sanitarium, from where she wrote a letter to Inez Melson, who looked after her for Marilyn. 'She is at peace and at rest now and May Our God bless her and help her always . . .'

When Sergeant Jack Clemmons telephoned Jim Dougherty, Marilyn's first husband, to tell him Marilyn had died, his call was taken by a sleepy Dougherty. Remarried, he turned to his wife and said, 'Say a prayer for Norma Jean. She's dead.' Dougherty, by that time serving as a police officer, was approached by reporters for a comment. He responded simply, 'I'm sorry.' And later he added, 'I was expecting it.' This was an unfortunate comment, reports of which made it easier for the publicity machine to promote the suicide claim.

Ex-husband Arthur Miller was not very forthcoming either. He said, 'It had to happen . . . It was inevitable.' Did he mean he expected her to commit suicide, or was he saying he was not surprised one of her overdoses had gone wrong? Or was he saying her previous 'cries for help' suggested she would one day be unlucky, and no one would be there for her? 'It would have been easy if she had been simple: you could have helped her,' he said. Neither Jim Dougherty nor Arthur Miller attended Marilyn's funeral.

When Joe DiMaggio was told Marilyn was dead he wept.

Robert Kennedy was only a few hundred miles north of Los Angeles when he was told by his press agent that Marilyn was dead. He was reported as saying, 'Yeah, it's too bad.' At Hyannis Port, the Kennedy family home, the Kennedy's elderly father, Joseph P Kennedy, who was recovering from a stroke, was exercising in his swimming pool. When someone said that Marilyn Monroe was dead, the old man said, 'No . . . no,' and a silence descended over those present. The pool was deserted and the silence became a gloom.

When Whitey Snyder was wakened with the news by his son that Sunday morning, he somehow knew before he was told that something had happened to Marilyn. He was devastated.

When Frank Sinatra heard the news of Marilyn's death he said he was 'Deeply saddened.' Kay Gable, Clark Gable's widow, responded by going to Mass and praying for her. Paula Strasberg wept and paid the finest compliments she could think of to Marilyn's acting ability. Pat Newcomb said she rushed to Marilyn's house as soon as she was told. She sobbed and was in hysterics and at one point had to be restrained by a police officer. She said, 'If I'd been here this would not have happened.' A mysterious thing to say, but as to what it meant,

The crypt at Westwood Cemetery where Marilyn was buried. Fans visit in droves each year. Photo Matthew Smith Collection.

we have never been enlightened.

The director of *Something's Got to Give*, George Cukor, by one means or another obtained in the course of time a firm grasp on what had been troubling Marilyn before she died. In 1979 he told Peter Harry Brown, co-author with Patte Barham of *Marilyn: The Last Take*, 'At the time I didn't realise how many emotional troubles she had and how the Kennedys were ruining her. If I had known I could have helped.' Anthony Summers, author of *Goddess, The Secret Lives of Marilyn Monroe*, reported that Cukor, on the day he died in 1983, had said, 'It's a nasty business, her worst rejection. Power and money. In the end she was too innocent.'

Cukor was greatly upset when he found out where Marilyn had been buried. Anthony Summers reported him telling someone, 'Do you know where the poor darling is buried? You go into this cemetery past an automobile dealer and past a bank building, and there she lies, right between Wilshire Boulevard and Westwood Boulevard, with the traffic moving past.' More recently, the small Westwood Cemetery has been scheduled for extention.

In what probably comes very close to Marilyn commenting on her own death, English reporter W J Weatherby, in his book *Conversations With Marilyn*, quotes her as saying, 'Sometimes I think it would be easier to avoid old age, to die young, but then you'd never complete your life, would you? You'd never wholly know yourself . . . ' I shall echo this later: she was robbed.

39

PERSONA NON GRATA

Another reason for believing that Marilyn had planned to remarry Joe DiMaggio was the readiness of her lawyer, Milton Rudin, to allow him to take charge of the funeral. Arthur Miller had been approached and had declined. Gladys, Marilyn's mother, was deemed not capable of handling the arrangements, and Bernice Miracle, her half sister, who would have found the cost of a funeral a burden, was happy to defer to Joe. Joe, conferring with Bernice and Inez Melson, Marilyn's business manager, took charge. He made all the arrangements, just as though he were still her husband. She was to be buried in a crypt at Westwood Memorial Park Cemetery, and a bronze plaque would declare, 'Marilyn Monroe — 1926–1962'. He made a statement: 'This will be a small funeral so she can go to her final resting place in the quiet she always sought.'

The body was prepared by her friends, Allan 'Whitey' Snyder, her make-up man, and his wife, Marjorie Plecher, her wardrobe mistress. This was the first corpse Whitey Snyder had had to make up and he found it difficult in the extreme, but he would not fail to keep the 'While I'm still warm' promise he had made to Marilyn. Marjorie negotiated with Inez Melson over the dress she would wear and it was agreed she would wear green, and clutch yellow roses. Her hair was a mess with formaldehyde, and they sent for the famed Sydney Guilaroff to do what he could. When he saw the body he fainted.

The funeral was a strange affair that reflected many of the conflicts that surrounded Marilyn in life. Her lawyers, Milton Rudin and Martin Gang, were there; Lee and Paula Strasberg, her acting coaches; her press people, Arthur Jacobs and Pat Newcomb; Eunice Murray, May Reis, her former secretary, and Ralph Greenson, her psychiatrist and his family were also there. Her masseur, Ralph Roberts and her hairdresser Agnes Flanagan were there. Whitey and Marjorie were included, as were hairdresser, Sydney Guillarof, Joe's son, Joe Jr, and Joe's friend, George Solotaire. A select few others were admitted to the ceremony. But the occasion was outstanding not so much for those who were there, but for those who were absent.

There was no invitation sent to Peter and Pat Lawford, Frank Sinatra or her leading man, Dean Martin and his wife; no invitation for Bob Slatzer, her long-time friend, or any of the stars Marilyn had worked with; no studio executives and no newsmen. Arthur Miller declined to attend and Jim Dougherty, Marilyn's 'boy next door' first husband — now a police officer — declined also as he was on duty at the time of the funeral. Pat Lawford, who had flown from the east to attend with her husband, was refused admission. Joe had instructed, 'Be sure that none of those damned Kennedys come to the funeral,'

Photo Matthew Smith Collection.

and Pat, though a good friend to Marilyn, was a Kennedy. She was in tears. Sinatra went but was kept out, and Sammy Davis Jr was also turned away. Of those who attended, it was pointed out that, though Marilyn numbered quite a few among her friends, they were almost all on her payroll. Ella Fitzgerald wanted to be at the funeral but was another who was turned away. Ella's memories of Marilyn included the time when she was being turned down by night-clubs that would not employ non-whites. Marilyn heard Ella's agent had tried the Mocambo Club and had, again, been unsuccessful, so she telephoned them, telling them that if they booked Ella she would attend every night she was there and take a table at the front where all could see her. Her irresistible offer was accepted and Ella was booked.

The organist played a little of Tchaikovsky's Sixth Symphony and, since Marilyn had been a fan of Judy Garland, 'Over the Rainbow' was played. The Reverend A J Soldan, a Lutheran minister, officiated, and Lee Strasberg gave the eulogy. A weeping Joe DiMaggio leaned over and kissed Marilyn saying, 'I love you, my darling, I love you.' A heartbroken Joe had spent the previous night kneeling by the coffin. As the cortege moved away, people who had gathered followed with a multitude of reporters and photographers. Hundreds of bouquets were sent.

Three times a week for the next 20 years, two red roses were sent to her crypt by Joe DiMaggio. He never remarried.

40

Cursum Perficio

Since childhood, Marilyn had suffered from an oppressive sense of insecurity and fatherlessness. As a young child she was fostered by the Bolender family, as her mother Gladys felt herself inadequate to raising a child. The Bolenders were responsible people who lived by a moral code engendered by their religious beliefs, and Norma Jean, as she was called as a child, found herself regularly attending Sunday School and sharing a strict upbringing with the other children in their home. But for all this, Norma Jean's abiding memory of that period was of a feeling of insecurity.

Eventually, her mother Gladys decided to make a home for her daughter and, with Gladys' friend Grace McKee taking an interest in her, life became less rigid and organised. Norma Jean had embarked upon a life in which 'pass the parcel' was no game but a serious matter in which she was the parcel, shunted around, deposited in one place, collected when it was convenient, and sent elsewhere when it was not. The swings from one lifestyle to another became part of her history and upbringing. She encountered years of change, order and disorder, according to whom she lived with or which

404

orphanage she was sent to. It was small wonder that after one of these moves she was said to suffer from stuttering.

This was the stuff of which insecurity was made and inbred. Norma Jean's mother, Gladys Baker, was a victim of insecurity also, surviving a tragic home life and several broken marriages. Her father had died insane, she believed, and her mother had been taken to hospital where she died of a heart complaint, though mood swings before she died indicated 'manic depressive psychosis', which was noted as contributory to her death. When she learned that her grandfather had hanged himself at the age of 82, Gladys went to pieces. She saw a clear pattern of insanity in her forebears that worried her intensely. Her first reaction was to try to find consolation in religion but she began a retreat into a netherland from which she would never return. This fear of insanity transmitted, not surprisingly, to the young Norma Jean, though it would be shown that neither she nor her mother had anything to be afraid of. Gladys' father, Otis, had contracted a form of syphilis while he worked in Mexico. This variety was not transmitted sexually, but resulted from the dire living circumstances experienced by many in those days in Mexico, and was by no means uncommon. It was, therefore, an organic cause that affected his brain. He was not insane. Della, Gladys' mother, may well have suffered from extreme depression, but she was not, by any means, insane, either.

Grandfather, Tilford Hogan, took his life as a consequence of the hopelessness that overwhelmed him because of the after effects of the 1929 Wall Street crash and the Great Depression that followed. A tenant farmer and a very sick man, he saw what little he had dissipate to the point he could no longer support his wife. Hogan, who might have been said to have 'taken his life while the balance of his mind was disturbed,' *was* certainly disturbed, but there was no insanity. But when Norma Jean became Marilyn Monroe, she could not escape from her mother's nightmare.

Norma Jean was not yet 16 when she was pushed into a marriage with Jim Dougherty. At that time she was living with her 'Aunt' Grace, Gladys' friend, who had taken a proprietary interest in her from the time she had lived with her mother, and eventually became her legal guardian. It was Grace who laid the foundation for her work in pictures. Jean Harlow was Grace's idol, and her enthusiasm for the 'blonde bombshell' soon infected Norma Jean. It was Jean Harlow that Norma Jean wanted to 'become', and Grace never lost an opportunity to encourage her ward in this ambition. Grace schooled Norma Jean in applying make-up, but stopped short of having her dye her hair the white that distinguished Harlow from other blonde stars of the time. Remarkably, it would be Pearl Porterfield, who originated Jean Harlow's 'hot platinum', who would originate the 'paler than white' colour for Norma Jean when she became Marilyn Monroe.

Grace's husband, 'Doc' Goddard, was transferred to West Virginia and that meant the family was to uproot again. Grace and 'Doc' could see their way clear to supporting Bebe, Goddard's daughter by a previous marriage, when they reached West Virginia but not Norma Jean. She was, once more, the parcel to be passed around. Grace's pressure for her to marry Jim Dougherty continued. Norma Jean had nowhere else to go except the orphanage, where she could stay until she was 18. It was Dougherty's mother who accurately read the situation and asked her son if he was interested in marrying her.

These were the days following Pearl Harbour and Dougherty expected to be going to war soon, though in fact he would not go overseas until 1944. He married Norma Jean in 1942, on the Sunday following her sixteenth birthday, knowing that if he was not there she would be safe with a loving family, and so the teenage girl began to grow up quickly. Bob Mitchum told me that before he got into pictures he and Dougherty worked at Lockheed Aircraft in Burbank, and he soon got to know Norma Jean. Out in a party at a company dance one night at the Palladium Ballroom, where the Dorsey Brothers Orchestra was playing, Norma Jean said she liked the young singer with the orchestra and Mitchum offered to introduce them. The singer was Frank Sinatra.

While Jim Dougherty was overseas, Norma Jean took steps to become a model, and the success she obtained eventually led to the beginning of her acting career and the creation of Marilyn Monroe. Her marriage to Jim Dougherty was lost in her bid for a career, which might also be said of her marriage to Joe DiMaggio and, to some extent, her marriage to Arthur Miller. Against the background and upbringing we have described, she strove to attain a 'Jean Harlow' status, independence and security. But while she achieved stardom, wealth, and adulation, she never obtained true independence, and the security she needed constantly eluded her. She once said, 'I don't like to talk about my own past, it's an unpleasant experience I'm trying to forget.'

As we saw from her secret tapes, it took little to take her back to the madness from which she was in flight. She believed her mother was crazy, and she did not know who her father was. She accepted the name Mortenson as her maiden name, though she really did not know he was her father. At points during her upbringing she revealed a deep need for a father, or a father figure, and this continued right through to the making of *The Misfits*, her last completed film, when she cast Clark Gable in the role. Towards the end of her brief life she sought a measure of independence through Ralph Greenson and psychiatry, which she may also have seen as a means of defence against the insanity she feared. Her tapes reveal she was still seeking a father, a family and security right until the end.

Immediately before she died, Marilyn was revising her household arrangements and taking charge of her domestic affairs. Whether her new arrangements would have brought her the added freedom and the degree of independence which she sought is a question to which there is no answer. It has been suggested her revised arrangements may have been intended to accommodate a new life in remarriage with Joe DiMaggio, but this is conjecture. Whether she would ever have remarried Joe — though there were strong indications to suggest the move — and found security in a new marriage with a man who adored her, we do not know. Her ambitions, we also saw from the secret tapes, lay in the direction of applying herself to a protracted period of hard work to achieve what she believed would be the demands of becoming a serious Shakespearean actress. Where this would have taken her we can only guess, but we know we were looking at the plans of a talented and very determined lady.

Marilyn was conscious of her illegitimacy throughout her life. It was a stigma thrust upon her just as the stigma of suicide was thrust upon her after her death. The former she could not change and she accepted it, even if reluctantly, with dignity. The latter was bestowed upon her through the unkindness and dishonesty of those around her, and she has had no redress.

When Marilyn bought her house in Fifth Helena Drive it bore a Latin inscription, 'Cursum Perficio'. This is taken from the New Testament, second epistle of St Paul to Timothy, chapter 4, verse 7, and means 'I have finished the course' or 'I complete the course.' There are those who would sagely find an element of prophesy in these words. I do not. She did not complete the course. Her life was stolen from her before she had the opportunity. And there is but one response open to us in the face of such monstrous plundering. Voltaire has it: 'To the living, one owes consideration; to the dead, only the truth.'

Select Bibliography

Brown, Peter Harry, and Patte B. Barham, *Marilyn: The Last Take*, Dutton, New York 1992

Capell, Frank A., *The Strange Death of Marilyn Monroe*, Herald of Freedom, Indianapolis 1964

Carpozi, George Jr., *The Agony of Marilyn Monroe*, Consul Books, London 1962

Dunleavy, Stephen, and Peter Brennan, *Those Wild, Wild Kennedy Boys!*, Pinnacle Books, New York 1976

Freeman, Lucy, *Why Norma Jean Killed Marilyn Monroe*, Global Right Ltd, Chicago 1992

Giancana, Sam and Chuck, *Double Cross*, Warner Books, New York 1992

Gregory, Adela and Milo Speriglio, *Crypt 33, The Saga of Marilyn Monroe: The Final Word*, Birch Lane Press, New York 1993

Guiles, Fred Lawrence, *Norma Jeane: The Life and Death of Marilyn Monroe*, Grafton Books, London 1986

Israel, Lee, *Kilgallen*, Delacorte Press, New York 1979

Jordan, Ted, *Norma Jean, My Secret Life with Marilyn Monroe*, William Morrow, New York 1989

411

Kennedy, Robert F., *The Enemy Within*, Harper and Row, New York 1960

Lawford, Pat Seaton, with Ted Schwarz, *Peter Lawford Mixing With Monroe: The Kennedys, The Rat Pack and the Whole Damn Crowd*, Futura, London 1990

Mailer, Norman, *Marilyn: A Biography*, Warner Paperback Library, New York 1975

Manchester, William, *Death of a President*, Michael Joseph Ltd, Michael Joseph Ltd, London 1967

Manchester, William, *One Brief Shining Moment: Remembering Kennedy*, Little Brown, Boston 1983

Melanson, Philip H., PhD, *The Robert F Kennedy Assassination*, Spi Books, New York 1991

Murray, Eunice, with Rose Shade, *The Last Months*, Pyramid Books, New York 1975

Noguchi, Thomas T., with Joseph Dimona, *Coroner*, Simon and Schuster, New York 1983

Otash, Fred, *Investigation Hollywood*, Regenery, Chicago 1976

Pepitone, Lena, and William Stadiem, *Marilyn Monroe Confidential*, New York 1980

Scheim, David E., *The Mafia Killed President Kennedy*, WH Allen, London 1988

Schlesinger, Arthur M Jr., *Robert Kenendy and His Times*, Andre Deutsch, London 1978

Sciacca, Tony, *Kennedy and his Women*, Manor Books, New York 1976

Shevey, Sandra, *The Marilyn Scandal*, Arrow Books, London 1989

Slatzer, Robert F., *The Life and Curious Death of Marilyn Monroe*, Pinnacle Books, Los Angeles 1975

Slatzer, Robert F., *The Marilyn Files*, Spi Books, New York 1992

Smith, Matthew, *JFK: The Second Plot*, Mainstream, Edinburgh 1992

Smith, Matthew, *The Men Who Murdered Marilyn*, Bloomsbury, London 1996

Smith, Matthew, *Say Goodbye to America*, Mainstream, Edinburgh 2001

Smith, Matthew, *Vendetta: The Kennedys*, Mainstream, Edinburgh 1993

Sorensen, Theodore C., *Kennedy*, Harper and Row, New York 1965

Spada, James, *Peter Lawford, The Man Who Kept Secrets*, Bantam, New York 1992

Speriglio, Milo, *Marilyn Monroe: Murder Cover-Up*, Seville, New York 1982

Speriglio, Milo, with Steven Chain, *The Marilyn Conspiracy*, Corgi, London 1986

Spindel, Bernard B., *The Ominous Ear*, Award Books, New York 1968

Spoto, Donald, *Marilyn Monroe, The Biography*, Arrow Books, London 1994

Steinem, Gloria, and George Barris, *Marilyn*, Victor Gollancz, London 1987

Strasberg, Susan, *Marilyn and Me*, Transworld, London 1992

Summers, Anthony, *Goddess, The Secret Lives of Marilyn Monroe*, Victor Gollancz, London 1985

Weatherby, W J, *Conversations with Marilyn*, Robson Books, London 1976

LIST OF ILLUSTRATIONS